Communication Inquiry:
A Perspective on a Process

Communication Inquiry:
A Perspective on a Process

Gerald R. Miller
Michigan State University
and

Henry E. Nicholson
Sangamon State University

ADDISON-WESLEY PUBLISHING COMPANY

Reading, Massachusetts • Menlo Park, California
London • Amsterdam • Don Mills, Ontario • Sydney

This book is in the
ADDISON-WESLEY SERIES IN HUMAN COMMUNICATION

Consulting Editor
C. David Mortensen

ISBN 0-201-04746-2
ABCDEFGHIJ-DO-79876

Foreword

Society is often described as an ongoing system of communication maintained by persons committed to the principle of consistent action. Similarly, this series in Human Communication is designed to explore the ongoing and pervasive impact of communication on the actions and patterns of everyday experience. The series provides a flexible and integrated discussion of key concepts, problems, topics, and issues related to "person-centered" subject matter. The books strive to be readable, nontechnical, and broadly based without sacrificing the depth needed to challenge serious students.

In developing such an important collection of texts, Addison-Wesley has called upon a well-known group of teachers whose competence is ideally suited to their texts. *Communication Inquiry: A Perspective on a Process* by Gerald R. Miller and Henry E. Nicholson introduces students to various ways of studying communicative behavior as an integral dimension of personal and social experience. *Dyadic Communication: A Transactional Perspective* by William Wilmot focuses on the complex and fascinating processes that shape the experience of communication in interpersonal social situations. *Communication and Social Influence* by Stephen W. King broadens the study of communication to the context of what is known about the potentials and hazards of using language to influence and persuade others. An overview of language and speech as communication codes, within and between individuals, is the subject of Larry Wilder's *Speech, Language, and Communication* (forthcoming).

The larger theoretical aspects of human communication are examined in *Pragmatics of Analoguing: Theory and Model Construction in Communication* by Leonard C. Hawes and in *Perspectives on Communication Theory* by Jesse G. Delia (forthcoming). *Analoguing* provides the first systematic treatment of the requirements of developing theories about the underlying nature of communicative experience. Delia's text will complement other books in the series by providing a broadly based synthesis of recent contributions to the study of communication theory.

These brief, integrated paperback texts are suitable for a wide range of purposes and courses within communication and the social sciences. Used in combination or alone with other texts and supplements, they will enhance and enrich the study of human communication.

C. David Mortensen

Preface

People's curiosity is seemingly insatiable. A questioning spirit certainly pervades their daily communicative activities: they seek to understand the outcomes of their communicative transactions, the motives of other communicators, the ethical choices that should guide their communicative conduct, their aesthetic preferences for certain types of messages, and a host of other communicative mysteries.

Paradoxically, however, many persons are wary of the more formalized manifestations of this powerful curiosity motive. Terms such as "statistical analysis," "aesthetic criticism," "operational definition," and "ethical criteria" have a foreboding, alien ring. Even mention of the hallowed term "research" is enough to cause some to shy away cautiously.

This book attempts to solve, or at least soften, this paradox. It treats the process of inquiry, in general, and communication inquiry, in particular, as an integral dimension of daily human experience. More specifically, it views communication inquiry as nothing more (fully realizing that "nothing more" embraces an area of marvelous complexity) than the process of asking interesting, significant questions about human communication and providing disciplined, systematic answers for them. The concepts and methodologies of formalized inquiry are but a means toward the end of asking more significant questions and providing more disciplined answers.

This is neither a book about philosophy of inquiry nor a volume on research strategy. Rather, it seeks to combine relevant aspects of both areas to engender a broadly based understanding of, and appreciation for, the process of communication inquiry. We believe that all readers can profit from such understanding and appreciation, whether or not they choose to pursue a career of scholarly inquiry. Understanding and appreciation of the process of inquiry results in heightened communicative responsibility and discernment, a goal well worth pursuing in its own right.

Many people contributed to our efforts, but brief books merit brief acknowledgments. Hence, our one expression of thanks is directed at those teachers, colleagues, and students who helped us discover, formulate, and refine the ideas found in these pages. They own shares in any of the book's assets; all liabilities must be assumed solely by us.

East Lansing, Michigan   G.R.M.
Springfield, Illinois   H.E.N.
January 1976

Contents

Prologue:
An Overview of Our Journey

This book represents an ambitious undertaking. Its purpose is not so much a detailed exploration of a single aspect of a problem as it is integration of the details of many aspects of a problem. Because of the nature of the subject, explorations and explanations are a necessary part of the process, but we hope that the strongest statement the book makes is the total integrative perspective it offers.

Although the title and the content of the book indicate a primary concern with inquiry into the human communication process, much of what we say could also be applied to any area that involves asking questions and seeking answers. Such areas include not only other social sciences, but also physical sciences, humanities, and, beyond that, much of the conduct of everyday living. We have divided the universe of questions into three types: definitional, factual, and evaluational. Others might suggest different divisions, but we feel comfortable with this scheme. We shall expose some of our own prejudices and preferences in order to explain our treatment of the subject and in hopes that it will help you form a relatively unbiased picture of what we are talking about from our biased treatment of it.

First, while believing in the value of specialization, we think it has inherent flaws. In the last ten years, our society has begun to turn slowly away from specialization and toward holistic examination of social issues. We no longer manufacture cars in the interest of production and profit alone—concern for the long-term effects of car production and use are part of the everyday life of both the consumer and the producer. Research into the uses of atomic energy has for years outdistanced research and concern for the effects of its use. Lately the lack of question-asking concerning this aspect of atomic energy has come under public discussion and government scrutiny, resulting in such events as shutdowns of nuclear power plants, attempts to limit nuclear weapons buildup, and efforts to eliminate concentrations of radioactive material in food products. Thus, specialized or, more appropriately, compartmentalized question-asking can defeat the purpose of asking questions in the first place: it can disrupt or retard the progress which research might be designed to provide. This, of course, is not to argue against specialization. Communication researchers (and all other professional question-askers) are highly trained people, and the extent of their training necessitates some kind of focus. Yet to concentrate solely upon their own favorite brand of question-asking seems outmoded in some respects and dangerous in others. Much question-asking by professional researchers deals directly with important social problems and often results in outcomes that have great potential for affecting society. Thus, the researcher mainly interested in factual questions would be remiss in ignoring the evaluative implications of inquiry.

Second, we may seem to place more emphasis on scientific inquiry. This results partly from our greater familiary with this approach to inquiry and partly from our belief that the methods employed by science provide the best overall model for inquiry. This is not to say that the quality of research conducted in one area is better or worse than that conducted in others, only that the scientific enterprise makes good use of objective research schemes and follows the tenets of sound question-asking. Thus, if one can grasp the logic and flow of scientific inquiry, he or she is well on the way to becoming an effective question-asker.

Third, we contend that good communication inquiry involves the application of common sense to communication problems. There is no substitute for clearly and sharply seeing the forest for the trees. Many everyday problems are simple and have simple solutions. No degree of technical sophistication or philosophical analysis makes a correct answer any more correct. We discuss some relatively sophisticated methods of inquiry here in order to familiarize the reader with them. All such methods were created for a specific purpose. Their indiscriminate application to every problem shows a lack of understanding by the inquirer. Some researchers habitually use unnecessary technical gymnastics in inquiry. They could well take a lesson from Sherlock Holmes, who could use a minimum of "clues" to reach a common-sense conclusion without resorting to abstract philosophy or mathematical gymnastics. If common sense has been formalized as a technique in certain situations, then when applicable it should be employed. We hope that an introduction to what may seem to be detailed techniques does not destroy your ability to see a problem clearly and simply, if indeed it is clear and simple. One oft-forgotten goal of inquiry is parsimony.

Fourth, we believe that inquiry is not a process that is the property of only an elite group to be applied only to abstract theoretical problems. Rather, inquiry cannot help but make us more alert and understanding participants in the world. In writing this book, we have attempted to "keep our feet on the ground." We have tried not to talk technically for the sake of talking technically. Thus, if you encounter unfamiliar or unusual terms in the text, they appear because we feel that they are key terms used in other treatments of the inquiry process and that it is wise to be familiar with their use.

Inquiry as we conceive it covers a great deal of territory. It invades the events of everyday life. Much of our behavior, thoughts, and communication is based upon the outcome of informal inquiries that we constantly conduct. We have several purposes in this book: to offer a reasonably detailed description of the inquiry process as used by persons interested in the process of human communication; to relate the specialized process of inquiry we describe to more familiar everyday situations so as to give perspective to our description; to break down the communication inquiry process into what we believe to be a set of reasonable and useful categories; and, finally, to reassemble the categories and to stress that the process of inquiry is not a collection of techniques or separable parts but rather a unified process.

These purposes may sound logically inconsistent, but we hope that as you read you will agree that they are not. While we feel, for instance, that it aids understanding to treat one aspect of inquiry at a time, we believe that application of this understanding is best achieved through a processual perspective where all parts are integrated by the user of the knowledge. Similarly, we do not feel that an analogy between what we might call "scholarly" inquiry and "everyday" inquiry either demeans scholarly inquiry or lowers the quality of our description. Rather, we think that the distinction between the two types is one of precision, not of kind.

As Caesar did Gaul, we have divided the realm of inquiry into three parts. More accurately, we have conceived of three basically different types of questions that an inquirer may ask.

If a question deals with the meaning of words or terms, we can reasonably expect its answer to fall (at least indirectly) upon the useful-not useful dimension. We call such queries *questions of definition.* If a question leads to answers or decisions on a true-false dimension, we call such queries *questions of fact.* Finally, if a question leads to answers or decisions such as "good-bad" or "beautiful-ugly," we call such queries *questions of value.* Such a conceptual scheme strikes us as adequately and concisely summarizing the domain of inquiry. It may initially seem that we have overlooked certain types of questions, but we trust that seemingly overlooked questions are merely translations of inquiries which fit this model. In the domain of factual inquiry, for example, we may conceive of questions beginning with "Who . . .?" and "How much . . .?" etc., which at first glance do not seem to lend themselves to yes-no or true-false answers. Our point is that a slight rewording of the question can be accomplished without destroying its essential meaning while at the same time allowing an answer of the type we have suggested. Example: Do men or women appear more credible when using strong fear-appeal messages? Answer: Men (women) Reworded: Do men exhibit more credibility than women do when both employ strong fear-appeal messages? Answer: Yes (no)

Again we feel that this scheme is useful *for purposes of explanation and discussion.* To be able to distinguish types of questions (and potential answers) aids greatly in furthering any inquiry. However, as we view the process of inquiry, it should be conceived as a collection of types of questions. Seldom should a single question stand alone.

An example of the problems inherent in a singular approach can be found in the examination of the influence of the mass media upon people's thoughts and attitudes. To answer questions such as whether the media do influence thoughts and attitudes of persons who use them or to find out if certain attitudes are more vulnerable to such influence than others, an inquirer must first define as precisely as possible what such terms as "attitudes," "influence," and "media" mean within the context of the question. Without such definitions the inquiry is, at worst, meaningless or, at best, difficult to interpret. Also, even when such definitional and factual issues yield answers, an implied question of value remains. Specifically, if the media do influence certain attitudes, what are the implications of this fact for decisions concerning the social responsibility of the media and possible restrictions (censorship) that might be imposed upon them? Should the media be subject to more stringent regulations? How do we weigh the value of free expression with the possible harmful consequences resulting from complete freedom? Or perhaps more realistically, what is the optimum balance between freedom of expression and regulation for the benefit of the society? To ask these value questions necessitates defining certain value terms such as "regulation," "free expression," etc. Moreover, the very act of choice in picking the original question for examination involves implicitly answering certain value questions concerning the relative value and importance of the factual inquiry. We point this out here as a prologue to a more detailed discussion of the issue in Chapter 5.

In Chapter 2 we discuss the use of theory as a launching ground for communication inquiry. We do not believe that inquiry without theory is sterile nor that well-constructed theory is always necessary for conducting inquiry. Such a belief entails a prescriptive approach. We do think, however, that regardless of prescriptions, little inquiry *is actually* conducted without some form of theory. Whether the theory is formal or informal, well-constructed or roughly formulated is irrelevant to this point. That it is difficult to conduct any inquiry without some form of theoretical underpinnings seems a fact, not a prescription.

In some cases, inquirers work from what might better be called a hypothesis—an expectation of an outcome which focuses inquiry upon a smaller range of potential answers. Sometimes hypotheses are derived from accepted laws, propositions, or generalizations; sometimes they stem from informal preconceptions based on past experience. To understand something about the principles of theory construction and its potential utility enables an inquirer to formalize, concretize, or extend the purpose of inquiry. Although theory is often associated with the domain of factual inquiry, it has its place in other areas of inquiry as well. Whether inquirers deal primarily with scientific or ethical "reality," they make use of a system of rules, laws, or principles which guide their thinking and their question-asking.

In Chapter 3 we argue that the beginning point of virtually all inquiry involves questions of definition. The recognition of the role of definition in inquiry places the question-asker on firmer footing at the outset. Poorly defined questions, theories containing poorly defined terms, and answers with ambiguous elements all detract from the value of communication inquiry. Our treatment of the definitional process as an interconnected series of translations hopefully sheds meaningful light on what may be erroneously considered as relatively unimportant preparatory work. In inquiry, as in all other activities, preparatory work determines the quality of the end product. The translational model we discuss delineates the goals of definition and assists in realizing maximum efficiency from this sometimes overlooked step of the inquiry process.

The discussion of observation in Chapter 4 betrays our scientific backgrounds. Scientific communication inquiry calls for repeated, carefully controlled, maximally unbiased observations. We attempt to familiarize the reader with the logic underlying the observational process. We intend no apology when we point out that observation has been the subject of many books and articles. To attempt to explore the numerous details of scaling and measurement, experimental design, and statistical analysis would constitute an unrealistic task. Instead, we have sought to impart an understanding of the general problems to be overcome in making observations and to reinforce the perspective which follows from such an understanding. More specifically, exposure to or learning of "powerful" observational and analytical techniques often blinds the inquirer to the central goal of all communication inquiry: providing useful answers to questions. Specialized techniques exist for specialized purposes, not as substitutes for creative imagination and common sense. Kaplan aptly calls a slavish commitment to a particular technique "the law of the instrument," comparing it to the behavior of a small child who sees a need for pounding everything when given a hammer.

Most of the problems to be overcome when making observations in communication inquiry can be summed up in one word: *error*. If we are about the business of seeking answers the last thing we want is a wrong answer. In the specialized methods that factual inquirers have developed for making observations, error has more than one meaning. We discuss the two major types of error (biased and unbiased) that can plague observation, trace their sources, and discuss methods for minimizing or eliminating them.

Finally, we provide a brief introduction to measurement, scaling, and statistics. Again, these topics have been the subject of countless books. We feel we have presented a reasonably adequate introduction to these topics without dwelling on them in detail. Overall understanding and appreciation is our limited goal, not a detailed grasp of these essential tools of observation.

In Chapter 5 we focus on the role of evaluation in communication inquiry. The acts of choosing a question for investigation, carrying out the inquiry (which in communication almost always involves dealing with human beings as subjects), and interpreting and disseminating the results all entail evaluative decisions, whether implied or explicit. Our first purpose is to bring to the fore those frequently hidden dimensions of evaluation which operate in domains of inquiry ostensibly concerned with other matters.

We argue that while value questions are a legitimate area for communication inquiry in their own right, there exists an extrinsic evaluative dimension to questions of definition and questions of fact. Obviously, value questions are not primary to investigators examining the persuasive appeal of various television commercials, but we suggest they should be one of their concerns, carefully considered before beginning the study.

One thesis underlying this chapter is that all value judgments are not equally "good". Rather, those based upon accepted general ethical or aesthetic premises or derived by cogent reasoning better reflect the term "value judgment" than do thoughtless emotional reactions. Yet we raise many more questions in this discussion than we answer. The reasons should be obvious.

Our final epilogue attempts to practice what we have been preaching throughout the book. As we have said, our goal is to demonstrate the interdependency of topics which we ourselves have treated independently and serially for reasons of clarity. While the epilogue is brief and non-textual, we feel it captures the complexity and interlocking nature of the topics covered in the preceding five chapters.

Throughout this book we use examples and dialogues to illustrate the concepts under consideration. In addition, each chapter contains several cases which acquaint the reader with actual instances of inquiry that have been carried out by communication researchers and other scholars—inquiries that demonstrate the application of the ideas and concepts discussed herein to real research situations. Hopefully, these examples, dialogues, and cases clarify and reinforce our major points. But it seems appropriate to end this prologue by restating our primary thesis once again: communication inquiry is best understood as a total process involving the intelligent asking and rigorous answering of questions. The chapters that follow seek to underscore this thesis.

1
Asking Questions

"Well, Miss Stein, what's the answer?"

"What's the question?"

—remark attributed to **GERTRUDE STEIN**
shortly before her death.

*The purpose of higher education is not
primarily to teach students how to answer
questions, but rather how to ask them.*

—MILTON ROKEACH

People incessantly ask questions. Whether their inquisitiveness stems from an instinctual curiosity motive, a learned realization that they must query in order to cope with life, or a subtle blending of these two causes remains itself an intriguing, unanswered question. Regardless of the precise reasons, the interrogative sentence is humanity's cradle-to-grave companion; an essential ingredient of the child's socialization, the statesman's decision-making, and the scholar's search for knowledge.

Generally, when people ask questions they sincerely seek answers to them. To be sure, there are other reasons for asking questions—or perhaps more accurately, pseudoquestions. Two common ones are the interpersonal bludgeon ("Well, you're just as big a liar as ever, aren't you?") and the ostentatious display of knowledge ("Do you think Sartre's *No Exit* or Camus' *The Stranger* more graphically captures the ultimate existential absurdity of the world in which we live?"). Usually we can spot instances where the motives of the inquirer deviate from a sincere quest for answers, though of course we can never be certain because motives are forever hidden from our sight.

We have chosen to call this posing of questions and seeking of answers the *process of inquiry*. Other labels are readily available; for example, the twin steps of question-asking and answer-seeking are frequently referred to as *research*. Although we have no personal quarrel with this term, we realize that for many persons "research" may connote a laborious, dry, uninspiring undertaking. Consequently, on the grounds that words often determine the way people think about things, we will avoid using the term "research" until later in this book.

Of course, the range of human inquiry is nearly infinite: people ask questions about atoms, molecules, rocks, other people, formal organizations, societies, solar systems, and countless other things. We are primarily concerned with people's questions about their communicative behaviors; we will focus on the *process of communication inquiry*. This does not mean that our remarks are inapplicable to other areas of inquiry; in fact, *we believe that the criteria for determining significant questions and the rules for arriving at reasoned answers to these questions are largely consistent across all problem areas.* What primarily distinguishes *communication inquiry* from *inquiry* in general is the substantive thrust of the inquirer;

his or her interests are riveted on human symbolic transactions, rather than the physical and chemical composition of Kohoutek's Comet or the genetic characteristics transmitted by DNA.

Since you, like all human beings, are an inveterate question-asker, you are probably thinking, "What do they mean by 'communication'?" Bear with us for a few pages. This chapter deals with the crucial first step of communication inquiry: asking questions. We will pin-point the kinds of questions that people ask about human communication and we will weigh some criteria for assessing the significance, or importance, of a particular question. And in the course of delving into these matters, we will also stipulate a working definition for the term *communication*.

THE QUESTIONS PEOPLE ASK ABOUT COMMUNICATION

People's curiosity about communication manifests itself in several domains. In this section we discuss three types of questions that are asked about human communication, question types that are central to the succeeding chapters of this book.

Questions of Definition

How many times have you witnessed, or participated in, a conversation that progressed along these lines?

KATE: "Boy did I see some effective communication today! Yesterday Professor Hunt wore a turtleneck sweater to the office. Today all four of his graduate assistants were wearing turtlenecks. Talk about persuasion."

FRED: "Well, it may or it may not have been 'persuasion,' but it certainly wasn't 'communication.' "

KATE: "What do you mean, 'wasn't communication?' That sweater Hunt was wearing communicated to his assistants and brought about a definite change in the way they dressed today."

FRED: "What you're talking about is 'prestige suggestion,' not 'communication.' I doubt that Hunt was consciously trying to persuade his assistants to wear turtlenecks. You didn't hear him tell them they should dress that way, did you?"

KATE: "No, but I don't see what that has to do with it. People can 'communicate' without intending to, and they don't have to use words either. In fact, most everything we come in contact with 'communicates' with us in some way or another."

FRED: "You don't have a clear concept of what 'communication' really is. I was reading a book by Miller and Steinberg the other day, and they say that 'communication is an intentional, transactional, symbolic process.' "

KATE: "Well, they're wrong! Watzlawick, Beavin, and Jackson, who know a lot more about communication than Miller and Steinberg, say you 'cannot not communicate.' "

FRED: "That's a lot of nonsense! Who are they . . . ."

Although the fun is apparently just starting, we will take leave of Kate's and Fred's dispute. Unless you have experienced a unique upbringing, you have been embroiled in enough of these controversies to be able to predict the approximate course of events.

People seemingly enjoy asking questions about what to call something and arguing about whether or not particular objects, acts, or situations should be included under a certain label. Should it be called "persuasion" when a viewer is enticed to purchase a tube of toothpaste by a network television commercial? Most people, though not necessarily all, would probably agree that it should. Suppose the same person buys stock in the company where he or she works because the boss threatens to fire anyone who doesn't. Is this an instance of "persuasion"? Probably there will be more disagreement about the latter case. And even if there is agreement to use the broad label "persuasion" for both events, should the analysis stop there or should further differentiations be attempted? Perhaps the first occurrence should be called "noncoercive persuasion" and the second "coercive persuasion." But can any act of persuasion ever be completely noncoercive; i.e., what is meant by the term "noncoercive"? Once the process of deciphering and deciding upon the labels for things begins, numerous problems are certain to arise.

Obviously, the task of deciding what to call things is central to human communication itself. Stated differently, effective communication is impossible unless the communicators have arrived at a body of *shared meanings*. This is not to say that each term or phrase must trigger an identical meaning for all those involved in the transaction (indeed, we would argue that this is an impossible goal), but rather that there must be some *commonality,* or *overlap,* in the meanings shared by the transactants. If we choose to call the general process of asking questions and seeking answers "inquiry," and if your meaning for that term is restricted to questions and answers that arise in a formal, legal setting, we shall all probably end up talking past each other most of the time.

To avoid this very problem, we began this chapter by stipulating our definition (and, hence, a dimension of our meaning) for the term "inquiry." Although our definition does not ensure communication fidelity (e.g., it may be so far afield from your definition that you experience problems plugging into it perceptually, or it may somehow seem ridiculous or "wrong" to you) it increases the likelihood that a severe communication breakdown can be avoided.

Successful solutions to the relevant questions of definition (the "What shall we call it?" questions) are vital to the process of communication inquiry, for *if terms are not clearly defined, an inquirer can neither know what question he or she is asking nor be reasonably certain when or how it has been answered.* Sometimes, of course, the definition of a term is at least partially contained in the question itself. Suppose, for instance, that you wished to pursue an answer to the following question: "How can I persuade my fiance(e) to go on a skiing trip this weekend?" In one sense, the definition of "persuade" can be found in the sentence: you will have "persuaded" your fiance(e) if he or she agrees to join you on a skiing outing this weekend.[1] To anticipate some of our remarks in Chapter 3, you have *operationally defined* a behavioral outcome that you are willing to call "persuasion."

But the term "persuade" refers not only to the outcomes of an influence attempt, it also refers to the strategies that may be employed to achieve these outcomes. When viewed from this context, the term's meaning is vague.[2] What strategies are you willing to employ to induce your fiance(e) to go on a skiing trip and what ones are you reluctant to use? Are you willing to threaten to break the engagement or to go skiing with another party? If so, you are apparently willing to resort to a *strong fear-arousing message;* i.e., you are willing to threaten your fiance(e) with harmful consequences if he or she refuses to go skiing. As a result, the question now could be more precisely stated, "Will a strong fear-arousing message persuade my fiance(e) to go on a skiing trip this weekend?" Even here, however, you may hesitate to put all of your communicative eggs in one basket, since you fear the consequences of a negative answer to your question. Perhaps you may then choose to state the question: "Will a strong *or* a mild fear-arousing message be more effective in persuading my fiance(e) to go on a skiing trip this weekend?" In each of the latter two cases, the question has been markedly narrowed from the original. Since most people would probably object to equating "persuade" with "a strong (or mild) fear-arousing message," the term appears to be too broad and ambiguous when used to refer to particular strategies that are potentially available to you. Although you might choose to lump all of these strategies and call them "persuasion," the goals of inquiry would likely be furthered by selecting a less global label, i.e., by focusing on a limited subset of strategies.

Perhaps, however, your concern lies not with a skiing trip, but rather with heightening your fiance(e)'s romantic feelings toward yourself. If this is your aim, you might pose the following question: "How can I persuade my fiance(e) to love me more intensely?" This question involves the same definitional problems regarding persuasive strategies that present themselves in the skiing example. But in addition, it will probably be much harder to specify a behavioral outcome or outcomes that you are willing to call "persuasion." Such actions as reporting intensified feelings to you or to others, interacting more enthusiastically with you, or spending more time with you may all be taken as evidence that you have "persuaded" your fiance(e) to "love you more intensely." On the other hand, none of these verbal and nonverbal behaviors may seem adequate to you. Obviously, what you will choose to call "persuasion" cannot be easily specified; still, if your meaning for the term cannot be delineated clearly, the answer to your question will continue to elude you.

The preceding examples may strike you as trivial or whimsical. Still, people do ask these sorts of questions about their daily communicative transactions and conscientiously seek answers to them. Often, the "research" conducted consists of applying social comparisons; e.g., "Bob's fiancee seems to love him very much; I'll have to watch him (or ask him) and see how he does it." Alternatively, books describing the techniques of history's great lovers may be perused on the premise that what worked for Casanova or Cleopatra may also pay off for the "researcher." Occasionally these quests bear relational fruit, but often they yield only frustration; the initial question remains unanswered. Although the causes of failure are many, lack of careful definition frequently plays a crucial role; the question is unanswerable because the meanings of terms are not clearly specified.

The importance of definitional issues can be underscored by looking at several questions of the type usually considered fair game for communication inquiry. For instance: *Will a high-credible communicator be more persuasive than a low-credible communicator?* Prior to seeking an answer to this query, the following definitional questions must be resolved:

1. *How shall we define "high-credible communicator?"* and, conversely,

2. *How shall we define "low-credible communicator?"* and, finally,

3. *How shall we define "more persuasive?"*

The answer to this last definitional question is particularly complex, since the inquirer must first stipulate a definition of "persuasion" and then specify a means for assessing the *relative amount of persuasion* attributable to the high- and low-credible communicators. In Chapter 3 we examine some approaches to these kinds of definitional problems.

Now consider a somewhat different kind of question: *Under what conditions, if any, is a communicator justified in lying?* Both the terms "lying" and "justified" must be carefully defined before inquiry can proceed, particularly since the meanings stipulated for them have a powerful influence on the direction taken by the inquirer. Contrast, for example, two possible approaches to defining "justified," one emphasizing the communicative effects of lying (e.g., "justified lying occurs when the falsehood furthers the communicator's desired outcomes") and one stressing the ethical aspects of the communication transaction (e.g., "justified lying occurs when the falsehood does not violate the moral obligations of the communicator"). If the inquirer opts for the first approach to defining "justified," his or her subsequent activities center on a *question of fact:* Under what conditions, if any, does untruthful communication aid the communicator in achieving his or her desired outcomes? If the inquirer chooses the second approach, a *question of value* becomes the focal point of the inquiry: Under what conditions, if any, do the moral obligations of a communicator permit untruthful communication? As we emphasize throughout this book, factual and value questions differ distinctly, and whether one or the other constitutes the focus of inquiry is often determined by the way the inquirer defines the key terms of the question.

Two crucial points emerge from the preceding examples. *First, whenever people engage in the process of inquiry, they must almost invariably deal first with questions of definition.* Putting it another way, the resolution of definitional questions is seldom an end in itself, but rather an indispensable means toward advancing inquiry into other types of communication questions. This chapter itself illustrates this fact. While most of our efforts are directed toward development of a conceptual framework (i.e., a series of related definitions) for viewing the process of communication inquiry, the framework itself is not the end product; *it is useful only insofar as it enables you to conduct communication inquiry more effectively.*

Second, concern for questions of definition is an integral aspect of the process of communication inquiry. This point follows directly from the first one; in fact, it might even be viewed as a corollary. No matter what kind of question people ask about human communication, they must always be concerned with defining their terms carefully. If they are not clear about the meaning assigned to terms, they can neither interpret the thrust of the question nor decide on the procedures they must employ to answer it. Moreover, other potentially interested inquirers will be saddled with the same handicaps. And since inquirers frequently wish to communicate their results to a larger audience, this fact is of upmost significance.

When has a question of definition been resolved satisfactorily? Unfortunately, this is a thorny question, for a great deal of nonsense and fuzzy thinking permeate disputes about definitional issues. Recall the hypothetical dialogue between Kate and Fred at the outset of this section. After Fred was caught up in the argument, he accused Kate of lacking a clear conception of what "communication *really is*" and cited a definition from a book to illustrate the error of her ways. Kate responded by branding the book's authors *"wrong"* and by pointing to a definition of "communication" that supported her viewpoint. From the dispute's direction, one could easily conclude that Kate and Fred were locked in controversy over the question: What *is* "communication"?

Such a conclusion would be erroneous. When someone stipulates a definition for a term—in this case, "communication"—he or she is not asserting what the term really "is," though the statement itself sounds as if that is what the speaker is about. Instead, the person is only saying, "When I use the term 'communication' I mean . . . ." Once one grasps this simple, yet profound, distinction, it becomes transparently clear that *it is meaningless to talk about the truth or falsity, the correctness or incorrectness, or the rightness or wrongness of a definition.* In short, except in one limited sense which we will mention later, definitions are neither true nor false.

The trap that lures the unwary into believing that words have *a* correct meaning was originally set by Plato and Aristotle. These two revered thinkers espoused an *essentialist* approach to definition; they contended that definitions are statements describing the essence of a thing. The term to be defined is *a name* for the essence of a thing, while the defining formula is *the description* of that essence. Both Plato and Aristotle, when faced with the obvious question concerning the source of knowledge of these essences, invoked a faculty of intellectual intuition that enables one to visualize essences and to find out which definition is the *correct* one.

It is difficult to exaggerate the mischief perpetrated by those who subscribe to this Aristotelian, or essentialist, view of definition. The British philosopher, Karl Popper, captures the difficulty nicely:

Aristotelianism and related philosophies have told us for such a long time how important it is to get a precise knowledge of the meaning of our terms that we are all inclined to believe it. And we continue to cling to this creed in spite of the unquestionable fact that philosophy, which for twenty centuries has worried about the meaning of its terms, is not only full of verbalism but also appallingly vague and ambiguous, while a science like physics which worries hardly at all about terms and their meanings, but about facts instead, has achieved great precision. (1966, pp. 18-19)

. . . The development of thought since Aristotle could, I think, be summed up by saying that every discipline as long as it used the Aristotelian method of definition has remained arrested in a state of empty verbiage and barren scholasticism, and that the degree to which the various sciences have been able to make any progress depended upon the degree to which they have been able to get rid of the essentialist method. (p. 9)

As we understand Popper, he does not contend that it is unimportant for us to know what we mean when we use a word, but rather: (1) that words do not have *a* correct meaning, and (2) that few, if any, significant problems can ever be solved solely by worrying about definitions of terms. To illustrate these points, consider the concept *attitude,* a term often encountered in questions dealing with communication inquiry. We have witnessed numerous long discussions about the meaning of "attitude." While such encounters make for lively, entertaining coffee shop dialogue, the participants usually appear to assume that there is *a* correct meaning for the term and that, if it could be unearthed, a host of problems could magically be laid to rest. Both assumptions are patently false. The term "attitude" does not have *a* correct meaning; it can be defined in many ways depending upon the purposes of the individual who does the defining. Moreover, if by some act of mystical fiat a "correct" definition could be established, and if everyone could agree on its "correctness," few important problems associated with the construct *attitude* would be solved. For most of the crucial issues center not on the term's meaning, but on the kinds of experiences, communicative and otherwise, that foster certain attitudes and, in turn, on the ways that these attitudes affect the individual's ongoing social transactions.

CASE 1:   *"Do as I say, not as I do!": The so-called attitudes-versus-behavior problem.*

Despite the time and energy that communication scholars have devoted to attempting to discover the meaning of "attitude," the term continues to create problems for inquirers. One of these problems—

the so-called attitudes-versus-behavior problem—illustrates the pit-falls of an essentialist approach to definition.

Typically, theorists have defined the term "attitude" so that it represents an intervening process that occurs inside a person after exposure to some stimulus and prior to the performance of some response. For example, if someone asks, "What do you think of Joe Blow?" (stimulus) and the person to whom the question is directed answers, "I think Joe Blow is a #&*$#!" (response), then the question-asker would probably *infer* that the question-answerer has a negative attitude toward Joe Blow. The term "infer" is stressed to indicate that as the term "attitude" is usually defined, it cannot be directly observed; rather, the existence of certain attitudes is inferred from observing a person's behavior.

To generate observations for making such inferences about attitudes, numerous "attitude scales" have been developed. All of these scales operate on the principle of asking people how they feel about things. Thus, if someone says that the feminist movement is "good, positive, and socially desirable," he or she is assumed to have a positive attitude about the feminist movement; but if he or she responds that the feminist movement is "bad, negative, and socially undesirable," a negative attitude is inferred.

Several decades ago a man named LaPiere (1934) formally documented something that everyone has known for thousands of years: people's verbal behavior does not always correspond with certain of their other actions. For instance, a person may say that he or she supports the feminist movement but refuse to contribute money to a fund-raising campaign for a feminist organization or to expend the energy needed to venture forth on a cold, winter night to hear a speech by Gloria Steinem.

This disparity between verbal behavior and other actions so plagues social psychologists and communication inquirers that they have coined a label for it: the attitudes-versus-behavior problem. This label is totally inappropriate for describing the problem, since it implies that the verbal responses obtained on attitude scales are, in some mysterious way, *the attitude,* while actions such as giving money or attending speeches are *behaviors.* Actually, of course, all of these responses represent behavior: *paper-and-pencil measures obtained on attitude scales are a form of verbal behavior.* Thus the problem, while real enough, centers not on the relationship of attitudes to behavior, but on the relationship of verbal expressions of an attitude to other classes of apparently consistent attitudinal responses.

Most important, confusion could probably have been avoided if students of communication had not fallen into the trap of thinking that "attitude" *means* "an individual's paper-and-pencil responses to an attitude scale." The consistency with which such scales were used to generate observations for making inferences about attitudes caused inquirers to perceive that the *essence* of an "attitude" is to be found in these scale-marking responses, even though their own conceptual writings point out the error of such an assumption.

The attitudes-versus-behavior problem has been extensively pursued, and the following references will give you additional information about the controversy:

Campbell, D. T. (1966). Social Attitudes and Other Acquired Behavioral Dispositions. In S. Koch (ed.), *Psychology: A Study of a Science*, Vol. 6, pp. 94–172. New York: McGraw-Hill.

LaPiere, R. T. (1934). Attitudes versus Actions. *Social Forces* **13**: 230–237.

Liska, A. E., ed. (1975). *The Consistency Controversy*. New York: John Wiley & Sons.

Miller, G. R. (1967). A Crucial Problem in Attitude Research. *Quarterly Journal of Speech* **53**: 235–240.

Wicker, A. W. (1969). Attitudes versus Actions: The Relationship of Verbal and Overt Behavioral Responses to Attitude Objects. *Journal of Social Issues* **25**: 41–78.

Thus, an inquirer cannot gauge definitional success by verifying the correctness of his or her choices, nor will much progress result from engaging in endless quibbles about the "true" meanings of words. How, then, is the soundness of a definition to be assessed? We subscribe to one overarching criterion: *the soundness of a definition is determined by its utility.* Hence, when engaged in the process of communication inquiry, a question of definition has been satisfactorily resolved when a useful definition has been stipulated.

We realize that when pitched at this level of abstraction our utility criterion may seem to beg the question; you may legitimately be asking how one determines the usefulness of a definition. Obviously, this is a functional issue; a definition is useful to the extent that it furthers the purposes of the defining party, or parties. When you are engaged in ordinary communication with someone else, your definitions are useful if they result in shared meanings. Consequently, in your daily communicative transactions, it is generally wise to use words in ways that conform to *standardized usage*. If you use the term "table" to refer to the object that most people designate as "chair," you are not necessarily wrong or incorrect, but you will have considerable difficulty obtaining a seat with a back rest, and you may find that people brand you as eccentric or even unstable.

Most of the matters discussed in this book relate directly or indirectly to factors that weigh on the utility of definitions. Consequently, we will limit ourselves at this point to a single illustration of the utility criterion. Specifically, we will stipulate our definition of "communication" promised earlier in this chapter.

When we use the term "communication" we mean "an intentional, transactional, symbolic process" (Miller and Steinberg, 1975). Our choice of a definition stipulated earlier by Miller and Steinberg does not imply that we judge this definition to be the "correct" or "right" one; instead, it suggests that since we have similar reasons for defining the term, the definition should be useful.[3]

Our purposes for defining "communication" are twofold: first, we wish to limit the problem area, or range of phenomena, with which we will deal; second, we seek to indicate what we deem the most advantageous perspective from which to view the process of communication inquiry. In respect to our first purpose, the key definitional terms are "intentional" and "symbolic"; in respect to our second objective, the relevant terms are "transactional" and "process."

By asserting that we will call an act "communication" only if it is intentional and symbolic, we rule out a number of our daily experiences. Thus, while passing by your house or your dormitory room, an acquaintance may overhear you singing in the shower and, as a result of this innocent eavesdropping, may change his or her estimate of your disposition. Do your singing and your acquaintance's subsequent change in attitude constitute an instance of communication? Only in the unlikely circumstance that you *intended* that your singing be overheard, either to cause someone to alter his or her estimate of you or for some other reason.[4] In a similar vein, while hurrying to class you may round a corner and painfully smash into another student. Have the two of you "communicated"? Not under the terms of our definition, for none of the actions of either party can be characterized as intentional or symbolic.

Contrast these situations with the opening night performance of a professional singer or the threatening gesture of a clenched fist brandished by a demonstrator at a police officer. Here the behaviors involved appear to be both intentional and symbolic. Hence, the definition we have stipulated dictates that we call these events "communication."

Certainly, we would not accuse you of being "wrong" or "incorrect" if you chose to call your shower serenade or your untimely collision "communication"; in fact, under certain circumstances, you might find it useful to think of these events in this way. All we have advanced is the relatively modest proposal that we find it useful to restrict the range of phenomena encompassed by the term "communication." Our definition specifies the grounds for inclusion or exclusion of specific phenomena.

The terms "transactional" and "process" impose a particular perspective for viewing the process of communication inquiry. By making them part of the definition, we go on record as favoring a continuous, mutually interdependent conception of communication, rather than a temporally-bounded, linear view. Historically, most definitions have been linear, not transactional: "communication" has been defined as an activity involving the transmission of messages by a source to a receiver for the purpose of affecting the latter's behavior. Our decision to abandon this perspective mirrors our belief that the goals of communication inquiry are better served by adopting a transactional perspective, a perspective that stresses the relational interdependence of communicators and their reciprocal influence on each other.

Note that at this time our commitment to the greater utility of a transactional approach stands largely as an article of faith. We are saying that if inquirers think about communication transactionally and frame questions from a transactional perspective, knowledge about human communication will increase at an accelerated rate.

Obviously, our belief reflects a "proof of the pudding is in the eating" dimension of utility; communication inquiry must proceed along these lines, and at some future time an informed judgment concerning progress must be made. Put differently, the question of whether a linear or a transactional view of communication will yield greater knowledge returns is itself an empirical one. Thus, as evidence accumulates, we may be forced to concede that we made the wrong definitional choice.

We have illustrated how the utility criterion applies to the formulation and stipulation of a definition. The resultant product represents only one of many possible definitions of "communication." *For our purposes,* our definition seems useful. Other inquirers—and for that matter, we ourselves—faced with different circumstances might opt for a different answer to the question: "What shall I call 'communication'?" Regardless of the precise definition, thoughtful inquirers are cautioned to avoid pointless arguments over its correctness and incorrectness and to focus instead on its probable utility.

Earlier we indicated that there is one limited sense in which one can meaningfully speak of the truth or falsity of statements regarding the definitions of particular terms. Suppose someone queries: "In our society, what are the most frequent meanings that people have for the term 'communication'?" After investigating this question, he or she reports an answer. Others may legitimately question the truth or falsity of this knowledge claim. They may even replicate the study to see if they come up with similar results.

CASE 2:   *How people feel about words: Dimensions of meaning.*

In 1957, three researchers at the University of Illinois, Charles Osgood, George Suci, and Percy Tannenbaum, reported a classic series of studies concerning the dimensions of meaning that people have for words. Every person who participated in the studies was given a number of concepts (e.g., "Mother," "Federal Aid to Education," "Prostitute") and was asked to respond to each one on a series of seven-interval scales bounded by polar adjectives such as "honest-dishonest," "good-bad," "fast-slow," "active-passive," "strong-weak," and "potent-impotent." Using a correlational technique known as factor analysis, Osgood, Suci, and Tannenbaum were able to see how the various sets of scales grouped together to comprise dimensions of meaning.

Three primary dimensions were identified: an *evaluation* dimension, an *activity* dimension, and a *potency* dimension. The evaluation dimension reflected a measure of attitude toward the concept; in fact, the scales that grouped on that dimension have since been widely used by persuasion researchers to index attitudes and attitude change. The activity dimension, represented by such scales as "fast-slow" and "active-passive," reflected a movement or energy-expending continuum, while the potency dimension focused on the perceived power of the concept.

The instrument developed in these studies is known as the *semantic differential,* and Osgood, Suci, and Tannenbaum argue that it measures three dimensions of meaning which people have for concepts. Although a number of complicated methodological issues have been raised about the semantic differential, it does appear that these three dimensions of meaning emerge rather consistently and, as we indicate in Chapter 3, these same dimensions of meaning generally hold from culture to culture. The following references will give you a more detailed description of this useful method for measuring the meanings that people share for words and concepts.

Block, J. (1957). Studies in the Phenomenology of Emotions. *Journal of Abnormal and Social Psychology* **54**: 358–363.

DiVesta, F., and R. Walls (1970). Factor Analysis of the Semantic Attributes of 487 Words and Some Relationships to the Conceptual Behavior of Fifth-Grade Children. *Journal of Educational Psychology Monograph* **61**: Whole No. 6.

Osgood, C. E. (1952). The Nature and Measurement of Meaning. *Psychological Bulletin* **49**: 197–237.

Osgood, C. E., and Z. Luria (1954). A Blind Analysis of a Case of Multiple Personality Using the Semantic Differential. *Journal of Abnormal and Social Psychology* **49**: 579–591.

Osgood, C. E., G. Suci, and P. H. Tannenbaum (1957). *The Measurement of Meaning.* Urbana, Ill.: University of Illinois Press.

This exception causes no trouble as long as the following distinction is kept in mind: *Questions concerning the meanings that people have for words are questions of fact, not questions of defini-*

tion. In other words, the question, "What key concepts are included in *my definition* for the term " 'communication'?" is distinctly different from the query, "What key concepts are included in *most people's meaning* for the term " 'communication'?" Contrary to popular belief, dictionaries operate in the latter domain; they do not *stipulate* definitions for terms, rather, they *report* the meanings most commonly shared by members of our society. Consequently, such commonplaces as "The dictionary gives us the correct meanings of words," and, "Webster defines 'communication' as. . . ." miss the mark: *the dictionary is a factual compendium of shared meanings or standardized usages, not a supreme arbiter of the "correct" meaning of terms.*

In the realm of communication inquiry, however, there is an important intersection between the definitional and the factual aspects of language. Questions about human communication usually contain terms that are found in the ordinary language. By contrast, concepts of physics such as "quantum particle" and "friction coefficient" have little meaning for the nonphysicist. The correspondence between ordinary language and the language of inquiry offers both advantages and disadvantages for the student of communication. On the one hand, it ensures that assertions about human communication will make at least some intuitive sense to the layman. On the other hand, the use of ordinary language poses potential hazards for inquirer and layman alike. Since the terms used are part of everybody's vocabulary, they sense that they know what the terms mean. Should the inquirer stipulate a definition that does not jibe with the ordinary meaning of the term, twin risks are encountered: those who are not students of communication may think they understand the intended meaning of the inquirer when in fact they do not; or, even more likely, they may accuse the inquirer of using language incorrectly, of "not knowing" the meaning of a particular term. We will comment further on these risks in later chapters.

Questions of Fact

Kate and Fred are at it again:

KATE: "Boy, we sure need everyone's cooperation if we're going to ride out this energy crisis. I wonder how the government can convince people to observe fuel-saving measures?"

FRED: "I favor a get-tough approach. Government officials ought to devote a lot of their time to informing the people what these measures are and making it quite clear what will happen if they're not obeyed. Loss of driving privileges, reduction of fuel allotments, even jail sentences—that's the way to handle it."

KATE: "I don't think threats and fear are effective ways to persuade people. They resent that kind of bullying, and they rebel when they have the chance. Or they just distort what you're trying to tell them, so all your communication doesn't make any difference."

FRED: "People may not like coercion, but it sure works. My dad says the main reason people went along with rationing during World War II was that the government made it clear what would happen to them if they didn't."

KATE: "I don't buy that! I think people felt a sense of patriotism and pride during that war and that they observed rationing measures because they felt it was their duty as American citizens. If your theory is correct, why was prohibition such a failure?"

FRED: "Well, for one thing, I don't think the government followed through vigorously enough; while they communicated what would happen to violators, they didn't back their threats up. Then, too, there were other factors. . ."

At this point, we will leave Kate and Fred to their argument. As with their previous conversation, you undoubtedly have a feel for the direction their dialogue will take.

Unquestionably, the two antagonists are throwing words around loosely. To determine areas of assent and dissent, they would find it useful to define terms such as "threats," "fear," "coercion," and "pride." Still, the crux of Kate's and Fred's disagreement is not a question of definition; rather, their controversy centers on a *question of fact*—or, perhaps more accurately, on several related factual questions.

Much communication inquiry concerns questions of fact. *A question of fact poses an inquiry about some property, or proper-*

ties, of the objects, acts, or situations it mentions. Moreover, depending upon the observations that are made of these properties, questions of fact are logically amenable to "yes" or "no" answers. Stated in a declarative rather than in an interrogative sense, statements that purport to provide answers to questions of fact are either "true" or "false."

To say that questions of fact concern "properties" of the objects, acts, or situations they mention is to assert that the locus of interest for such questions resides "out there" in the external world. Consider this trivial question as an initial example: Will Smith wear a tie when he speaks to the Rotary Club tomorrow night? The question has to do with the presence or absence of a particular property of Smith at a specific point in time: a property of "tiedness" or "tie wearing." How do you answer it? You attend the speech (or send a delegate) and *observe* Smith. If you observe a property of "tiedness," you respond to the question affirmatively; if not, you respond negatively.

Although we branded as trivial the question about Smith's sartorial choices, an amazing amount of controversy is generated by such mundane issues. How many times have you heard people argue about what movie is playing at a particular theatre? About the score of last year's Super Bowl? About the winner of the Best Male Actor Award at the 1963 Academy Awards? Whether Franklin Roosevelt said "the only thing we have to fear is fear itself"? People seem to relish quibbling over these matters even when the properties in question lend themselves to easy, unambiguous observations. Perhaps when the issue centers on a past or present occurrence, most individuals are reluctant to admit that they have forgotten, or are mistaken about, their original observations.

Of course, not all questions of fact are this simple. Harken back to the central point of conflict in Kate's and Fred's dialogue: are messages containing threats and/or fear-arousing appeals effective instruments of persuasion? This is a factual question; it concerns the behavioral outcomes that will result in a communication situation blessed with certain properties. But when compared to the query about Smith's tie, it is incredibly complex. Think of all the other things that go into a message besides fear-arousing appeals. Consider the impact of the message's source; perhaps threats and fear appeals work better for some communicators than for others. Reflect on the many types of people who constitute a potential audience; might not their prior learning experiences, their personality makeups, and their beliefs and attitudes influence their perceptions of fear-arousing messages? Once an inquirer begins to inventory all the variables that may conceivably influence the answer to this question, the list quickly becomes formidably long. Indeed, while the question fits the logical requirements for factual inquiry, it is probably so broad and complex that a simple yes or no answer is next to impossible.

We can illustrate the difference in a somewhat different way by referring to a second key term in our definition of questions of fact, the term "observations." The truth or falsity of a factual statement is determined (and hence, the answer to a question of fact is provided) by making the relevant observations. Obviously, answering some questions requires more observations than are demanded for answering others. To determine if Smith is wearing a tie during his Rotary Club address necessitates but a single observation. Moreover, only Smith himself must be observed. How many observations are necessary to determine if fear-arousing messages are effective instruments of persuasion? If an inquirer wanted to know whether they are *always* effective, he or she would need to make an infinite number, assuming that communicators will continue to use fear-arousing messages. But an infinite number of observations are impossible; this is one of the logical problems associated with induction which we will cover later. Furthermore, an inquirer cannot precisely assess the persuasive impact of a message containing fear-arousing appeals without *comparing* responses to it with responses to a message devoid of such appeals and/or with responses of a group of people who receive no message at all. It is unnecessary to look at Jones to determine whether Smith is wearing a tie; it is necessary to look at the persuasive effects of a mild fear message and/or of no message at all if one wishes to assess the impact of a message containing strong fear appeals. This concept of *control*, or of using the appropriate *control groups*, will be discussed in Chapter 4.

Note also that the relevant observations may concern *past events, present events,* or *future events* (e.g., "Did Smith wear a tie yesterday?"; "Is Smith wearing a tie now?"; "Will Smith wear a tie tomorrow?"). When questions of fact deal with present or future events, *direct observation* is frequently possible, i.e., the observer may witness the event first-hand. But when questions of fact concern past events, direct observation is impossible; instead, the inquirer *observes indirectly,* usually by consulting the reports of others who have witnessed the event. Thus, while you probably believe that Abraham Lincoln said, "Four score and seven years ago . . . ," you did not directly observe a message called the Gettysburg Address—nor, for that matter, did the authors of most of the history books from which your observations concerning this event were culled.

For many questions, of course, the limitations imposed by indirect observation are trifling, at least if those conducting the inquiry are willing to grant that the writers who provided chronicles of the past have not engaged in deliberate falsehood. Suppose, however, that you are interested in the question, "What was the persuasive impact of the Gettysburg Address?" To be sure, you will encounter no shortage of historians and other witnesses who testify that the speech had an electrifying impact on the Union's supporters, that it bolstered the morale of the North, etc. Conversely, however, you will come across historians who argue that the speech received a lukewarm reception, and even a few who assert that it was an outright failure. Faced with this mixed bag of testimony, you may despair of ever answering the question.

Your problem lies not with the veracity of the various observers; it stems, rather, from a basic limitation of dealing with factual questions historically. *When attempting to reconstruct factual answers from the past, the observer has little or no opportunity to structure and to control the conditions of observation.* One cannot systematically determine how people felt before hearing Lincoln's speech, nor compare their initial feelings with their post-speech attitudes. One cannot control for other factors that may have influenced their attitudes toward the war. One cannot compare the opinions of a group who heard the speech with a comparable group who did not. Thus, when investigating questions of fact, there are inherent limits to the power of historical inquiry.

The many issues associated with question-complexity and with number and conditions of observations lead us to a third aspect of our definition of questions of fact. We have asserted that factual questions are logically amenable to yes or no answers. Here the crucial term is *logically;* it implies that when a question is factual, there are no *in principle* reasons why it cannot be answered either affirmatively or negatively.[5] But to say there are no *in principle* barriers does not deny that it may be practically impossible to provide a definitive answer at this time. Thus, an inquirer may ask: Will there be a greater number of messages sent in 1978 than there were in 1977? Certainly, there are no logical reasons why this question does not warrant a yes or no answer. Nevertheless, a definitive response must await the 1979 New Year. On the basis of observations presently available, the inquirer may project a trend and assert that 1978 will probably eclipse 1977 in number of messages sent, but it is impossible to be positive. Suppose that the energy crisis peaks early in 1978, or that the paper shortage grows even more severe. Perhaps 1978 will bring the ultimate catastrophe, a nuclear war. These, as well as a host of other political, social, and economic developments, could drastically curtail the number of messages sent in 1978.

Thus, because of the empirical constraints imposed on inquiry, most factual questions of greatest import to communication inquirers can only be answered *"probably yes"* or *"probably no."* This is particularly true when the questions concern *empirical generalizations*—i.e., statements that assert what will usually occur under some particular set of communicative circumstances—rather than *singular facts*. Thus, the question, "Does Miller perceive Nicholson as a highly credible source?" deals with a singular fact and can probably be answered yes or no. Still, while the question may be vital to Nicholson if he is trying to get Miller to do something for him, it has little import for the general process of communication inquiry. By contrast, the question: "Are high-credible communicators more persuasive than low-credible communicators?" focuses on an empirical generalization of great significance to communication inquiry.[6] Here, only a reckless student of communication would respond to this query with an unqualified yes or no; instead, a more cautious answer would be, "Usually," "It depends," or most likely, "Yes, other things being equal." The rub is that our inquirer does not presently know if other things *are* equal, or, for that matter, *what* other things must be equal, for such knowledge is one of the hallmarks of a *deterministic system,* an objective far from realization in the domain of communication inquiry.

One other aspect of our definition merits brief scrutiny. To many of you, it may seem strange to talk about the truth or falsity of *facts.* If so, you are on the right wave-length, for even though people sometimes erroneously speak this way ("Now I'll give you the *true* facts of the case"), facts are neither true nor false—*facts just are.* In the process of conducting communication inquiry, however, the questions asked and the answers offered are structured linguistically; while inquirers observe *"the facts,"* they report their observations via *"statements of fact."* And, of course, any statement that alleges a fact can be either true or false; to use an improbable example, the assertion, "Most human communicators have two heads," represents a false statement of fact, while the statement, "Most human communicators have one head," conforms with our observations of the property of "communicator headedness."

Having explored some of the implications of our definition of questions of fact, we want to return to Kate's and Fred's dialogue. An analysis of the structure of the dialogue reveals the complex process involved in conducting inquiry about factual questions.

KATE: Raised a question of fact about a specific matter of policy. She asked what communication strategies the government could employ to persuade our citizens to observe fuel-saving measures. (Note that the question dealt with present and future communication events.)

FRED: Responded with a statement of fact intended to answer Kate's question. He said that the government's most effective communication strategy involves the use of messages containing threats and fear-arousing appeals.

KATE: Took issue with Fred's statement by questioning the truth of the empirical generalization. She said that messages containing fear-arousing appeals are not effective instruments of persuasion. (Note that this statement of fact concerns past, present, and future events.)

FRED: Attempted to support the truth of the empirical generalization by advancing a statement of fact concerning a past event. He stated that the government's use of fear-arousing messages during World War II persuaded citizens to observe rationing programs.

KATE: Denied the truth of Fred's statement of fact and attacked the empirical generalization by advancing a contradictory statement of fact concerning another past event. She said that the government's use of fear-arousing messages during prohibition was ineffective in persuading citizens to obey the law. (Note that Kate referred to the empirical generalization as "Your [Fred's] theory." Although the term "theory" is often used this way in daily discourse, such a usage does not conform with the definition of theory stipulated in Chapter 2 of this book.)

FRED: Disputed Kate's statement of fact by asserting that the conditions necessary to ensure the effectiveness of fear-arousing messages were not met during prohibition. In other words, he did not deny the truth of Kate's factual statement; instead, he argued that the conditions present did not permit a valid test of the empirical generalization.

Several features of the structure of the dialogue deserve emphasis. First, observe that while the discussion commenced with Kate raising a factual question about a specific matter of policy, the dispute quickly centered on the truth or falsity of the type of factual statement we have called "empirical generalization." Moreover, if Kate and Fred could agree on the truth or falsity of the generalization—or perhaps more accurately, on the conditions under which the generalization will hold and the conditions under which it will not— they would be likely to have less difficulty reaching accord on the questions that relate to singular facts.

Questions of fact involving empirical generalizations are of crucial import to the process of communication inquiry.[7] Another, better-known label for such statements is "*law.*" In the domain of factual inquiry, laws are descriptive statements about the way phenomena behave. Laws have typically been defined as "If . . . then" statements; e.g., "If a message contains strong fear-arousing appeals, then its audience will be persuaded." Laws may also be defined as "statements concerning the ways in which specified objects will behave in specified environments" (Miller, 1972, p. 28). Using this definition, a law might be stated as follows: "When persons are placed in a communication environment where they are exposed to messages containing strong fear-arousing appeals, they behave by changing their attitudes and behaviors to conform with the recommendations found in the message."

Much communication inquiry concerned with questions of fact proceeds along the lines illustrated in Fig. 1.1. The inquirer starts with a question based on the truth or falsity of an empirical generalization. The inquirer usually assumes the truth of the generalization and from it *deduces* a factual statement about what will happen in a specific situation that conforms with the empirical generalization. The product of this deduction, which is an *anticipation statement* about a future event, is called a *hypothesis*. The inquirer tests the hypothesis by making the appropriate observations, reaches a conclusion regarding its probable truth or falsity, and relates his or her conclusion to the original empirical generalization.

The process we have just described is sometimes called the classical, or hypothetico-deductive approach to science. Naturally, things do not always proceed this neatly. In some cases, an inquirer may begin with a number of related observations, state an empirical generalization that seems to capture the similarities inherent in the observations, and then test the generalization systematically, using the procedures outlined in the preceding paragraph and illustrated in Fig. 1.1. Thus, someone might observe a child being scolded by a parent, a college student being reprimanded by a professor, and a suspect being interrogated by a police officer; note that the child, the student, and the suspect all engaged in considerable nonfluent behavior; and formulate the empirical generalization that people placed in stressful situations are quite nonfluent. It would then be possible to test the generalization in a situation where the conditions of observation could be controlled to eliminate, or at least equalize, the possible effects of other variables.

Much of the content of succeeding chapters, particularly Chapter 4, focuses on the procedures for making observations which bear on questions of fact. Moreover, it will become clear that empirical limitations associated with the procedures used in gathering and interpreting observations require the inquirer to talk in terms of *probable* truth or falsity, even though there are no *in principle* obstacles to designating a specific hypothesis as either true or false. Finally, it will also become apparent that one of the chief tasks of inquiry is the refinement and extension of present empirical generalizations. In other words, existing generalizations may not

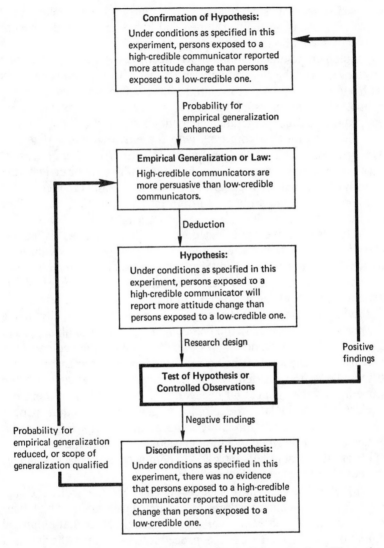

Fig. 1.1 *A Typical Approach to Factual Inquiry in Communication. (The authors would like to thank Dr. Theodore Clevenger, Jr., for his helpful suggestions.)*

specify the characteristics of the objects or the environments precisely enough.

CASE 3: *When to cry wolf: The persuasive efficacy of fear-arousing appeals*

In Book II of *The Rhetoric* Aristotle writes of the persuasive impact of fear. Certainly, persuaders in our society make extensive use of fear-arousing appeals. For instance, the socialization of many children rests largely on negative sanctions and threats imposed by parents and teachers. Each day the media contain many messages that rely on the persuasive efficacy of fear-arousing appeals.

But do such appeals work? In 1953 Irving Janis and Seymour Feshbach conducted one of the first studies designed to investigate this question. These researchers defined a strong fear-arousing appeal as one that stresses the harmful consequences of failure to conform with message recommendations. Groups of high-school students heard messages emphasizing the importance of proper dental hygiene. Strong fear-arousing messages contained a number of references to the painful effects resulting from improper tooth care, as well as several pictures of diseased gums and badly decayed teeth. These references and pictures were omitted from the mild fear message.

Janis and Feshbach concluded that the mild fear message was more persuasive than the message containing strong fear-arousing appeals. They attributed this result to a kind of Freudian repression mechanism: students who heard the strong fear message became anxious and fearful and to avoid such unpleasant feelings repressed, or "tuned out," the message content.

Initially, then, it may appear that Janis and Feshbach confirmed the following empirical generalization about persuasive communication: mild fear-arousing messages are more persuasive than strong fear messages. Actually the matter is not nearly this simple. Since Janis and Feshbach's original undertaking, literally scores of studies have been conducted to examine systematically the effects of other variables on the persuasive impact of fear-arousing messages. Although a complete inventory of the findings would require several pages, the following later results illustrate some of the restrictions that must be attached to the initial empirical generalization:

1. If the message recommendations are unambiguously stated and can be easily carried out, a strong fear message is more persuasive than a mild fear message.

2. If the source has high initial credibility, a strong fear message has greater persuasive impact than its mild fear counterpart.

3. If the strong fear message stresses harmful *social,* rather than *physical* consequences, it is likely to be more persuasive than a mild fear message. (Think, for instance, of all the television commercials underscoring the harmful social consequences that may result from failure to purchase the product.)

By now, the lesson should be clear: it is difficult to develop simple empirical generalizations about something as complicated as human communication. What usually happens is that researchers start with a simple generalization which is then refined and rendered more complex by subsequent research. The following references illustrate more fully how this process has worked in the arena of fear-arousing message appeals.

Higbee, K. L. (1969). Fifteen Years of Fear Arousal: Research on Threat Appeals: 1953–1968. *Psychological Bulletin* **72:** 426–444.

Janis, I. L., and S. Feshbach (1953). Effects of Fear-Arousing Communications. *Journal of Abnormal and Social Psychology* **48:** 78–92.

Leventhal, H. (1967). Fear: For Your Health. *Psychology Today* **1:** 54–58.

Miller, G. R., and M. A. Hewgill (1966). Some Recent Research on Fear-Arousing Message Appeals. *Speech Monographs* **33:** 377–391.

Powell, F. A., and G. R. Miller (1967). Social Approval and Disapproval Cues in Anxiety-Arousing Communications. *Speech Monographs* **32:** 152–159

Of course, as our hypothetical dialogue indicates, there are other ways of testing the truth of an empirical generalization. Rather than stating a hypothesis and structuring a situation designed to provide observations for testing it, the inquirer may look to the past and *may identify historical incidents that embrace the use of particular communicative strategies and then attempt to assess their effectiveness.* We will have more to say about the uses and limits of this historical approach in Chapter 4.

Kate's and Fred's dialogue illustrates another point worth underscoring: *most of the factual questions that interest communication inquirers bear upon the outcomes, or effects, of communication.* Stated differently, inquirers are usually concerned with the ways that certain features of the communication environment influence the ongoing or subsequent behaviors of the transactants themselves. Here the term "behaviors" is used broadly. Like Kate and Fred, most people often equate "behaviors" with the success or failure of a persuasive message: were the message recipients induced to believe or to act in ways consistent with the communicator's intent? Inquirers need not, and should not, restrict themselves to this limited sphere of factual inquiry. For instance, prior communicative behaviors undoubtedly influence present and future communication; prior messages may have an impact, both quantitatively and substantively, on future messages. In a similar vein, communicators develop expectations, or *rules,* about the ways they should communicate in certain situations, and these rules unquestionably exert a powerful behavioral impact on the transaction. Thus, Berger (1973) found that initial transactions—the "getting acquainted" stage—invariably center on a certain kind of content; specifically, biographical information such as age, home, marital status, academic major or job, and interests or hobbies. Even when the transactants are enjoined not to converse about these topics, they apparently cannot resist, suggesting that their initial needs and expectations demand the airing of certain information. The range of factual questions dealing with behavioral outcomes is almost limitless, and each is fair game for the communication inquirer.

A final point about factual inquiry provides us with a convenient transition to the next section of this chapter. We have already emphasized that our understanding of a question's thrust hinges on careful definition of its terms. This same injunction applies to statements offered as answers to a specific type of question. In particular, it is often hard to interpret statements which contain terms that can be used in a *factual* or a *value* sense. Consider the following four statements:

1. "Of all the fund-raisers you could hire, Rita is the *best.*"
2. "Joe is the *best* liar around."
3. "It is *best* not to gossip about people."
4. "Democratic group leaders are the *best.*"

Some persons would contend that all four statements are value judgments, since all contain the word "best." The way we have analyzed questions of fact and the way we will analyze questions of value causes us to reject this position; instead, we hold that terms such as "best" can be used in either a factual or a value sense. Thus, in the first sentence, "best" is used in a factual, "means-ends" sense; the sentence asserts that if you want to ensure maximum returns from a fund-raising campaign, you should hire Rita—an assertion it is possible to label true or false. Sentence 2 uses "best" in a factual, "of its kind" sense; it alleges that if one seeks to rate people's skill at the dubious art of lying convincingly, Joe rates highest. Again, procedures could be devised for determining the truth or falsity of the statement.

Sentence 3 is particularly ambiguous. If the person uttering the statement means that avoidance of gossip will enhance one's social and economic status, minimize interpersonal strife, etc., "best" is used in the factual, means-ends sense of Sentence 1; if the person means that it is ethically reprehensible to gossip, "best" is used in an intrinsic, value sense.

Finally, Sentence 4 most unambiguously meets the conditions for a value judgment. While the speaker may conceivably be using "best" in a means-ends sense (i.e., the group will get more done with less discord), it seems more likely that this is an expression of a value preference regarding leadership style, an assertion that the most moral, ethical approach to group leadership is manifested by the democratic leader.

The important point of these examples is that it is impossible to determine the intent of a question or a statement without considering it in context.[8] Factual questions may contain terms such as "good" or "best"; conversely, value queries need not necessarily employ these words. This distinction will become clearer as we move on to a discussion of questions of value.

Questions of Value

Our intrepid debaters, Kate and Fred, never seem to tire of controversy:

FRED: "I've been reading some of this research that supposedly shows there are genetic differences in intelligence between whites and blacks. I don't think that sort of material should be publicized."

KATE: "Surely, you wouldn't want to censor scientists. I think they should be allowed to do research on problems of their choice and to communicate their findings to others."

FRED: "But there are ways that science can conflict with our society's values, both in the ways it goes about research and in the results it reports. I suppose a lot of people in Germany in the thirties thought it would be unwise to put restrictions on scientific research, too."

KATE: "I don't think your analogy holds. Do you have evidence that the research you were reading was poorly done? If not, it seems we ought to weigh the findings carefully and think about their implications for our society."

FRED: "Maybe you think my analogy is wrong, but if you were one of those poor people in the South who were used for those venereal-disease studies, you might change your mind. Now as to my having evidence about the research's quality, I think you miss the point. I'm saying that *even* if it is done well, it should still be avoided, for it's dealing with problems and reaching conclusions that are repugnant to our democratic values."

KATE: "Oh, you're saying that there are certain areas where scientists shouldn't meddle, huh?"

FRED: "Right!"

KATE: "Well, I sure can't agree with that. Intellectual censorship is foreign to our values, too. Moreover, maybe if there are genetic differences, we're being unfair . . . ."

This exchange between Kate and Fred differs from their two previous conversations. Once again, some terms are used loosely, and some factual assertions are introduced into the dispute. But neither questions of definition nor questions of fact constitute the crux of Kate's and Fred's disagreement; instead, they are at odds over a *question of value*.

People constantly dispute questions of value. *A question of value poses an inquiry concerning the ethical or aesthetic judgment of an object, act, or situation; it asks what moral or artistic value should be assigned to something. Since questions of value concern the ethical and aesthetic assessment of objects, acts, or situations rather than properties of the objects, acts, or situations themselves, they are not logically amenable to yes or no answers. Stated declaratively, statements that purport to provide answers to questions of value are neither true nor false.* Whereas the locus of disputes about factual questions lies "out there" in the objects, acts, or situations themselves, the locus of disputes concerning value questions lies within the conflicting mental judgments of the disagreeing parties.

Those of you who are familiar with the study of ethics will recognize that our position embraces the commonsense core of *ethical relativism*. A conflicting position, *ethical absolutism*, argues that value judgments are either true or false, that they do not differ from questions of fact in this respect. We disagree with this position, opting instead to view value judgments as *prescriptive* (i.e., mandating the ways people *ought* to behave) and statements of fact as *descriptive* (i.e., detailing the ways people *actually do* behave). Although a thorough analysis of the two positions transcends the scope of this book, we will attempt to illustrate why we find the relativistic position more useful and more compelling.

Suppose you make two statements: (1) "Johnson is wearing a gray suit," and (2) "Johnson is an evil man." The two statements *sound* similar, but their apparent similarity is misleading. The first assertion is a statement of fact; it refers to an alleged property of Johnson: his graysuitedness. The second sentence, however, is a value judgment; while it *appears* to refer to a quality of Johnson (his "evilness"), it actually describes your predispositions and attitudes toward, your moral assessment of, Johnson. Perhaps the difference between the two statements can best be understood by contrasting the situations that would exist should people disagree about them.

For one thing, people are less likely to disagree with you about the first statement. When you say someone is wearing a gray suit, has brown hair, or is wearing glasses—i.e., when you make factual assertions about various properties of the person—there is usually general assent. To be sure, arguments may arise over conflicting observations; e.g., "His suit looks more like it's light blue to me." When they do, it becomes necessary to sharpen relevant definitions or to refine relevant observations. Or perhaps the other party may yield to your greater observational acuity; "It still looks light blue to me, but you've always had a sharper eye for colors, so if you say it's gray, it must be." Though such disputes do arise, agreement is usually negotiated.

But what if one party continues to disagree? Suppose you are in a room with 20 people when you make your observation about Johnson's suit. Nineteen of them agree with you, but the remaining individual responds, "You're wrong, Johnson is wearing a maroon suit." Immediately, everyone in the room seeks to show the dissenter the perceptual error of his ways. He is told to look again, to get his eyes tested, to point out whom he believes to be Johnson, to lay off the bottle for the rest of the evening—in short, to get his observational wits about him. Should he stubbornly continue his dissent, the others in the room, including yourself, will conclude that he is hopelessly color blind, incredibly drunk, or suffering from some mental disorder.

Now switch roles for a moment and assume that you are the only dissenter in such a situation. How are you likely to feel? We would predict that you will be frightened, anxious, and perhaps even believe that you have suddenly lost touch with reality. In a classic experiment dealing with the effects of group pressure, Asch (1951) asked subjects to match a stimulus line with another line of the same length which was presented among a set of other lines unequal in length to the stimulus line. The judgments were made in a group setting, and the other group members were actually confederates, rather than naive subjects. On some of the trials, the confederates deliberately responded incorrectly. Not only did the subjects' responses often conform with the erroneous judgments, many of them also reported that they felt confused and anxious when their own perceptions did not jibe with the group's.

Now consider the kind of situation that exists if there is disagreement about the assertion, "Johnson is an evil man." Certainly, such value pronouncements often spark conflict. Still, there are times when almost everyone will assent to a value judgment, for our culture ensures some commonality in the value preferences that are learned. Thus, if a man beats his children, steals from the poor, and cheats friends, most of his neighbors are likely to call him "evil." But unlike "child-beating," "evilness" is not a property of the man nor his actions; it is a shorthand moral assessment based upon the assessor's attitudes and beliefs concerning the man's behavior.

Consequently, should nothing change about the conditions in our hypothetical crowded room except the statement that you make about Johnson, the situation would still be altered drastically. Our lone dissenter will still endure a great deal of social pressure to change his view—i.e., to agree that Johnson is an evil man—but a persistent dissent will not cause others to perceive the dissenter as perceptually unbalanced.[9] Under certain conditions (though probably not in this case), continued recalcitrance may even be viewed as an act of courage, rather than a psychological aberration. Caws (1967) captures the contrast between the two situations nicely, asserting that "we would all admit that a lone dissenter who insisted that a course of action was wrong when everybody else said it was right would exhibit a kind of human dignity, whereas somebody who insisted that something was green when everybody else said it was blue would merely look silly" (p. 64).

If the answers to factual and value questions were logically identical, these situational differences would not exist. At an intuitive, commonsense level, people usually realize that when they ask a question of fact, they are inquiring whether something does or does not exist "out there," seeking answers that are either true or false. By contrast, they sense that when they ask a question of value they have deserted the external world of properties and have instead requested someone's moral or ethical assessment of an object, act, or situation. Such assessments, while sometimes of great import, are incapable of being verified as true or false.[10]

Still, people are occasionally lulled into believing that both factual and value statements refer to things that are "out there." Why does this happen? Typical linguistic structures are one of the chief culprits. As we have already indicated, people ask value questions and utter value judgments in the same linguistic ways that they deal with the realm of facts. They say, "That is a beautiful picture," rather than, "Something about that picture causes in me a sense of aesthetic appreciation." Or they declare, "Jane is immoral," instead of, "Something about Jane causes in me a sense of moral revulsion." This is probably not surprising, since the former statements are more crisp and vivid. Surely, you will be more successful in galvanizing public opinion against Jane by calling *her* immoral than by saying she inspires a sense of moral revulsion in *you*. But if the goal is careful analysis rather than practical persuasion, it is important to underscore the difference in the way that statements about the two types of questions should be structured.

Two possible reservations about our definition of value questions should be anticipated. First, it may appear that words such as "evil," "noble," "ugly," or "beautiful" are nothing more than summary labels for a number of properties. After all, it becomes laborious to say repeatedly that a man assaults others, cheats, lies, hoards, etc. Are people not just eliminating this verbal drudgery by condensing these many behaviors into the succinct statement, "He is evil"?

It must be granted that observation of certain socially unacceptable behaviors by a person often causes others to render a moral assessment of that person. Nevertheless, when we say a person is evil, we are saying *something more* (or perhaps more accurately, *something different*) than when we say that the person has been known to assault, rob, and cheat. After all, many people concede that Robin Hood was a thief, yet call him noble, not evil. Moreover, if two people disagree about a value question, one may grant the other the truth of numerous factual statements and still dispute the central value judgment. Thus, someone may respond to your assertion concerning Johnson's evilness thus: "I agree that Johnson sometimes beats his children (but they deserve it); I grant that he often cheats his friends (but if they are so stupid, they deserve it); and I know that he lies frequently (but I think his lying is justified), *still,* I do not think that Johnson is an evil man." As you may recall, this very approach was used by Fred in his most recent disagreement with Kate. She suggests by her questioning that if the research on genetic differences in intelligence is well conducted, there is nothing morally objectionable about doing it. Fred retorts that even if the research were scientifically impeccable, it would still be morally reprehensible. In short, though facts may provide evidence to fuel a value dispute, the answer to a value question is something other than a summary statement of properties. *Instead, it is the person's self-report of his or her own ethical or aesthetic assessment.*

Second, what of statements that describe the values held by a particular person, or group of persons? Suppose, for example, that someone makes the following assertion: "Eighty-five percent of the citizens of the United States are opposed to any form of government censorship of the news media." Is not this statement either true or false? And is it not a value judgment?

The answer to the first query is yes; to the second, no. While the statement can be verified as true or false, it is not a value judgment. *Statements that describe the values held by a person, or persons, are statements of fact.* In this particular example, the statement is not responsive to the question, "Is government censorship of the news media wrong?" but rather to the query, "What percentage of United States citizens feel that government censorship of the news media is wrong?" In a sense, inquiry about such factual questions serves a similar purpose to that of the dictionary: just as the meanings that people have for words can be reported, so can their ethical and aesthetic assessments of various persons or actions. Nevertheless, someone may know that 99 percent of the populace opposes government censorship of the news media and still argue that such censorship is morally justified.

Having enlarged on our definition of value questions, it remains for us to consider the import of such questions for communication inquiry. The best way to begin is with twin disclaimers. Although we accept the relativistic position that value judgments are neither true nor false, we do not think that all value judgments are equally defensible nor do we believe that value judgments are unimportant. Let us consider each of our disclaimers in turn.

One extreme view of ethical relativism holds that the answers to value questions are nothing more than emotional outbursts; that when individuals make value judgments, they are only enthusiastically shouting "Whee!" or "Boo!" Since one emotional outburst is as good as another, all value judgments are, therefore, equally tenable.

We reject this position. *Instead, we hold that answers to value questions which are supported by valid evidence and sound reasoning are vastly preferable to answers which are arrived at unthinkingly.* In other words, we subscribe to the value judgment that value judgments should be grounded in cogent argument. *Thus, when dealing with value questions, the major task of the communication in-*

quirer is to formulate a position on the question and to argue it cogently. Caws (1967) emphasizes this centrality of argument to the area of values forcefully.

> Apart from insane persons . . . everybody can in principle be brought into a community of agreement about matters of fact, provided there is sufficient evidence, and so on. What would be needed to create a similar community of agreement for judgments of value? Evidence will not do, at least not by itself; if there is to be such a community of agreement it must . . . be constructed on a basis of argument. That is why the problem of value is at bottom a philosophical one while the problem of fact is at bottom a scientific one. *The resolution of a scientific disagreement always rests, in the end, on evidence; the resolution of a philosophical disagreement always rests, in the end, on argument.* (p. 65, italics ours)

What procedures are employed by the communication inquirer to argue about questions of value? We discuss this question in somewhat greater detail in Chapter 5. For now, it is sufficient to say that the inquirer pursuing value questions must, at a minimum, accomplish three steps: (1) definition of the important terms of the question; (2) specification and defense of a set of criteria upon which the ethical or aesthetic assessment is to be based; and (3) development of a set of arguments to support a particular moral or artistic stance, with the original criteria used as one of the bases for argument. Given powerful, cogent argument, the end product should create a *sense of belief* on the part of at least some of those privy to it.

The need for thoughtful pursuit of value inquiry is underscored by our second disclaimer: even though people can never know the truth or falsity of value judgments, this does not mean that they are unimportant. Quite the contrary, some of the most vital questions about communication concern human values. Although people cannot *know* that their value preferences are correct, they must *believe in, and act upon them.* Both as students of human communication and responsible citizens of a democracy, they have a duty to formulate well-reasoned positions on the limits and practice of free speech, the management of information, the social responsibilities of the mass media—in short, they are required to make ethical and aesthetic judgments about the quality of the communication environment. The possibility that communication scholars have sometimes been remiss in discharging this moral duty is reflected in a recent presidential address by one of the leaders of a national learned society of communication. Lamenting Watergate and other acute national problems, Jeffrey (1973)* asserts:

> As communication critics and educators, we failed in our responsibilities to officially oppose those practices [of the Nixon Administration] when they became so blatantly evident. We persist in that failure today. In the ten hours of deliberation of the Legislative Council at this convention [Jeffrey was speaking at the 59th Annual Meeting of the Speech Communication Association], not a single resolution was introduced to condemn the unethical practices of the Nixon Administration for withholding information from the public for political and private purposes; for deliberately deceiving the public with false statements as in denial of bombing in Cambodia when, in fact, it occurred; for refusing to supply tapes, notes and correspondence relating to possible criminal activities; for taping private conversations without the knowledge of the parties being taped; for other acts relating specifically to the free flow of information and privacy of communication that should be the central concern of teachers and scholars in speech communication.
>
> . . . Henry Wieman and Otis Walter wrote in 1957, ". . . Ethical Rhetoric has the promise of creating those kinds of communication which can help save the human being from disintegration, nourish him in his growth toward uniquely human goals, and eventually transform him into the best that he can become." That should be our paramount goal as teachers and scholars in communication. (16)

One need not ponder the personalization of Jeffrey's remarks nor even agree with his arguments about the Nixon Administration to appreciate his general tenor. Preservation and advancement of a

---

* From R. C. Jeffrey, "Ethics in Public Discourse," SPECTRA 9: 3 and 15–16. Quoted by permission of the publisher.

free society demands constant stocktaking about fundamental communication values. The communication inquirer should be in the forefront of those seeking to formulate reasoned value positions concerning public and private communication.

We will close our discussion of value questions by reemphasizing a key point. We have defined questions of value so that they concern only intrinsic ethical and aesthetic matters. Ours, of course, is only one possible definition. Some writers have defined value questions so broadly that almost any human act involving a decision can be labeled a value judgment. We do not deem this a useful approach, since it so universalizes the term "value" as to rob it of any functional significance: *if every human choice reflects a value judgment, then the term "value" has little utility; one might better use the label "behavior."* The importance of this point emerges clearly in Chapter 5, where we discuss the role of value judgments in the conduct of factual inquiry. Obviously, the pursuit of factual questions entails many choices. Some persons have pounced on this fact to support the argument that scientific inquiry about human communication can never be value-free. We counter by contending that the decisions involved in factual inquiry do not usually stem from ethical or aesthetic considerations; instead, they embody instances of the "means-ends" sense of factual assertions discussed earlier in this chapter. This argument will be stated more clearly in Chapter 5.

CASE 4: *No one is an island: The role of self-disclosure in human communication*

Since we have considered the importance of three types of questions for communication inquiry, it seems useful to underscore the relationships among them. We will do this by examining a concept of current interest to students of communication, the concept of *self-disclosure*.

How is the term "self-disclosure" to be defined? Typically, it is defined as the act of revealing personally private information to another. Such revelations involve some degree of risk, since the person to whom the information is disclosed might conceivably use it in ways that would have harmful consequences for the self-disclosing party.

But how can it be determined that information is personally private, particularly since matters that are privy to one individual may be items of open record for another? Usually information is considered personally private if it concerns topics that *most people* in our society would be reluctant to discuss with others. Thus, topics like sexual hangups and economic problems are thought of as self-disclosing areas. It should be obvious, however, that this approach creates some problems, since *some people* are apparently willing to talk about these topics with anyone.

Once the task of defining self-disclosure has been completed, many factual questions can be raised about its relationship to other communication variables. Do people self-disclose more to persons they like? Does self-disclosure strengthen or intensify the bonds of a communication relationship, and if so, to what extent? How do people react to being confided in; i.e., how do people react to being entrusted with personally private information?

Finally, the very idea of self-disclosure carries with it a number of value implications. In contemporary society, many persons seem to view the notion of "self-disclosure" as synonymous with "genuineness" and counsel that self-disclosure should be a universal communicative commodity. But is it desirable that people open their souls and bare their psyches to everyone? Perhaps the overall quality of our communication environment can best be enriched by reserving self-disclosing acts for those few "special" relationships of primary significance.

Certainly, we have not explored all the intricacies of self-disclosing communication. What we have said, however, ought to give you a flavor of the interrelationships of questions of definition, fact, and value. Your understanding of these relationships, as they relate to self-disclosure, can be enriched by exploring the following references:

Culbert, S. A. (1967). *Interpersonal Process of Self-Disclosure: It Takes Two to See One.* Washington: N. T. L. Institute for Applied Behavioral Science.

Jourard, S. M. (1971). *The Transparent Self.* Rev. Ed. New York: Van Nostrand.

Miller, G. R., and M. Steinberg (1975). *Between People: A New Analysis of Interpersonal Communication,* esp. Chapter 10. Palo Alto, Calif.: Science Research Associates.

Pearce, W. B., and S. M. Sharp (1973). Self-Disclosing Communication. *Journal of Communication* **23**: 409–425.

SOME CRITERIA FOR ASSESSING THE SIGNIFICANCE OF COMMUNICATION QUESTIONS

We have devoted considerable time to differentiating the types of questions that can be asked about communication. Still, regardless of question types, there are important questions and trivial ones. What criteria should be used to assess the significance of a question for communication inquiry? Although we will not dwell on this question at length, we will mention three yardsticks for gauging the potential import of questions. Our meanings for these criteria, as well as their relevance to inquiry, should become clearer as your reading progresses.

1. *Personal interest.* At a basic level, any question that interests or perplexes a person is personally significant. When Charlie Brown frets about ways to communicate with the new girl in class so as to create a favorable first impression, no one can doubt the question's significance to Charlie. Moreover, at a more general level, the continued success of such enterprises as the Dale Carnegie course reveals that questions about "winning friends and influencing people" concern many members of our society. In fact, we would argue that any question which interests the inquirer is fair game for communication inquiry.

There are, however, severe limitations associated with employing personal interest as the sole criterion of significance. In particular, the idiosyncratic interests of an individual often fail to coincide with issues of general import. Since only so much time and energy are available for communication inquiry, it would be nice to put our fingers on questions with potentially broad ramifications. This objective suggests two additional criteria.

2. *Social importance.* Communication is a uniquely social activity; consequently, most significant questions about communication are of general social import. Our previous remarks have included exam-

ples of such queries; e.g., "How can we communicate with people to foster their support of a particular national policy?" (question of fact) or, "What ought to be the intrinsic characteristics of our society's communication environment?" (question of value). The answers to such questions exert a powerful impact on our daily lives.

Sometimes students of communication assert their indifference about, or even disdain for, the social importance of a question.[11] We do not accept the position that the *potential* social import of a communication inquiry is irrelevant; if no argument can be made for the eventual social application of the inquiry, then the question is trivial. We do agree, however, that other matters may sometimes take priority over *immediate* social application. Our assent leads directly to our third criterion.

3. *Theoretical significance.* A primary goal of some communication inquirers is to be able to explain and predict human communicative behavior as simply and parsimoniously as possible. Although this objective is stated in a deceptively simple way, it embodies a number of complex, thorny problems that are discussed in later chapters of this book. For our present purpose, we need only say that the development of *theory* is a necessary condition for realizing the ability to explain and predict; consequently, any question that furthers the construction of communication theory is a significant one. This pronouncement marks an appropriate stopping point, as well as an entry into our next chapter, which deals with the role of theory and theory construction in communication inquiry.

NOTES

1. We do not want to exhaust you or ourselves by extending analyses on and on. Our reluctance will sometimes result in over-simplification. In this example, for instance, "successfully" has dimensions other than mere physical compliance. Thus, if your fiance(e) said, "I'd really like to go!" and seemed to enjoy the entire weekend, you would perceive greater persuasive "success" than if he or she angrily replied, "Oh, all right, if you insist!" and then complained incessantly throughout the trip.

2. To achieve stylistic economy, we will sometimes use phrases such as "the term's meaning." You should keep in mind that

our position makes it impossible for terms or words to have a property of meaning; rather, people have meanings for terms and stipulate definitions for them.

3. Moreover, when an extant definition will do nicely, it is counterproductive to saturate the literature with additional definitions. We will have more to say about this problem in Chapter 3.

4. We recognize that the determination of intent is itself a knotty definitional problem. There are at least five operational approaches: one may ask the message source, ask the message receiver, ask outside observers, examine the message itself, or use some combination of the first four.

5. "In principle": it is not something to be acted upon, but rather a provision governing our analysis. Thus, there are no *in principle* barriers to verifying the statement "There are mountains on the moon's dark side" as either true or false, but until recently verification was practically impossible.

6. In ordinary usage, "credible" means "believable"; consequently, this question is almost circular or tautological. By "credible" we mean the extent to which a communicator is perceived as competent, trustworthy, and dynamic—to mention but three components of interest. Thus we are not relying on ordinary usage in the question, nor is the question circular given our definition of "credible."

7. The importance of such questions can be underscored by putting it this way: statements of a singular fact are *descriptions* of a particular situation; empirical generalizations are *explanations* of *why* certain events, or outcomes, occur in an entire class of particular situations. Thus, the statement, *"This* water boiled at 212 degrees Fahrenheit and at standard pressure," is a *description,* while the statement, "If the temperature is 212 degrees Fahrenheit and the pressure standard, then water will boil," is an explanation.

8. Moreover, concepts are neither true nor false, only statements are. Consequently, a concept such as "nice" has no truth status until placed in a statement such as, "It is nice outside today." If the person making the statement is referring only to certain climatological properties—e.g., the temperature is above 65

degrees and the sun is shining—the statement is factual; if he or she is rendering an aesthetic assessment of the outdoors on this particular day, the assertion is a value judgment.

9. Of course, the person may be considered "morally corrupt," or "a moral deviant." But this assessment is itself a value judgment and refers not to a property of the dissenter but rather to the other group members' judgments of the ethical desirability of the person's beliefs.

10. Of course, at phenomenological bedrock, the one thing we are always certain we know is our own mental states. Thus, you *know* that you believe that Johnson is evil. But to say that you know that you feel this way is not the same as saying that the statement, "Johnson is an evil man," can be verified as either true or false.

11. This tendency of scholars to view practical matters and mundane creature comforts with disdain can be traced back as far as the ancients, as witnessed by the following amusing, yet revealing, comment of Plutarch about Archimedes: "Archimedes possessed so high a spirit, so profound a soul, and such treasures of scientific knowledge, that though these (engineering) inventions had obtained for him the renown of more than human sagacity, he yet would not deign to leave behind him any commentary or writing on such subjects; but repudiating as sordid and ignoble the whole trade of engineering, and every sort of art that lends itself to mere use and profit, he placed his whole affection and ambition in those purer speculations where there can be no reference to the vulgar needs of life." (Plutarch. (1959). *Lives of the Noble Romans,* E. Fuller (ed.). New York: Dell-Laurel.

QUESTIONS AND EXERCISES

1. For one day, keep track of how many times people apparently confuse questions (or statements) of definition, fact, and value. Observe conversations with roommates or friends and listen to professors in class. Try bringing several of these confusions to the attention of the person who is talking. What happens?

2. Obtain the text of a recent political speech; e.g., a national Presidential address. Count the number of statements of defini-

tion, fact, and value that appear. Which type of statement appears most? How do you think these frequencies compare with everyday conversation?

3. Exchange your findings with a classmate who has chosen the same address. Compare counts. On what statements do the two of you disagree? Discuss the disagreements and try to see why you differ. (Hold this exercise for further analysis in Chapter 4.)

4. Search for instances where people confuse questions of definition with questions of fact. Notice particularly how often confusion results from statements such as "A neurotic person is . . .," or "A good student is . . . ." What kinds of interpersonal problems result from this confusion? How might these problems be alleviated?

5. Analyze each of the following questions and demonstrate how each might become a subject for *either* factual or value inquiry depending upon the way key terms are defined:

    (a) Is logic or emotion a more important element of communication?
    (b) Can a bad person make a good speech?
    (c) Is Andrew Wyeth the world's greatest living artist?

REFERENCES

Asch, S. E. (1951). Effects of Group Pressure upon the Modification and Distortion of Judgments. In H. Guetzkow (ed.), *Groups, Leadership, and Men,* Pittsburgh: Carnegie Press.

Berger, C. R. (1973). The Acquaintance Process Revisited: Studies in Initial Interaction. Paper presented at the Speech Communication Association Convention, Nov. 1973, New York.

Caws, P. (1967). *Science and the Theory of Value.* New York: Random House.

Jeffrey, R. C. (1973). Ethics in Public Discourse. *SPECTRA* 9: 3 and 15–16.

Miller, G. R. (1972). *An Introduction to Speech Communication.* Indianapolis: Bobbs-Merrill.

Miller, G. R., and M. A. Hewgill (1966). Some Recent Research in Fear-Arousing Message Appeals. *Speech Monographs* 33: 377–391.

Miller, G. R., and M. Steinberg (1975). *Between People: A New Analysis of Interpersonal Communication*. Palo Alto, Calif.: Science Research Associates.

Popper, K. R. (1966). *The Open Society and Its Enemies*. 5th rev. ed., Vol. 2. Princeton, N.J.: Princeton University Press.

2
Using Theory

Nothing is more practical than a good theory.

— **KURT LEWIN**

Theories are nets cast to catch what we call
"the world."

— **KARL POPPER**

The term "theory" is no stranger to everyday conversation; probably few days pass without the word popping up in your own conversation. Like Humpty Dumpty, people engaged in daily discourse make the term "theory" mean exactly what they want it to mean, nothing more nor less. Consider the use of "theory" in each of the following sentences:

"That's a good *theory,* but it won't hold up in practice."

"I have my own *theory* about why he started smoking dope."

"That's merely a *theory* and not a fact."

"What's the *theory* behind that scheme?"

"During the 20th Century, the reigning *theoretical* paradigm of classical mechanics has been replaced in physics by relativity *theory.*"

We are primarily concerned in this chapter with the uses of theory in communication inquiry. For our purposes, most of the preceding usages, as well as others like them, are of limited utility. A possible exception might be found in the final sentence concerning the current state of affairs in theoretical physics, but before we have finished we hope to show that the present status of theory-building differs drastically in the physical and behavioral sciences. Moreover, although most of our remarks will focus on the role of theory in dealing with factual questions, we will also have something to say about the development of theories designed to deal with ethical and aesthetic issues.

Thus, our concern with theory centers on its use in statements such as these:

"Explanations of attitude change derived from dissonance *theory* are sometimes circular."

"A useful *theory* should not allow for the prediction of all possible outcomes."

"Information-processing *theories* and stimulus-response *theories* take a radically different view of the process of human communication."

"Ethical *theories* are either absolutistic or relativistic."

"One way to construct an aesthetic *theory* is to posit the existence of ideal forms."

The fact that we can largely ignore some meanings of the term "theory" and focus our attention on others does not imply that we can exhaustively explore the topic of theory in this chapter. Theory is a complicated topic; scholars from a variety of disciplines continue to analyze, to discuss, and to argue about many complex issues relating to theory and theory construction. Our goal is not to unravel their numerous sophisticated arguments, but rather to show how theory is a useful—perhaps we should even say indispensable—tool in conducting communication inquiry. Consequently, we will be primarily interested in arriving at some of the *uses*, or *functions*, of communication theory, rather than specifying its precise meaning or developing an exhaustive set of criteria for evaluating it.[1] More specifically, we will first explore how theory intrudes on inquiry about factual communication questions and then consider its utility in the domain of value controversies. As an illustrative starting point, let us first consider how people behave as theoreticians in their everyday communication activities.

THE THEORIST IN US ALL: OUR DAILY
COMMUNICATION WITH OTHERS

Our hypothetical acquaintance, Fred, has developed an interest in Kate's attractive roommate, Jane. Unfortunately, Jane seems engrossed in her relationship with another party, Jack. Craving advice or information which will help him bridge the barriers, Fred seeks out his old friend, Kate, for counsel:

FRED: "Have you got any ideas about how I can get a date with Jane? I've just about exhausted all the approaches I know."

KATE: "I'll tell you one thing I've noticed and even pointed out to Jane. Jack really puts her down a lot; most of the time he acts like a super-chauvinist. But rather than getting angry, Jane almost seems to thrive on it. Why the other night at a party, he was saying things to her that I wouldn't have taken from anybody."

FRED: "I wonder *why* some women like to be talked down to that way. Do you suppose they just naturally crave domination by some man?"

KATE: "I doubt if there's anything 'natural' about it, because I'm a woman and it sure doesn't turn me on. I suppose it is possible that a lot of women have learned to assume the submissive role because of the sexist nature of our society."

FRED: "Well, if that's true, and given the things you've been telling me, maybe I've been using the wrong strategy. I wonder *what* would happen if I just called her tonight and told her in no uncertain terms that I'm tired of fussing around and that I expect her to go out with me this weekend."

KATE: "I really can't say, because I don't know a lot of things: what she thinks of you, how deeply she's involved with Jack, what her plans are for this weekend, or for that matter, how well you can pull that approach off."

FRED: "Well, I suppose it's worth a try. If it *works,* or even if I get the feeling it *might work* if things are right, I'll be way ahead of where I'm at now—which is nowhere!"

Certain aspects of Fred's conversation with Kate reveal that he is wearing his theoretical hat. When he asks *why* some women seem to find condescending communication from men rewarding, Fred is searching for an *explanation* of Jane's favorable reactions to Jack's messages. Moreover, he then attempts to provide an explanation of sorts by asserting that it may just be "natural" for women to respond in this way. Unsatisfactory as Fred's explanation may be, it is not unlike some early instinct theories of social psychology which sought to explain all kinds of human behavior by positing underlying, innate instincts. We will have more to say about these theories shortly.

When Fred asks *what* will happen if he employs an aggressive, one-up communication strategy with Jane, he is trying to make a *prediction;* i.e., he wants to determine the probable outcomes, or consequences, of presenting certain types of messages. Kate's response to his query illustrates that successful prediction depends on knowledge about certain other relevant conditions: to predict the probable outcomes of Fred's strategy, one must know, among other things, how Jane feels about Fred, how much she is attracted to Jack, what her commitments are for the weekend, and how adept Fred will prove to be in using this particular communication style.

Finally, Fred ends the conversation by speculating about the likelihood that his aggressive, one-up communication strategy will *work*. These remarks underscore Fred's concern for *control*. More specifically, he is interested in controlling one limited, but important aspect of his environment, Jane's responses to his persuasive messages. In fact, Fred even distinguishes between two senses of control: *actual control* ("it works") and *potential control* ("it might work if things are right").

In their daily communicative activities, most people behave as if they shared Fred's preoccupation with explanation, prediction, and control. They seem to strive to understand the reasons for their own communicative behaviors, as well as the communicative behaviors of others. They appear to make predictions about the probable ways that people will respond to various message strategies and then select the strategy most likely to trigger the desired responses. In addition, they seek to control their environments so as to derive certain physical, economic, and social rewards from them.[2] Obviously, these three objectives are inextricably bound together. Thus, if Fred's explanation of Jane's attraction for Jack is correct— namely, that she enjoys being dominated and put down—then his prediction that this strategy is likely to bear fruit for him has a good chance of being on target, thereby permitting him to exercise control over an important aspect of his environment.[3]

To be at least partially triumphant in their daily efforts to explain, to predict, and to control, people avoid behaving in a random, haphazard fashion. Instead, they develop theories about ways to communicate effectively with others. In this context, what we mean by "theory" is one or more propositions about the behavior of people in general that enable a person to deduce how he or she should communicate with particular individuals. In their simplest form, then, the theories that guide most daily communicative transactions are synonymous with the concept of "empirical generalization," discussed in Chapter 1. For example, the assertion, "Women prefer domineering men," is an empirical generalization. It is also a theoretical proposition, since from it can be deduced the appropriate way for a man to communicate with a particular woman he wishes to impress favorably.

Unfortunately, as people go through life testing their favorite theories, they discover many disconfirming instances. Rather than becoming infatuated with them, certain women treat arrogant, domineering men coolly, even disdainfully. Obviously, the original theoretical proposition must be modified, or "toned down." Perhaps only a particular kind of woman is likely to fall prey to an aggressive, one-up strategy: a quiet, retiring, unassuming woman. If so, the theoretical proposition should be modified to assert, "Submissive women prefer domineering men."

This modification of the original theoretical proposition is likely to improve the communicative effectiveness of men who wish to subscribe to it, *providing* they can discover valid ways of identifying submissive women before engaging in a great deal of communication with them.[4] On the other hand, if valid ways of identifying submissiveness are not unearthed, the proposition can be used to provide an after-the-fact, circular "explanation" of these men's communication failures. In other words, each time their aggressive, one-up strategy fails to bear fruit, they can rationalize the failure by asserting that the woman in question was not submissive. The problem with such reasoning can be illustrated by considering two forms of the argument, one valid and one invalid. We will state the valid form first:

All submissive women prefer domineering men.

This woman is submissive.

Therefore, this woman prefers domineering men.

An alternative to the argument which, while logically invalid, is often used in everyday communication theorizing, goes as follows:

All submissive women prefer domineering men.

This woman is not submissive.

Therefore, this woman does not prefer domineering men.[5]

In the preceding valid and invalid forms, the content of the premises is used to deduce the conclusion—although the conclusion deduced is logically erroneous for the invalid form. Moreover, given the valid form, it is possible to disconfirm the theoretical proposition, "All submissive women prefer domineering men"; i.e., an instance may be observed where a submissive woman does not prefer a domineering man. But the original reasoning makes disconfirmation impossible, because the failure to respond positively to domineering men is used as a datum to infer the woman's lack of submissiveness. Obviously, the entire process is circular: the theoretical proposition asserts that submissive women prefer domineering men, but what is used as evidence for the presence or absence of a particular woman's submissiveness is her preference or lack of preference for domineering men. What is necessary to disconfirm the original theoretical proposition is an independent measure of submissiveness that can be used to categorize any particular female *before* a male embarks on an aggressive, one-up communication strategy.

The preceding example illustrates an important point about theories; *if a theory is to be useful, it must be logically possible to falsify it*. In other words, it should be possible to observe outcomes that would lead to the conclusion that the theory is wrong. Obviously, the muddle-headed reasoning discussed above makes it impossible to falsify the theoretical proposition, "Submissive women prefer domineering men," since every time a disconfirming instance is observed, it is "explained" away by arguing that the woman was not submissive. We will have more to say about this falsification criterion later in the chapter.

Other illustrations of the use of theory in people's daily communicative activities abound. For example, several social scientists (e.g., Thibaut and Kelley, 1959; Homans, 1961; Blau, 1967; Gergen, 1969) have explored numerous issues surrounding a perspective called *social exchange theory*. Social exchange theories hold that people's behaviors are governed by the perceived payoffs associated with each alternative. Certainly, the language of such theories is part and parcel of the common parlance: persons often speak of "fair exchanges" and "mutual back-scratching," and most individuals do not hesitate to talk about communicative exchanges in terms of "outcomes," "profits," "rewards," or "costs." Blau uses the label "social exchange" to refer to "voluntary actions of individuals that are motivated by the returns they are expected to bring and typically do in fact bring from others" (1967, p. 91). Thus, people who base communicative decisions on general propositions of social exchange theory will usually select their communication strategies and evaluate their probable outcomes by considering the question: "What's in this for me, and how much will it cost me?" In fact, the answer to this question will probably determine whether the individual decides to enter into communication relationships with particular others.

CASE 1: *When first we meet: Social exchange dynamics in forming acquaintanceships.*

It is commonplace that when people first meet they strive to engender favorable reactions, particularly if they find each other attractive. Phrases such as "putting your best foot forward" and "creating a favorable first impression" attest to the pervasiveness of this phenomenon. Verbally, new acquaintances share information calculated to paint them in the best possible light; nonverbally, they are attentive, alert, and eager to communicate.

The propositions of social exchange theory provide one possible explanation of the energy and commitment devoted to such early exchanges. Blau (1967) argues that when people are attracted to others and want to appear attractive to them, their ability to gain the benefits expected from an association depends on their skill at persuading others to find them attractive and in creating the desire for interaction. Thus, attempts to appear impressive and desirable permeate the early stages of acquaintance formation.

Social exchange theories suggest, however, that success in making favorable initial impressions demands a number of subtle communicative skills. Although the process involved is actually a form of bragging, artful students of impression management appear so natural that they do not seem to be bragging at all. Moreover, if an individual seems too impressive, others may perceive some conflict in the situation: on the one hand, they believe it would be socially rewarding to associate with such an impressive person, but on the other hand, they fear that these same impressive qualities may doom them to a clearly inferior social position. This is one sense in which the phrase "coming on too strong" is relevant to the outcomes of initial interactions.

The same kinds of social exchange dynamics apply to early expressions of regard for the other person. When compliments seem sincere ("from the heart") they are socially rewarding and create a favorable impression of the complimenter. Still, there are several potential pitfalls associated with expressing regard. For instance, if one consistently gives compliments but they are not reciprocated by the other party, the compliment-giver clearly assumes a socially inferior posture in the relationship. Furthermore, the social-reward value of a compliment is partially determined by the frequency of its occurrence: we value a compliment more highly when it originates from someone who is known to express regard grudgingly, rather than from one who showers praise profusely on everyone. Finally, too frequent expressions of regard may be perceived as insincere (Berger, 1975), or as indicative of an effort to ingratiate oneself (Jones, 1964), thus reducing the value of these expressions as a social exchange commodity.

The following references, plus those cited above in the text, will provide the interested reader a more comprehensive treatment of the position taken by social exchange theorists.

Berger, C. R. (1975). Judgments of the Sincerity of Compliments as a Function of Their Frequency of Their Occurrence in Initial Interaction. Unpublished manuscript, Department of Communication Studies, Northwestern University.

Blau, P. M. (1967). *Exchange and Power in Social Life*. New York: John Wiley & Sons.

Jones, E. E. (1964). *Ingratiation*. New York: Appleton.

We hope our excursion into the realm of everyday communication has dispelled the anxieties you may harbor about the concept of theory. Theories are not esoteric, mystical things; most daily communication is governed by rough, inductively derived theoretical propositions. Moreover, since everyone communicates with a wide variety of other people, theories are essential tools for achieving the communicative goals of explanation, prediction, and control. When communication inquirers conduct systematic inquiry, they employ theory in a similar fashion and toward similar ends. The major differences lie in the degree of rigor that is exercised and the extent to which the theory is clearly and explicitly articulated: in everyday communication, theories are used roughly and intuitively and often remain implicit and unstated; in systematic inquiry, theories are developed and tested with logical and empirical rigor and are stated clearly and explicitly. We are now ready to capture the flavor of this latter process.

THEORY AND THE SCIENTIFIC CONDUCT OF COMMUNICATION INQUIRY

Thus far, we have avoided the ambiguous, and somewhat pretentious, term "science." Still, when people conduct communication inquiry about questions of fact, they are usually cast in the role of scientists. Moreover, theory is an invaluable ally of scientific inquiry, as we shall attempt to demonstrate in this section.

As a starting point, how are such terms as "science," "scientist," and "scientific inquiry" to be usefully defined? It seems appropriate to define them functionally, i.e., to assign meaning to them in terms of the purpose that communication scientists have in mind when conducting inquiry. *We argue that the purpose of scientific inquiry in communication is to develop statements containing empirical content that have truth value outside the situation, or situations, in which the original observations were made.* Let us next consider some of the key aspects of this statement.

To say that a statement contains empirical content is to classify it as a factual assertion. Thus, the statement, "The mean length of sentences in this book is 29.7 words," contains empirical content, though whether the statement is true or false we do not know, since we have not taken the trouble to verify it. Similarly, the empirical generalization discussed in Chapter 1, "High-credible communicators are more persuasive than low-credible communicators," also contains empirical content.

In one important respect, however, the two statements differ drastically. The assertion pertaining to the mean sentence length of this book has no scientific import, for it makes no claim for truth value outside the situation in which the original observations were made. Stated differently, the statement pertains only to this book; it does not pertain to other books that have not been observed. To be sure, someone might use the information in the statement to draw inferences about other books or about the authors—e.g., "Books about communication inquiry have long sentences," or "Miller and Nicholson like to use long, involved sentences"—but such inferences would surely be criticized on the grounds of inadequate sampling.

By contrast, the statement concerning the greater persuasive power of high-credible communicators does purport to have truth value outside of the situations in which the original observations were made. Obviously, no one can observe all the high-credible and low-credible communicators in the world and determine their relative persuasive effectiveness.[6] Consequently, the communication scientist observes a sample of these communicators and then makes an empirical statement that transcends the sample; i.e., he or she generalizes to similar situations in which observations have not been made. Thus the statement has scientific import; whether it also has scientific utility depends on the extent to which the generalization holds true in unobserved situations.

Thus the goals of communication scientists are similar to the aims of persons engaged in everyday communication: they strive to improve their ability to explain, to predict, and to control. Their ultimate objective is the discovery of a set of logically related general propositions which enable them to deduce correctly some outcome, or some characteristic, of a particular communication transaction. *This set of logically related general propositions we label a "theory."*

One of the major values of a theory is its synthetic power; it permits the communication scientist to capture relevant dimensions of a large number of communication phenomena in a relatively small number of general propositions. Without a theory, the scientist must flit from one situation to another, making and recording observations. With a theory, it is possible to make advance predictions about the outcomes of particular communications and then check to see if these predictions are correct. Each empirical check constitutes a test of the theory. As the checks continue to confirm the theory, the scientist develops greater confidence in its explanatory and predictive power.[7] Furthermore, if the theory has a good explanatory and predictive batting average, its potential as an instrument for control is also high.

Although a theory can be composed of a set of logically related empirical generalizations, most of those employed by communication scientists rely on propositions dealing with *intervening variables,* i.e., processes or constructs which refer to things that are going on inside of persons when they communicate. In turn, these intervening variables are assumed to exercise an effect on overt behavior; they are expected to influence the way an individual encodes, decodes, or responds to messages.

CASE 2. *Booming, buzzing confusion: Making sense out of others' behavior.*

Eaton Rapids

Slade, Luman 2221 S Canal Rd.	663-4129
Slentz, Jerry 624 Jennie	663-3576
Slusser, M L 420 W Plain	663-8277

If you are like most persons, you are probably wondering why in the world Miller and Nicholson began this case by listing numbers from the Eaton Rapids, Michigan, telephone directory. Though our communicative openers are perhaps bizarre and far-fetched, your likely response to them illustrates an important point: people are strongly motivated to discover (or at least to *feel* they have discovered) the reasons for others' behavior. So intense is this quest for social causality that a family of theories has been developed to deal with the processes by which individuals attribute reasons for other people's behavior. Those theories are called *attribution theories,* and they all stress the fact that persons constantly seek to understand and to assign meaning to others' behavior.

Frequently we are faced with the problem of identifying reasons for another's communicative behavior. If someone pays us a compliment, does it stem from sincere admiration or from a desire to curry our favor? If a poor person proposes marriage to a wealthy companion, does the proposal really reflect undying devotion or an attempted shortcut to wealth and status? Do politicians actually believe in their campaign promises or are they merely seeking to amass votes? Obviously, the list of such questions is almost endless.

The three steps in the attribution process are: observing an action or behavior ("You are really an intelligent person!"), making a judgment of the actor's intent ("You are trying to curry my favor"), and making a dispositional attribution ("You are an obsequious—or ingratiating—person"). Note that only one step of this process deals with observable behaviors, while the other two center on what we have called *intervening variables*. A person's "true" intent is always hidden from our scrutiny; we can only make inferences about intent by observing someone's behaviors and the situational context in which they occur. Likewise, we attribute dispositional attributes after observing someone's behavior in a variety of situational contexts. Thus, if we observe ten of an individual's behaviors and make only one judgment of obsequious intent, we are not likely to assign a dispositional attribute of obsequiousness to the person, but if eight of the ten behaviors are judged obsequious, the attributional label will almost certainly follow.

Attribution theories deal with the variables that influence the intentional judgments we make and the dispositional attributes we assign. Following are some references that provide a more detailed analysis of these theories:

Heider, F. (1958). *The Psychology of Interpersonal Relations*. New York: John Wiley & Sons.

Jones, E. E., D. E. Kanouse, H. H. Kelley, R. E. Nisbett, S. Valins, and B. Weiner (1972). *Attribution: Perceiving the Causes of Behavior*. Morristown, N.J.: General Learning Press.

Shaver, K. G. (1975). *An Introduction to Attribution Processes*. Cambridge, Mass.: Winthrop.

By way of illustration, consider one family of theories that has enjoyed considerable popularity among communication researchers: *cognitive consistency theories* (e.g., Newcomb, 1953; Osgood and Tannenbaum, 1955; Festinger, 1957). Although various cognitive consistency theories differ in many details, they all rely upon the

same set of logically related general propositions. These three propositions are as follows:

1. Persons prefer a state of psychological equilibrium or cognitive
   consistency.
2. The presence of cognitive inconsistency triggers an aversive, or
   unpleasant, motivational state, and,
3. As a result, the individual is motivated to behave in some way
   calculated to restore consistency.

To understand the implications of cognitive consistency
theories for communication inquiry, some of the important constructs found in the propositions must be defined. As indicated in
Proposition 1, the term "cognitive consistency" refers to a state of
psychological equilibrium; it describes a situation where all of the
individual's beliefs, attitudes, and values (cognitive elements) are
linked in a psychologically consistent manner. Suppose, for example, that you have independently decided this book is very dull and
uninteresting. While talking to a friend and fellow classmate whose
opinion you value, you request an assessment of the book. If your
friend also finds it dull and uninteresting, you experience no cognitive inconsistency; both of you dislike the book. But if your friend
enthusiastically responds that it is a most interesting book, you are
likely to experience some inconsistency, for we usually expect
friends whose opinions we value to share most of our likes and
dislikes (Newcomb, 1953). Furthermore, this cognitive inconsistency should be unpleasant (which is about all that is meant by
"aversive motivational state"), and consequently, you should behave in some way calculated to restore consistency. Some of your
behavioral alternatives include reevaluating your assessment of the
book ("I guess it's better than I originally thought"), reconsidering
the judgmental acumen of your friend ("I must have overestimated
his or her good sense"), or, what is more likely, readjusting your
attitudes toward both the book and your friend—i.e., you end up
liking the book a little more and valuing your friend's opinion a little
less.

How can communication be related to this situation? Consider
two possible responses of your friend: "It's the best book I've ever
read!" and "It's a good, run-of-the-mill text." If you dislike the
book intensely, both responses should produce some cognitive in-

consistency, but the first should generate more than the second, since your friend disagrees more strongly with you. Hence, the theory predicts that attitude change toward the book and/or your friend will be more pronounced when he or she heartily endorses the volume, and it would be possible to conduct a study to check this prediction.

Furthermore, you have other alternatives at your disposal for restoring cognitive consistency, or avoiding cognitive inconsistency.[8] Message distortion constitutes one option; you may not "hear" your friend's enthusiastic endorsement of the book. Of course, distortion occurs more readily when a response is not extremely intense: it is easier to "hear" someone express dislike of the book when calling it a run-of-the-mill text than when claiming it is the best book he or she has ever read. Again, this theoretical implication could be tested by varying the intensity of your friend's endorsement and then measuring your estimate of his or her attitude toward the book.

Finally, if you have a hunch that your friend likes the book, you may perhaps avoid an unpleasant attack of cognitive inconsistency by steering clear of any conversation about its merits. In other words, you may circumvent the negative psychological effects of belief-discrepant information by avoiding situations where the information will come to light. As a matter of fact, this is a general theoretical implication of cognitive consistency theories: people usually seek out information that conforms with their beliefs and avoid information that conflicts with them—the so-called *selective exposure* hypothesis (Festinger, 1957; Freedman and Sears, 1965).

Notice what has transpired in the last few paragraphs. We have taken a specific communication situation and employed a set of theoretical propositions to derive predictions about a variety of possible behavioral outcomes. Without the assistance of theory, many of these outcomes might have remained unnoticed; theory constitutes a means for organizing and directing our expectations about communicative antecedents and consequences. Moreover, the construct of cognitive consistency provides a *unifying explanatory mechanism* for dealing with many diverse behavioral outcomes and a vehicle for *predicting* probable future outcomes.

This is not to imply that all is scientific sweetness and light with cognitive consistency theories. If these theories are to be useful explanatory and predictive tools for communication scientists, at least two major problems must be faced. The first involves the detection of inconsistency arousal. Recall that cognitive consistency theories deal with psychological, not logical consistency. There is no reason to presume that people are guided by the rules of formal logic when organizing their cognitive storehouses. Thus, cognitions or behaviors which seem inconsistent to others may appear quite harmonious to the actor concerned, and when this is the case, no cognitive consistency will be produced.

What is needed, then, is a means of measuring inconsistency arousal. In the past, some researchers have been guilty of the sort of *post hoc,* circular reasoning discussed earlier in this chapter. They have reasoned that if a person experiences cognitive inconsistency, he or she will behave in a certain way. Next, they have looked to see whether the person does engage in the particular behavior: if so, they have assumed that he or she has experienced cognitive inconsistency; if not, they have assumed that no inconsistency arousal occurred. This approach makes it impossible to disconfirm, or falsify, the theory. The measure of inconsistency arousal must be *independent* of the anticipated subsequent behavior to conduct adequate tests of the theory.

A second key problem associated with cognitive consistency theories is captured by the phrase, "behave *in some way,"* found in the third general proposition. As we have already indicated, a variety of behavioral alternatives are usually available for reducing inconsistency. Another way the sanctity of the theory can be ensured is by predicting that the individual will perform a certain behavior to reduce inconsistency, and, when this fails to occur, arguing that some other behavioral means of inconsistency reduction was used. When conducting inquiry from a cognitive consistency perspective, it is insufficient to predict that *some* consistency-restoring behavior will occur; rather, the *preferred behavioral mode* of inconsistency reduction must be specified.

In order to clarify our argument, we have summarized the minimal conditions for an adequate test of hypotheses based on consistency theories in Fig. 2.1. *If* these conditions are met, consistency theories permit the derivation of numerous hypotheses that are of interest to students of communication: hypotheses concerning the information-seeking behavior of individuals, hypotheses concerning attitude change that may occur when a person is induced to say something he or she does not believe (Festinger and Carlsmith, 1959; Miller and Burgoon, 1973), and hypotheses concerning the ways people will evaluate two or more alternatives after choosing one of them (Festinger, 1957; Brehm and Cohen, 1962). On the other hand, if these conditions are not met, consistency theories may become tautological and may allow a *post hoc* rationalization of any possible outcome.

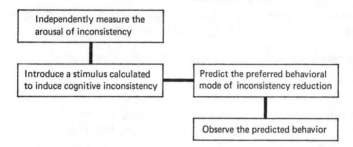

Fig. 2.1   *Minimal Conditions for an Adequate Test of Hypotheses Based on Cognitive Consistency Theories.*

The purpose of our fairly detailed examination of cognitive consistency theories has not been to advocate their theoretical supremacy for dealing with communication questions, but rather to illustrate some general considerations bearing on the nature of theory and to underscore some problems associated with using theory in scientific communication inquiry. We will have occasion to discuss other theories in the next section of this chapter, when we consider some specific issues relating to the use of theory in communication inquiry. Since we have touched upon several important points in this section, it seems wise to conclude with a summary of them:

1. A communication theory can be defined as set of logically related general propositions which permit the deduction of some outcome, or some characteristic, of a particular communicative transaction.

2. A communication theory provides a unifying explanatory mechanism which can be used to impose coherence on numerous, diverse behavioral outcomes.

3. A communication theory provides a means for predicting future behavioral outcomes.

4. If a communication theory is to be tested effectively, it is necessary to specify the *initial conditions* required to trigger the theory and to ascertain that these conditions have been met.

5. If a communication theory is to be tested effectively, it is necessary to specify behavioral outcomes unambiguously.

SOME SPECIFIC ISSUES RELATING TO THE USE OF THEORY IN COMMUNICATION INQUIRY

Finality versus Tentativeness: Balancing the Scales

We have repeatedly emphasized the importance of theory as a unifying explanatory mechanism. But in using such words as "explain," it is important to avoid the trap of imparting an air of finality that, in the eyes of the less cautious or more committed, renders the theory inviolate.

Such a trap is easily sprung. For, in most of their daily activities, including those involving communicative interchanges, people assume that once an event is explained to their satisfaction, the dialogue is ended. Granted, individuals may differ widely in their initial explanations of an event. Suppose a person known to favor the legalization of marijuana attends a meeting where the speaker argues against this measure. Following the meeting, our erstwhile supporter of legalized marijuana changes his or her position dramatically and begins to oppose such a move. One person may explain this changed behavior by pointing to the logical cogency of the arguments contained in the speech. A second observer, who happens to know that the speaker holds the mortgage on our erstwhile supporter's house, may remark that the latter's changed behavior represents an attempt at ingratiation. A third, psychoanalytically-minded individual may suggest that the speaker projects a strong parental image to the former supporter of marijuana legalization, and that the latter is trying to identify with the speaker. Obviously, in any subsequent attempt to agree on the "correct" explanation, or motive, for our supporter's changed behavior, a lively controversy may ensue.

But if all three observers can agree on one explanation, the argument ceases. In addition, all of them feel the sense of psychological security which accompanies the belief that they have "found the answer." By the same token, unqualified acceptance of the explanatory power of a particular theory also implies discovery of the correct answer. Such an implication represents a gross oversimplification, and in some instances this oversimplification may retard the search for knowledge and understanding.

An example of this unfortunate situation occurs when the so-called theory does not provide a real explanation at all, but only a pseudoexplanation. Early psychological instinct theories, mentioned previously, represent one instance of pseudoexplanation. Why, it was asked, do people seek to amass vast fortunes? The "explanation" given by the instinct theorists was that individuals have an *acquisitive instinct*. Or, when asked why human beings come together in groups and communicate, the instinct theorists answered that people have a *herding instinct*. As a result of many similar queries, an elaborate list of human instincts was compiled, each of which purported to explain some human action.

Surprisingly, numerous people were lulled into believing that such lists actually did explain the behaviors of interest. Actually, of course, these verbal appeals to instinct were nothing but pseudoexplanations. To say that people have a herding instinct only restates in different words the already accepted observation that they organize together in groups. Unless one believes that humans are born with a herding instinct and that socialization and maturation contribute nothing to the development of organizational and communication behaviors—a position not likely to withstand close scrutiny—the statement, "Human beings form groups because they have a herding instinct," is nothing but a tautology, a repetition of the same phenomenon using a different phrase. In this form, instinct theory explains nothing; it offers only a facade of explanation.

Our purpose is not to poke fun at these early theorists, but rather to stress that theories, while indispensable to inquiry, should be viewed as tentative formulations, not final answers. Many contemporary theorists, each swearing that her or his particular theoretical viewpoint lays bare the secrets of human behavior, erroneously believe that they have explained an event if they can translate it into their preferred language. For example, some learning theorists, when asked why people engage in a whole host of behaviors, answer that the behaviors are performed because they are *reinforcing*. The philosopher of science, Michael Scriven, has labeled this tendency to invoke vocabulary the "translation trick." He asserts:

> When we start talking . . . about certain aspects of general social behavior, we are really performing the translation trick, not the explanation trick. This might lead us to think we have explained but it is really "the disease of the jargonier." It is important to be able to distinguish between being able to talk about something in a particular vocabulary and understanding it in that vocabulary. The test as to whether a vocabulary "imparts new and genuine understanding" is its "capacity to predict new relationships, to retrodict old ones, and to show a unity where previously there was a diversity," not its capacity to produce an 'aha' feeling.[9] (1964, p. 190)

While the causes for engaging in the translation trick are undoubtedly multiple, slavish commitment to the ultimate explanatory power of a particular theory is probably one major reason for such semantic gymnastics.

Consider now a second reason why scientific communication theories must be treated as tentative formulations, not final answers. The causes for behavioral events can be analyzed at various levels. At each level, satisfactory explanations of the event can frequently be developed. Imagine that one evening shortly before a Presidential election you drop in on a firmly committed Democratic friend. In the midst of an intriguing discussion about the explanatory function of theory, your friend decides to watch a televised address by the Democratic candidate. How might the occurrence of these particular behaviors be explained; i.e., what theories may account for your friend's desire to interrupt the conversation and to turn on the television? For since you have not expressed interest in the telecast, the interruption represents a departure from social convention.

Next morning, still piqued by the events of yesterday evening, you mention the incident to several coffee-drinking companions. Included in the group are an anthropologist, a sociologist, a psychologist, and a physiologist. Suddenly you are witness to a lively discussion of the cause of your friend's behavior, a discussion that proceeds in the following manner:

ANTHROPOLOGIST: "Well, I think it's all a matter of cultural values. When a society places a premium on political participation, it's not surprising that the individual feels certain pressures to govern his or her behavior accordingly. Now if we look at societies where participation is not a value. . . ."

PHYSIOLOGIST: "Nonsense, you anthropologists always get so global that your so-called theories don't explain anything. Now if we want to explain why that person turned on that campaign speech, we've got to talk in terms of certain neuro-physiological events. After all, the reasons for an individual's overt behavior can be reduced to the firing of certain neurons. Theoretically, we can derive. . . ."

SOCIOLOGIST: "But when this question was first raised, no one was interested in things like neurons. What we need to look at are forces in the environment that impelled the person to turn on the TV. Reference group theory. . . ."

PSYCHOLOGIST: "Aha, here we go! Now I'll agree that we aren't interested in neurons, but we're about to fall into the abyss of the sociologist's group laws. Why don't we avoid that fallacy and talk about individual behavior? It seems to me that certain drive-reduction learning theories provide a parsimonious way to explain this behavior. Take the Hullian notion that the probability of the occurrence of a particular behavior is a function of habit strength multiplied by drive. . . ."

ANTHROPOLOGIST: "Well, we're on the elegance and precision kick again. The only trouble is that we've removed the problem so far from the real world. . . ."

PHYSIOLOGIST: "Yes, but if you want real elegance and precision, you've got to reduce to the physiological level. . . ."

SOCIOLOGIST: "I want to get back to that group laws point. . . ."

Enough of our imaginary conversation. The crucial point is that each participant has sought to explain the same behavioral event from a different analytical context; each has created concepts that suggest a particular level of explanation. There is no disagreement about *what* event has occurred; each participant has accepted the veracity of your report. Instead, the dispute centers on the way to best *explain* the occurrence of the event. Perhaps a cynical observer might even suggest that this particular dispute reflects little more than four individuals performing the translation trick discussed above.

Assume, however, that the controversy involves something more than semantic tricks. One must conclude that any decision that an event has been explained is, first of all, somewhat arbitrary and, second, based on numerous complex factors. In the classical sense of *explanation,* to which we have previously had recourse, a particular event has been explained if its occurrence could have been predicted from a more general theory. It is entirely possible that with sufficient information the anthropologist, the sociologist, the psychologist, and the physiologist could *all* have predicted that your friend would turn on the television. If so, each of their theories satisfactorily explains the behavior. To argue that one of them explains it best implies certain pragmatic choices, value judgments, and psychological commitments on the part of the person doing the arguing. Indeed, some of these choices and judgments are illustrated in our hypothetical dialogue: terms such as "parsimony," "elegance," and "precision" are bandied about by the antagonists.

To further complicate matters, these kinds of disagreements exist at each level of analysis; they are not confined to between-level disputes. For example, there are numerous psychological theories. A learning theorist, a perception theorist, and a cognitive consistency theorist would choose to explain your friend's decision to watch television from different theoretical perspectives. In some cases, these differing theoretical preferences may be of real significance; in others, they may represent nothing more than a commitment to a particular vocabulary. But if all three theorists arrive at the same prediction, and if this prediction is subsequently verified, then each theory explains the behavior. Moreover, one of the theories may provide the most useful explanation in one set of circumstances, while another may prove more useful in a second set. In other words, theories have a *functional* dimension: a theory may be useful in one situation but not another. Once this fundamental premise is accepted, it becomes obvious that no theory should be viewed as the last word in explanation.

A final caution against absolute endorsement of a theory relates to the logical apparatus employed to test the soundness of theoretical propositions. When a hypothesis about a particular communicative outcome is derived from a theoretical proposition, it is tested inductively. That is, the outcome is observed, and if it conforms with theoretical expectations, it is taken as confirming evidence for the theory. Conceivably, however, the particular outcome of interest could be observed an infinite number of times. In making these observations, one could never be logically certain that a different outcome would not occur on the next occasion. Granted, if the same outcome was observed 10,000 times, one would become psychologically certain of its occurrence. But logically, it is possible that on observation 10,001 the outcome would change. And if it did, an instance would exist where the hypothesis and, in a broader context, the theory from which it was derived had been disconfirmed.

The problem we have just described is central to inductive logic and has long been of interest to philosophers of logic and science. When applied to the question of theory validation, it denies the possibility of verifying a scientific theory as *true*. For since it is impossible to exhaust the number of tests that can be conducted of any hypothesis derived from a theory, the validity of the theory must always be couched in probabilistic terms. If after repeated tests no negative instances are observed, confidence in the theory's validity increases. But by its nature, inductive logic deals with the probability, rather than the certainty, of a theory's validity.

It is, however, logically possible to verify a theory as *false*. In a few cases, when a theory is grounded in categorical, invariant universal generalizations, one disconfirmation is logically sufficient to spell the theory's doom. Of course, communication scientists do not impose such a demanding criterion for at least two reasons. First, there are many opportunities for error to enter into an observation, and theories about communication are almost always qualified by the *ceteris paribus* (all other relevant things being equal) assumption. Taken together, these two considerations cause the communication scientist to be cautious about rejecting a theory, even if its propositions are framed as categorical universals. Second, many communication theories are *stochastic*—i.e., they specify what *probably* will happen—rather than deterministic—i.e., they do not specify that a particular prediction is *certain* to happen. For stochastic theories, a single disconfirming observation does not constitute sufficient grounds to label the theory false, since the instance observed may be one of the minority of cases when the predicted result does not occur. Still, for either deterministic or stochastic theories, a number of disconfirming observations may force the theorist to conclude that a pet theory is in error.

The logic of this situation explains why we have stressed the importance of avoiding hypothesis testing situations that permit *post hoc* rationalization of all possible outcomes and why we have emphasized that a useful theory must be capable of falsification. Karl Popper has argued persuasively that the minimum criterion of a viable scientific theory is the potential falsification of its propositions. After asserting that "Theories are, therefore, *never* empirically verifiable," Popper goes on to say:

> But I shall certainly admit a system as empirical or scientific only if it is capable of being *tested* by experience. These considerations suggest that not the *verifiability* but the *falsifiability* of a system is to be taken as a criterion of demarcation. In other words, I shall not require of a scientific system that it shall be capable of being singled out, once and for all, in a positive sense; but I shall require that its logical form shall be such that it can be singled out, by means of empirical tests, in a negative sense: *it must be possible for an empirical scientific system to be refuted by experience.* (1959, pp. 6–7)

Here, then, is a final, telling blow for those who would accept the veracity of a particular theory without pause or question. Logically speaking, the validity of a theory is always tentative. This is not to suggest that one theory is as good as another or that people should not develop theoretical preferences based on sound scientific criteria. What we are cautioning against is unthinking commitment to the inviolability of a particular theory. Communication inquiry is a continuous search for new knowledge and enriched understanding. When viewed properly, theories are invaluable allies in our quest; when accepted dogmatically as ultimate truth, they equip us with intellectual blinders that narrow our vision and impede scientific progress. The wise student of communication maintains an open mind, while at the same time making tentative commitments to promising theoretical positions. By so doing, the scales of inquiry are balanced.

Inside versus Outside: Two Sources of Explanation

When attempting to explain the occurrence of a particular behavior, students of communication have two major explanatory avenues at their disposal. They may choose to explain the behavior primarily in terms of the perceptions, needs, and motivations of the behaving party, or they may search for an explanation grounded largely in the forces imposed on the behaving party by the external environment. In other words, the inquirer may look *inside* the actor or *outside* at the actor's environment for most explanatory clues.

Which of these approaches has greater merit? Scholars from numerous disciplines have filled the pages of many books and journals with spirited debate about this question. The opposing positions have been given a variety of labels: "action" theories versus "motion" theories, "cognitive" theories versus "stimulus-response" theories, "push" theories versus "pull" theories, "phenomenologists" versus "behaviorists," etc. But no matter what we call the antagonists, the fundamental issue remains the same: *should theories about communication be grounded primarily in the perceptions and motivations of the actor or in the relevant conditions of the external environment?*

Since we have thus far discussed the issue in abstract terms, a specific example of the differing emphases involved in the two approaches may help to clarify things. Let us return to a problem area mentioned briefly in Chapter 1, receiver responses to persuasive messages containing strong fear-arousing appeals. Suppose a communication scientist wished to test the hypothesis that a message containing strong fear-arousing appeals will be more persuasive than one containing mild appeals.[10] Moreover, assume that this scientist conceptually defines "strong fear-arousing appeals" as appeals emphasizing the harmful consequences that will result for receivers if they fail to conform with the recommendations contained in the message. In other words, a strong fear-arousing appeal would look like this:

If you do not quit smoking, you will have to suffer the consequence of lung cancer, with the attendant coughing, internal bleeding, excruciating pain, and ultimately, death.

In contrast, a mild fear message would not detail these harmful consequences.

What theoretical grounds might lead the scientist to predict the persuasive superiority of the strong fear message? A scientist inclined toward an action theory, or "inside" perspective, will probably focus on the different ways that receivers perceive and interpret the two kinds of messages. Thus, in prior research conducted on this problem, Miller and Hewgill* used cognitive consistency theories as the basis for deriving their hypotheses:

> These [cognitive consistency] theorists hold that individuals strive to maintain cognitive balance among the many covert and overt behaviors that comprise their response repertories. Since balance is the preferred psychological state, any perception of imbalance will be tension-producing, and the individual will subsequently act . . . in a manner calculated to restore cognitive balance.
>
> Application of these assumptions to the process of persuasion suggests that any persuasive message has at least two functions: (1) the arousal of cognitive imbalance, and (2) recommendation of specific means for restoring cognitive balance; i.e., advocacy of a particular set of . . . behaviors that will eliminate imbalance.
>
> Furthermore, it seems probable that persuasive messages vary in the extent to which they produce cognitive imbalance in message recipients; or, stated another way, that the magnitude of the cognitive imbalance generated will depend on message variables. [We assume] that, *ceteris paribus* [all other things equal], a message containing strong fear-arousing appeals will result in greater cognitive imbalance than will a message containing mild appeals. The grounds for this assumption are found in the fact that strong fear-arousing appeals explicitly emphasize the harmful consequences of failure to comply with message recommendations and mild appeals do not. Message recipients exposed to strong fear appeals should therefore experience greater tension . . . and in turn, this greater tension should strongly predispose the message recipient to behave *in some way* calculated to restore cognitive balance. (1966, 377–378)

* From G. R. Miller and M. A. Hewgill (1966), "Some Recent Research in Fear-Arousing Message Appeals," *Speech Monographs* 33: 377–391. Quoted by permission of the publisher.

Notice that this theoretical perspective places emphasis on the perceptions and motivations of the message recipients, and that it posits an intervening variable of cognitive balance, or consistency, to explain possible differences in recipient responses to strong and mild fear-arousing messages. Unless these mediating, internal processes are activated, the message containing strong fear-arousing appeals would be expected to have minimal persuasive impact.

The preceding assertion underscores another important characteristic of inquiry conducted from an action theory perspective: the scientist must use measures designed to determine whether the expected mediating processes were triggered. In the Miller and Hewgill studies, it was necessary to obtain a measure of perceived fear on the part of message recipients and to compare the self-reports of recipients exposed to the strong and mild fear messages. If the recipients who heard the strong fear-arousing appeals report a significantly higher level of perceived fear (and, fortunately, they did), the initial conditions for generating differing amounts of cognitive consistency have been satisfied; if not, the theoretically derived hypotheses cannot be tested adequately.

Now consider how a motion theorist, or "outsider," would approach this problem. Rather than focusing on the motivational states of the message recipients, a motion theorist would concentrate on the observable characteristics of the messages. For instance, he or she might reason that the message containing strong fear-arousing appeals explicitly spells out the consequences of a particular sequence of responses, while the mild fear message does not. Armed with the Skinnerian (1953, 1971) proposition that behavior is shaped by its anticipated consequences, and knowing that the strong fear message details these consequences more explicitly, the motion theorist might also predict that the strong fear message will have greater persuasive impact.

The major advantage of the motion theory approach lies in its total concern with observable behavior; the theorist does not have to measure how the recipients perceived the message and can avoid any speculation about unobservable intervening constructs and processes. The most distinguished contemporary advocate for a strict motion theory viewpoint, B. F. Skinner, has repeatedly criticized the behavioral scientist's zeal for such speculation. Typical of his remarks is the following:

Almost all our major problems involve human behavior, and they cannot be solved by physical and biological technology alone. What is needed is a technology of behavior, but we have been slow to develop the science from which such a technology might be drawn. *One difficulty is that almost all of what is called behavioral science continues to trace behavior to states of mind, feelings, traits of character, human nature, and so on.* [italics ours] Physics and biology once followed similar practices and advanced only when they discarded them. The behavioral sciences have been slow to change partly because the explanatory entities often seem to be directly observed and partly because other kinds of explanations have been hard to find. . . . As the interaction between organism and environment has come to be understood, however, effects once assigned to states of mind, feelings, and traits are beginning to be traced to accessible conditions, and a technology of behavior may therefore become available. It will not solve our problems, however, until it replaces traditional prescientific views. (1971, 24–25)*

Thus, Skinner contends that communication scientists would be ahead if they could quell the urge to speculate about intervening processes and adhere to a strict motion theory perspective.

CASE 3. *What are the consequences? Two views of reinforcement.*

Most behavioral scientists agree that behavior which is positively reinforced tends to be repeated. Thus, if a small child correctly responds "ball" when shown a round, inflated, rubber object, presentation of a positive reinforcer such as, "Very good, Mary!" or a piece of candy increases the likelihood that the child will say "ball" the next time she is asked to name a similar object. Similarly, if our hypothetical friend, Jack, tries a particular communicative approach with Jane and manages to obtain a date with her, the probability that he will use this approach the next time is increased, not only for his dating requests to Anne but with other women as well.

* From B. F. Skinner (1971), *Beyond Freedom and Dignity*, New York: Alfred A. Knopf. Quoted by permission of the publisher.

Action and motion theorists disagree, however, on the best way to conceptualize the process of reinforcement. Among action theorists, a *drive-reduction* position is frequently advocated. Theorists such as Hull (1943) and Spence (1956) hold that *drive* is a generalized energizer that increases the vigor of response tendencies. If certain stimulus conditions exist, drive increases; for instance, if Jack finds Anne highly attractive, he will be driven to seek contact with her and will behave in ways calculated to establish such contacts.

If Jack is unsuccessful, his drive state will not be reduced. But if Anne accepts his invitation for a date, her acceptance and anticipated companionship will be *drive-reducing* for Jack. *It is this drive-reducing characteristic that makes an event reinforcing for the drive-reduction theorist,* or stated differently, an action or event is a reinforcer if it results in a decreased drive state. Moreover, since drive is an intervening variable that is closely linked to, or even synonymous with the motivations of the actor (remember, Jack is motivated to establish a relationship with Anne), this conception of reinforcement falls within the action theory perspective.

By contrast, a motion theorist such as Skinner (1938) views reinforcement differently: for Skinner, a reinforcer is simply any event that increases the probability of a particular response. Thus, if it is observed that the presentation of candy following a specific response (e.g., "ball") increases the probability of that response under similar stimulus conditions, then candy is, by definition, a reinforcer. The drive-reduction theorist would agree that candy is often reinforcing but would attribute it to the fact that sweets are drive-reducing. The motion theorist's approach permits him to avoid speculating about such intervening processes as drives, needs, and motivation.

Still, it is probably not an accident that Skinner chose M&Ms rather than broccoli as a possible reinforcer for children, or that he uses grain instead of dirt clods with pigeons. Obviously, most children like M&Ms better than broccoli. But when one starts speculating about what people like and dislike, one begins to move toward an action theory perspective. Moreover, while certain things and actions—e.g., candy and social approval—are reinforcing for many people, it is also apparent that people vary in what they *perceive* to be reinforcing. The old chestnut, "Why do you keep hitting yourself in the head with a hammer?" "Because it feels so good when I stop," illustrates this point.

There are many complex issues associated with the process of reinforcement. Many of these issues are detailed more fully in the following references:

Hull, C. L. (1943). *Principles of Behavior.* New York: Appleton-Century-Crofts.

Miller, N. E., and J. Dollard (1941). *Social Learning and Imitation.* New Haven: Yale University Press.

Skinner, B. F. (1938). *The Behavior of Organisms.* New York: Appleton-Century-Crofts.

Spence, K. W. (1956). *Behavior Theory and Conditioning.* New Haven: Yale University Press.

This disdain for intervening variables has caused many behavioral scientists to attach the label "atheoretic" to the work of Skinner and other radical motion theorists. We believe this is a mistake. The tendency to invoke the label "atheoretic" stems from the erroneous assumption (discussed extensively in Chapter 1) that there is *a* correct way to define the term "theory." Instead of being atheoretic, Skinner, and others of his persuasion, have a different conception of theory than the one shared by most behavioral scientists. Specifically, the action theory conception has dominated the behavioral sciences in general, and communication science in particular: *most behavioral scientists think of theories as sets of logically related propositions concerning certain intervening variables.* By contrast, the motion theorist is more likely to conceive of theories as *sets of logically related empirical generalizations concerning the environmental antecedents and consequences of behavior.*

As yet, few full-blown motion theories have entered the arena of communication science. There are several reasons why. First, it is difficult to discover ways of logically linking empirical generalizations without resorting to intervening variables. What is more likely is that numerous empirical generalizations will be unearthed but stand in isolation until someone comes along and pulls them together by devising a set of intervening constructs. To say that this is the typical happening does not necessarily imply the impossibility of logically relating empirical generalizations without recourse to mediating processes; it only recognizes that most communication scientists have thought about theory from an action framework.

Moreover, it is hard to maintain a "pure" motion theory vocabulary; in fact, ordinary language predisposes us to think about the causes of human behavior in action theory terminology. Even though Skinner chooses to define a reinforcer as "any event that increases the probability of a response," thereby bypassing any concern for mental events, it is almost inevitable that someone will ask, "*Why* do most children find M&Ms reinforcing?" Whether or not the question is relevant, it immediately transfers our attention to the internal predispositions of the child, rather than the relevant characteristics of the child's environment. Similarly, social approval (e.g., "Um-hmm," or "Good idea!") is a reinforcer that can be used to control and shape communication behavior (e.g., Greenspoon, 1955; Verplanck, 1955; Hildum and Brown, 1956), and it is commonplace to query, "*Why* do people find social approval reinforcing?" Commenting upon the style of his own book, *Beyond Freedom and Dignity,* Skinner notes these pitfalls of everyday language:

The text will often seem inconsistent. . . . The English language contains many more expressions referring to human behavior than to other aspects of the world, and technical alternatives are much less familiar. The use of casual expressions is therefore much more likely to be challenged. It may seem inconsistent to ask the reader to "keep a point in mind" when he has been told that mind is an explanatory fiction, or to "consider the idea of freedom" if an idea is simply an imagined precursor of behavior, or to speak of "reassuring those who fear a science of behavior" when all that is meant is changing their behavior with respect to such a science. The book could have been written for a technical reader without expressions of that sort, but the issues are important to the nonspecialist and need to be discussed in a nontechnical fashion. (1971, pp. 23–24)

We think Skinner underscores the problem nicely, although we are less sanguine than he about the possibility of purging such language from technical treatises.

What is our own conclusion about the relative merits of action and motion theories as intellectual signposts for conducting communication inquiry? At the risk of being accused of sidestepping the issue, we believe both approaches can expand the available knowledge of communication phenomena, that both action and motion theorists should grab a piece of the communication action (or motion, if you prefer). In opting for this position, we wish to stress that both theoretical approaches employ behavior as the basic datum. Even though action theorists emphasize intervening variables such as "need," "value," and "attitude," they can never directly observe these constructs.[11] Instead, they observe behavior, and as a result of their observations, make inferences about those mediating processes that compose the core of their theory. Thus, an action-oriented attitude change theorist, upon hearing you exclaim, "This book is atrocious!" would probably infer that you have a negative attitude about the book, or about communication inquiry in general. But any conclusions drawn about your attitudes are not reports of observations; rather, they are inferences based upon some sample of your observed behaviors.

Therefore, we do argue strongly for the primacy of behavior in developing a science of communication. Our position mandates that action theorists be willing to abandon their pet theoretical constructs if they are not supported by their own, and others' observations. However, as long as action theories and motion theories are properly utilized by the communication scientist, both have potential for providing useful explanatory and predictive frameworks. At this time, it would be presumptuous to say that one offers a scientific panacea, the other only an empty platitude.

All versus Some: How Much to Explain

We have pointed out that a theory provides a unifying explanatory mechanism for explaining diverse communication phenomena. In this section we will consider the issue of how much phenomena one should attempt to explain.

The classical goal in theory building is the discovery of *universal* lawlike generalizations, a goal pursued and realized in many areas of physical science. This approach is sometimes called the *covering law model*. A covering law involves the type of categorical universal statement discussed in the earlier section on finality versus tentativeness of a theory. Consider the lawlike generalization: water boils at 212 degrees Fahrenheit under standard pressure. The two relevant variables in the law are temperature and pressure. As long as these two variables can be measured and controlled, a mixture of two parts hydrogen and one part oxygen will demonstrate the molecular behavior commonly labeled "boiling" in the United States, India, the tropics, the polar regions, or any other area of the world. For that matter, given the ability to control the two relevant variables, water should also boil on the moon or on other planets. In other words, the lawlike generalization is universal; it is a covering law that does not admit to exceptions when the variables are accurately measured and adequately controlled.[12]

To a great extent, behavioral scientists, including the communication scientist, have aspired to the discovery of similar universal lawlike generalizations. These aspirations have not, however, been realized, largely because their realization would require the solution of several formidable, if not insoluble, problems. Let us briefly examine two of these problems, using as an illustrative vehicle the empirical generalization: high-credible communicators are more persuasive than low-credible communicators.

How many relevant variables affect the validity of this generalization? Intuitively, it seems obvious that the number far exceeds the two variables governing the boiling of water. Suppose someone wishes to believe the arguments of a low-credible communicator and finds the arguments of a high-credible source unpalatable. Certainly Geppetto and the Blue Fairy are more credible communicators than the Fox and the Cat, yet Pinocchio spurns the good advice of the former and falls prey to the blandishments of the latter, literally making an ass (or at least a half-ass) of himself in the process. Or suppose the message recipients are masochistic types who gain morbid satisfaction from being deceived and misled. Or perhaps there are external constraints against acting on the arguments of the high-credible communicator but not on those of the low-credible source. Our list of qualifying conditions seems limited only by the scope of our imagination.[13]

These myriad limiting conditions necessitate the attachment, overtly or by implication, of the phrase, "other things equal," to empirical generalizations concerning human communication. By contrast, it is hard to imagine a physicist saying, "Other things equal, water boils at 212 degrees Fahrenheit under standard pressure." Physicists do not have to say this because they know all the relevant variables that must be "equal" if the law concerning boiling water is to hold. Communication scientists are in a much less enviable position; they have not begun to discover all the relevant variables that influence a generalization about the persuasiveness of high-credible communicators. Thus, as noted earlier, the generalizations made by communication scientists are stochastic—based on probabilities—not deterministic—based on universal regularities.

If this were the only difficulty, the communication scientist might not have great cause for concern. After all, particle physics is presently restricted to probabilistic, rather than deterministic statements. But communication scientists face another problem not shared by their colleagues in the physical sciences. Even if the empirical generalization that high-credible communicators are more persuasive than low-credible communicators is universally valid (i.e., if it holds in all societies throughout the world) it does not necessarily follow that the behavioral and demographic components of credibility are constant from one social system, or situation, to another. Stated differently, water is universally defined as two parts hydrogen and one part oxygen. Temperature and pressure are measured the same way in China, the United Arab Republic, and the United States. But credibility may not be *perceptually defined* in the same way in all social systems. In one, it may consist of three parts age and one part educational attainment; while in another, it may consist of zero parts age (or, stated differently, age may not be a relevant variable) and four parts educational attainment.

This point can be made more vividly by contrasting several diverse social systems. In a street gang, the difference between high credibility and low credibility may hinge on one's ability with his fists or a switchblade. Among the members of a scientific society, the extremes may be captured by a Nobel Laureate and a suspected fabricator of data. Stockbrokers' credibility may be assessed by their economic hits and misses; an advertisement trumpets, "When E. F. Hutton speaks, people listen." In a traditional society, advanced age may confer wisdom and high credibility; in a modern society, advanced age may be viewed as a sign that the individual is handicapped by an inadequate blood supply to the brain. Unlike water or temperature, credibility is a slippery construct to nail down.[14]

Some may argue that the preceding problem constitutes no *in principle* barrier to the communication scientist's search for universal lawlike generalizations. After all, we have admitted that the generalization may hold universally, so the unique task is one of determining the empirical dimensions of the relevant theoretical constructs in differing social systems. Although perhaps cogent, this argument seems too pat, for no matter how one views the logical roots of the problem, it is still onerous. In particular, variability in the empirical loading of constructs—i.e., in the ways that different variables, or values of variables, enter into measurement of the construct—across social systems severely limits the communication scientist's potential for control. When physicists know how to control the molecular behavior of water in the United States, they are confident that they can also exercise control in India. But the communication scientist's ability to control responses of message recipients to sources in Great Britain does not ensure comparable control in Nigeria, for the relevant theoretical constructs may have different empirical loadings in the two countries.

How can we temper the thorny problems associated with the search for universal lawlike generalizations concerning human communication? One possible solution lies in seeking explanations that are of more limited scope. Rather than searching for universal lawlike generalizations, the communication scientist could pursue the more modest task of developing explanations of the communicative behavior of specifically delineated portions of the total universe.

Systems theory approaches to explanation constitute a valuable aid for the communication scientist who wishes to travel this path. Much could be said about the differences between covering law and systems views of explanation. Since the arguments are complex, we will summarize briefly several of the more important distinctions.

First, explanations grounded in universal lawlike generalizations combine logical and empirical considerations, while systems paradigms separate the two: the system is logically modeled, tested empirically, and then remodeled to conform with the test outcomes. The system itself is a logical, not an empirical creature. As Meehan puts it:

A system is not defined by its capacity to predict or explain but by its internal logical structure; no system is necessarily useful in explanation though all explanations make use of systems. Any set of two or more variables and one or more rules of interaction is a system. Given two variables (A and B) and one rule of interaction (A is the inverse of B), the system is complete and there are two entailments: if the value of A does not change, the value of B will not change; if the value of A is stipulated, the value of B is the inverse of the value of A. (1968, pp. 53–54)

Second, an explanation derived from covering law models is either right or wrong, but an explanation grounded in a systems perspective is evaluated in terms of its utility. In other words, systems theory explanations are assessed *functionally,* with the paramount function usually the communication scientist's ability to control:

> The quality of the explanation can be evaluated in terms of the purposes for which it is used. A weak explanation provides minimal control over a limited part of the environment, control that may be in various degrees unreliable; a strong explanation provides accurate and reliable control over substantial parts of the environment. The scope, power, reliability, and usefulness of an explanation can vary greatly, and *each explanation must be evaluated separately in terms of specific purposes.* (Meehan, 1968, p. 23, italics ours)*

Finally, with the exception of general systems paradigms, the explanational scope of systems theories is more restricted than the scope of covering law models: the two approaches differ on the all-versus-some question.[15] A communication system may be comprised of a family circle, two persons engaged in task-directed communication, the students, faculty, and administrators of a large university, an athletic squad, the members of a sorority, or a host of other human components. After modeling the system of interest, communication scientists load the constructs empirically and then attempt to develop explanations of the communication characteristics of the system, explanations that increase their capacity to control. Universal lawfulness is not a criterion for evaluating the explanation, rather, the explanation is "good" if it enhances understanding and control of the system.

---

* From E. J. Meehan (1968), *Explanation in Social Science: A System Paradigm,* Homewood, Ill.: The Dorsey Press. Quoted by permission of the publisher.

We have been discussing the systems approach to explanation rather abstractly; once again, a specific example may clarify some of our points. Fontes (1973) became interested in the problem of how particular communication networks may affect adolescents' educational and occupational aspirations. More specifically, he sought to assess the influence of three networks of potentially significant others: the adolescent's peers, relatives, and teachers and counselors. In order to investigate the problem, Fontes constructed the structural-functional systems model found in Fig. 2.2.

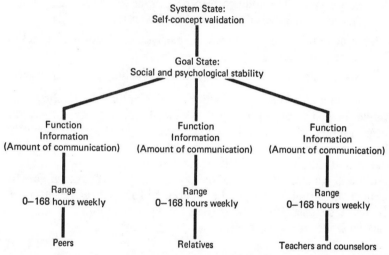

Fig. 2.2 *Fontes' Structural-Functional Model of the Communication Networks Influencing Adolescents' Occupational and Educational Choices (from Fontes, 1973).*

Note that the *system state* posited is self-concept validation, and that the *goal state* is social and psychological stability. The system state describes the focus of the research; Fontes was interested in studying the way adolescents validate an important dimension of their self-concepts; specifically, their occupational and educational choices. The goal state describes the end sought by the system, which in this case is the adolescent's social and psychological stability.

The *function* contributing to this goal state is information, defined as amount of communication. The system is limited to the three communication networks, or groups of significant others, mentioned earlier; peers, relatives, and teachers and counselors. In other words, the system is, by definition, *logically closed*. This does not mean that other sources of information may not exert a powerful impact on the adolescent's occupational and educational choices. For instance, should research reveal that the mass media play an important role in determining occupational and educational choices, the model could be revised to include this information source.

Three key propositions underlie this modeled system:

1. The adolescent's self-concept is the composite of his information about his relationship to objects of his experience and is directly causative of his conscious behavior.

2. Social and/or psychological disparity is a function of a lack of communication.

3. Stress is a function of social and/or psychological disparity.

From these three propositions and Fontes' relatively simple model of a structural-functional system, literally scores of hypotheses can be derived. Confirmation of these hypotheses supports the logical soundness of the system model, while disconfirmation indicates that modifications of its logical structure may be necessary. Although we cannot list all of the potential hypotheses available for empirical testing, a few will be mentioned for illustrative purposes. It might be useful and interesting for you to attempt to generate further hypotheses yourself:

HYPOTHESIS 1:   The network which engages in the greatest amount of communication with the adolescent concerning occupations and education will exert the most influence upon the adolescent's short-term realistic occupational expectations.

HYPOTHESIS 2:   The network which engages in the greatest amount of communication with the adolescent concerning occupations and education will exert the most influence on the adolescent's *perception* of his or her significant others' short-term realistic occupational expectations for the adolescent.

HYPOTHESIS 3:   The greater the amount of communication between the adolescent and his or her significant others, the lower the amount of stress the adolescent will experience.

HYPOTHESIS 4:   The smaller the disparity between the adolescent's short-term realistic occupational expectations and the adolescent's significant others' short-term realistic occupational expectations, the lower the amount of stress the adolescent will experience.

Notice that none of these hypotheses specify universal lawfulness; they are empirical implications of the logical system that has been modeled. The explanations contained in the system and its derived hypotheses are useful to the extent that they permit better control of the adolescent's development of self-concept. As hypotheses are confirmed or disconfirmed, the logical parameters of the system are maintained or modified. In short, the entire enterprise seeks an explanatory mechanism for dealing with a relatively limited domain of communication phenomena.

Although a detailed discussion of this point is beyond the scope of this book, the theoretical foundations of, and the methodologies associated with systems theory also permit more complex formulations of questions and more adequate tests of data bearing on the questions. One problem facing communication theorists who seek covering laws lies in the possibility that such laws depend upon so many parameters that the only way to express them is from a systems theory perspective. In fact, aside from the all-versus-some criterion, a very complex covering law may be impossible to distinguish from a systems theory statement.

Should communication scientists confine their theoretical search to the universal lawlike generalizations demanded by the covering-law model or should they pursue the more modest explanatory aims embodied by the systems theory approach? Again, we assume a laissez-faire stance, since we believe that both approaches can presently be used profitably in communication inquiry. Until recently, the covering-law model has received the most attention, but an increasing cadre of communication scientists are framing their research problems within a systems theory context. As time passes and more research verdicts are posted, it may be possible to pass judgment on the relative merits of the two positions. For the moment, however, the question of all-versus-some can remain open, and communication scientists can be encouraged to avail themselves of both types of explanatory mechanisms.

USING THEORY IN THE DOMAIN OF VALUES

Although much remains unsaid about the role of theory in dealing with factual communication questions, we will now turn to some of its uses in conducting value inquiry. More specifically, we will examine some of the characteristics of so-called ethical or aesthetic theories and consider how they assist students of communication in probing value questions.

We have chosen the label "critic" to describe those individuals whose primary concern is the development of reasoned arguments about value queries. Thus, just as scientific theories are invaluable allies to the communication scientist, ethical and aesthetic theories provide powerful assistance for the communication critic. Moreover, like the impromptu scientific activities mentioned earlier, criticism is an integral part of our daily communicative undertakings. Perhaps we can best illustrate this fact by tuning in on yet another conversation between Kate and Fred:

FRED: "Well, getting that date with Jane was a lot of hassle for nothing. I wouldn't go out with her again on a bet!"

KATE: "Oh, why not?"

FRED: "All night long I felt like I was being used. She never seemed to relate to me as a person, but just appeared interested in what she could get out of me."

KATE: "What leads you to that conclusion?"

FRED: "Well, first she ordered the most expensive item on the menu. Then she spent the whole meal talking about her problems with Jack and asking me for advice about how to handle them. After dinner, I suggested a movie, but she said she preferred to drop by the Airliner for a few drinks. Of course, Jack just happened to be drinking there with some friends and we just happened to get seated close to his table. Then all of a sudden she started coming on strong for the first time all evening; you know, hanging on my every word, doing a lot of touchy-feely, all that stuff. But just as soon as we left the bar she turned it off again. And believe it or not, all she talked about on the way home was whether I still had the term paper I wrote in that basic communication course last term."

KATE: "That's interesting. I know she hasn't been doing well in that course, and the other day I mentioned that you got an "A" in it last term. She didn't say anything about it then, but her asking you about your term paper starts me to wondering. In fact, I've noticed that she sometimes is pretty self-serving in the things she asks of me."

FRED: "It doesn't surprise me a bit. If I were you, I'd be careful about getting into a one-down position with her. She really knows how to use people to her own benefit."

Throughout this conversation, Fred is *criticizing* Jane's interpersonal behavior, including, of course, the motives underlying her communication with him. Although Fred details numerous happenings to Kate, his primary concern is not with the facts of the situation, but rather with the ethics of Jane's behavior. The things that transpired during his date with Jane are used by Fred as inductive instances to support a value-oriented generalization: Fred concludes that Jane is an unethical communicator, that she uses communication as a tool to manipulate others in satisfying her own ends.

Such critical evaluations of others' communicative behavior are common transactional commerce. Every day we make value judgments about communication, both in terms of the ends sought by communicators and the means employed to achieve these ends. Under what conditions, if any, is it ethically defensible for the government to withhold information from our citizenry? What are reasonable ethical standards for achieving truth in advertising? What, if any, are the ethical limits of pornographic communication or communication depicting violence and bloodshed? Is persuasion inherently unethical? Is deceit or lying ever justifiable, and, if so, under what conditions? What are the ethical responsibilities of the individual communicator to others? The list of possible issues is almost limitless.

A primary task of the communication critic is to arrive at reasoned judgments about such ethical issues and to convince others of the wisdom of these judgments.[16] *Usually, critics base their reasoning on some universal normative generalization, or generalizations.* These generalizations are not unlike the universal lawlike statements of the communication scientist, with the important exception that their content is *prescriptive,* not *descriptive.* Stated differently, a normative generalization expresses a value judgment, not a statement of fact, and as a result, it cannot be verified empirically.

We can illustrate this distinction by returning to Fred's indictment of Jane. In criticizing her behavior, Fred reasons from the following normative generalization: ethical communicators should not manipulate other persons nor treat them as objects. Obviously, this is a prescriptive statement detailing the way people *ought* to behave, rather than a descriptive statement indicating how they *do* behave; in fact, the social exchange theories mentioned earlier in this chapter suggest that people often do engage in reciprocal manipulation. Furthermore, the truth or falsity of this normative generalization cannot be ascertained empirically. Granted, it might be possible to point out occasions when manipulation and the treatment of persons as objects produced calamitous results, both for the object of manipulation and for the manipulator. By the same token, however, situations could undoubtedly be identified when all the parties involved apparently profited from such a relationship; again, social exchange theories have something to say about this. Most important, no matter what the factual consequences of such behavior, it could still be argued that it is unethical and demeaning.

Armed with this normative generalization, the critic employs it as a yardstick for assessing the ethical quality of the communicative acts of a particular individual, or individuals, and on the basis of his or her assessment, arrives at a judgment or verdict. The formal structure of this critical process can be illustrated by returning to Fred's criticism of Jane:

NORMATIVE GENERALIZATION:
Ethical communicators should not treat other persons as objects.

INFERENTIAL DATA:
Jane (1) gouged Fred for a great deal of money at dinner, (2) used Fred as a sounding board for working out her problems with Jack, (3) used Fred to try to get to Jack at the bar, etc.

JUDGMENT:
Jane is an unethical communicator.

Thus, normative generalizations provide a theoretical foundation from which to launch arguments about the ethics of particular communicators or specific communicative acts. But although they are arrived at differently, these generalized norms share another characteristic with the empirical generalizations of the communication scientist: universal agreement about such norms is hard to come by. Consider, for instance, the normative generalization: ethical communicators should not lie; and then attempt to evaluate each of the following communicative acts by applying this generalization:

1. A person compliments an insecure friend on a new suit, in spite of actually considering it hideous.
2. A man manages to seduce a woman by promising marriage although he has no intention of fulfilling his promise.
3. A business executive compliments a partner's wife on a fine dinner while covertly taking a Rolaid.
4. A doctor tells a patient he or she is progressing well, knowing that the patient is terminally ill with cancer.
5. A con artist promises an elderly gentleman to deposit his savings in a bank, successfully pulls a handkerchief drop on him, and leaves him penniless.
6. A rich industrialist promises financial support for a competitor's business only to renege and leave the competitor bankrupt.

Did you reach an identical ethical judgment for each of these six communicative acts? We suspect that you were quickly conscious of some differences among them. Numbers 1 and 3 represent a class of communicative acts sometimes labeled "white lies"; these are statements that enable the prevaricator to spare the feelings of the other party or to avoid an unpleasant transaction. Numbers 2, 5, and 6 embody situations where harmful consequences accrue for the liar's victim, yet persons often attach differing ethical judgments to them. Contempt for the con artist is usually expressed; the lover's duplicity is condemned by some but viewed as justifiable by others, and the business executive's actions are actually applauded by some as smart practice. What seems to be involved are varying levels of sympathy for the liar's victims: the elderly gentleman is usually seen as a gullible, trusting person who has been ruthlessly victimized; the seduced female may be seen as an unwary lover who did not play her cards too skillfully, and the bankrupt industrialist as a stupid competitor not well-suited for a career in industry.

Finally, Number 4 appears difficult to evaluate without requesting more information. What are the probable consequences of the doctor's deception for the patient? For the patient's friends and family? In addition, the act raises other questions. Does the doctor's primary ethical responsibility lie in being truthful with patients or are there times when there is greater responsibility to the psychological well-being of these patients, even if it necessitates lying? If so, is the psychological well-being of this particular patient really promoted by deception or is the long-range trauma likely to be magnified?

These examples suggest that the sovereign normative generalization, ethical communicators should not lie, demands qualification if it is to provide the foundation for cogent communication criticism. There are several ways critics may approach this task. For instance, they might qualify the generalization in the following manner:

NORMATIVE GENERALIZATION:
Ethical communicators should not lie.

QUALIFIER:
Unless the undesirable consequences of not lying outweigh the desirable consequences.

Such a qualifier recognizes that there are times when truthfulness may produce more undesirable consequences than lying, though it suggests that these instances constitute a definite minority. In arriving at a judgment, critics must weigh the consequences of the falsehood. If they perceive the consequences as predominantly positive and if they believe the truth would have produced more undesirable consequences, they may conclude that the deceit was ethically justified. But if the opposite circumstances prevail, their ethical judgment of the communicator will likely be negative.

Thus, an ethical theory usually consists of one or more normative generalizations along with the qualifiers that are attached to them. Of course, different theories may yield diametrically opposed arguments and conclusions, even though the inferential data are the same. If a critic begins with the normative generalization that any communication that furthers one's self-interest is ethically justified, he or she will reach a different judgment, given the same inferential data, than the critic who starts with the generalization that ethical communicators should not manipulate other people.

This fact suggests that the critic's first argumentative task is often a defense of his or her normative generalizations. Why should people accept the moral superiority of the avoidance of manipulative communication over the doctrine of Machiavellian self-interest? If persons can further their own interests by manipulative communication, why not do so? If the critic does not anticipate and counter these kinds of questions, it will be impossible to convince others that his or her chosen theoretical posture is preferable to other alternatives.

Note that our view of ethical theories is itself rooted in a value judgment: *we hold that even though value judgments about communication cannot be verified as true or false, they should be given greater credence if they are based on rational, reasoned argument.* As we indicated in Chapter 1, there is a school of thought about ethics that takes exception to our viewpoint, arguing that value judgments are nothing more than statements of individual preference. Obviously, such statements need not be justified by an elaborate framework of normative generalizations and complex argumentation. If the assertion, "Louie Bender is a good person," means only, "I like Louie Bender better than most persons," or even, "Louie Bender behaves the way I like people to behave," then a complicated web of justificatory discourse is unnecessary.

We do not question that people often reflect only their own personal preferences with the value judgments they utter in daily life. Nevertheless, our primary concern in this volume is with the process of communication inquiry. Purposeful, systematic inquiry demands that the inquirer provide reasoned support for any value judgments made. The terms "critic" and "criticism" do not imply mindless complaining and carping, even though they are often used this way in everyday discourse. Rather, "criticism" connotes expert judgment, and expertise in the realm of ethical inquiry is enhanced by a firm theoretical foundation.

Finally, we will touch briefly on the place of theory in aesthetic inquiry. Just as we often question what is moral in communication, we often ask what is beautiful. In other words, we seek to make aesthetic judgments—judgments about the artistic merits of a communicative act or event.

Again, the role of aesthetic critic is common to our daily experience. We argue about the relative merits of one movie or another, or of this book versus that one. We express our opinions about classical and semiclassical, modern jazz, Dixieland, hard rock, country and Western, and a host of other musical forms. We discuss the stylistic merits of the speaking of Adlai Stevenson, Martin Luther King, or George Wallace. In short, we are constantly called upon to cope with, and to make judgments about, the aesthetic quality of our communication environment.

How is theory employed in the reasoned pursuit of aesthetic questions? For the most part, the critic preoccupied with aesthetic issues uses theory in much the same way as the critic whose concern is ethical issues. Isenberg (1948) imposes the following formal structure on aesthetic criticism:[17]

NORMATIVE GENERALIZATION:
Any work which has x quality is aesthetically pleasing.

INFERENTIAL DATA:
This work has x quality.

JUDGMENT:
This work is aesthetically pleasing.

Thus the normative generalization is a theoretical proposition containing a generalized aesthetic judgment. Using this judgment as a starting point, the critic examines the relevant works of interest to determine whether they contain the quality mentioned in the normative generalization, and on the basis of this examination renders an aesthetic judgment concerning them.

Of course, a careful aesthetic criticism usually demands more than a single normative generalization. Suppose, for instance, that a critic wished to pass aesthetic judgment on Martin Luther King's "I Have A Dream" speech. Probably he or she would bring to the task a set of normative generalizations describing the stylistic qualities (i.e., the symbolic and structural forms) that contribute to the aesthetic excellence of a speech. The critic would then examine King's address carefully to discover which of these qualities are present and which are not and, finally, on the basis of the entire body of inferential data, would make an aesthetic judgment of the speech.

Like the critic concerned with ethical issues, the aesthetic critic of communication must often defend his or her normative generalizations. Why are these particular qualities most vital to a work's aesthetic merit, rather than others that might have been selected? In order to convince others of the soundness of his or her judgments, the critic's initial arguments usually focus on this issue.

As we have indicated, the concept of theory is relevant to each of the following chapters. We have devoted some time to sketching out scientific and critical conceptions of theory and to suggesting some of the uses of theory in communication inquiry. We believe that our subsequent discussions of definition, observation, and evaluation will reveal that the time was well spent, for theory plays a leading role in the expansion of our knowledge and understanding about human communication.

NOTES

1. Consistent with Chapter 1, we should reemphasize that the term "theory" does not have one precise meaning. As we hope to show, different definitions of the term are useful for varying approaches to inquiry.

2. For many, the term "control" has a negative, manipulative connotation. When we say that people seek to control their environments, we mean nothing more than that they prefer and seek one set of outcomes over another. Viewed in this light, there is nothing unethical about seeking environmental control.

3. Some philosophers of science treat the terms "explanation" and "prediction" as equivalent, since they are characterized by essentially identical logical structures. We will distinguish between the two processes for pragmatic reasons; i.e., we think some useful points can be made by treating explanation and prediction separately.

4. One reader of this chapter suggested that this example is chauvinistic. We do not agree. We are not advocating that males communicate with females in a domineering way, even if such a style might be effective. We do believe that the sexist aspects of our society have traditionally functioned to reinforce submissiveness on the part of many females and that the empirical generalization we are discussing has some current validity. To ignore this fact does not strike a blow against male

chauvinism; in fact, the best way to change things may be to admit the present applicability of the generalization and to strive to eliminate its applicability in the future.

5. Although logically invalid, such reasoning probably has merit in everyday prediction-making. If there is reason to believe that attraction to domineering men is largely confined to submissive women, it makes sense to avoid a domineering communicative style upon encountering a woman who is not submissive. Moreover, the argument can be recast validly by employing strict implication: If *and only if* a woman is submissive, then she prefers domineering men. This woman is not submissive. Therefore, this woman does not prefer domineering men.

6. Also, it is impossible to observe all the high-credible and low-credible communicators who came before and all those who will come in the future.

7. We shall indicate later that while the scientist may become increasingly confident of the theory's validity, it is logically impossible to verify a theory as true.

8. The phrase "restoring cognitive consistency, or avoiding cognitive inconsistency" reflects something more than mere verbosity. One problem faced by cognitive consistency theorists is the identification of those situations where inconsistency is triggered and then reduced by performing some behavior as opposed to those situations where inconsistency is not even triggered.

9. The sociologist, Arthur Stinchcombe, remarks that one understands something when he can "summarize in a sentence the guts of a phenomenon" (1968, v). Although we do not expect such an astute observer as Stinchcombe to fall prey to the translation trick, we believe such scientific "antics with semantics" often do create a powerful illusion of understanding.

10. As indicated in Case 3 of Chapter 1, the persuasive efficacy of fear-arousing appeals has been extensively studied. For a good review of the findings. see Higbee (1969).

11. Unless, of course, they define them as nothing more than behaviors. But should they adopt such a strategy, they would no longer be operating from an action theory perspective.

12. For an interesting discussion of explanation as it relates to water boiling, see John Waite Bowers (1970, pp. 4–19). Note also that our earlier advocacy of a falsification criterion precludes the labelling of such covering laws as true.

13. Some may argue that Pinocchio actually perceived the Fox and the Cat as the more credible communicators, perhaps because he wanted to believe their messages. Again, this kind of argument, which could always be invoked, returns us to the realm of *post hoc* circularity discussed earlier.

14. Some may contend that the same general dimensions of credibility—e.g., competence and trustworthiness—underlie all of these examples. Even if this is true, it does not solve the basic problem: the behavioral and demographic components of these dimensions differ from situation to situation.

15. General systems paradigms seek laws that hold across systems of varying levels; in short, such paradigms seek to unify the laws of a variety of biological and behavioral disciplines. By contrast, cybernetic systems and structural-functional systems usually carve off a limited domain of phenomena for study.

16. That we assign the critic the role of convincing others of the wisdom of his or her position indicates our view concerning the question: Is persuasion inherently unethical?

17. We have taken some liberties with Isenberg's labels to maintain consistency with our own terminology. Isenberg's categories are "norm" (our "normative generalization"), "reason" (our "inferential data"), and "verdict" (our "judgment"). We believe, however, that the critical processes described by these two sets of labels are essentially the same. We should also point out that Isenberg presents an interesting, persuasive argument defending the possibility of eliminating the normative generalization from the critical schema. Although we will not pursue the issue here, interested readers are urged to examine his paper.

QUESTIONS AND EXERCISES

1. Having read Chapter 2, return to the introductory quotation of Kurt Lewin. What do you think he means by the assertion, "Nothing is more practical than a good theory"?

2. Think of an effective communicator with whom you are acquainted. How would you explain this person's effectiveness? Are you an "insider" or an "outsider"; i.e., is your explanation grounded primarily in the person's personality traits, attitudes, etc., or in certain objective aspects of his or her communication behavior? Or have you mixed the two approaches in your explanation?

3. Assuming you relied primarily on either an "inside" or "outside" explanation in Question 2, go back and translate your explanation into the other approach. For instance, if you said the communicator is effective because he or she is *warm* or *empathic,* try to identify communication behaviors that correspond to these inner states. Conversely, if you attributed effectiveness to a high proportion of interrogatives—e.g., "How do you feel about . . . ?"—as compared with declaratives—e.g., "You seem to feel . . ."—try to relate these differences in communication behavior to some inner state. Can you now see how the two approaches are (or at least can be) related?

4. Reexamine the conversation (Page 75) of the anthropologist, sociologist, psychologist, and physiologist. Using this conversation as a starting point, try to explain some event you have observed at several levels of analysis. How would your *purpose* for explaining the event influence the level of analysis chosen?

5. Indicate whether each of the following propositions represents an "all" (universal lawlike generalization) or "some" (systems) approach to theory construction:

   (a) As a communicator's language intensity increases, his or her persuasive effectiveness increases.

   (b) As a member's status increases in a formal, task-oriented organization, the member's sending and reception of messages increase.

   (c) As the number of negative comments exchanged by family members increases, members' satisfaction with the family relationship decreases.

REFERENCES

Blau, P. M. (1967). *Exchange and Power in Social Life*. New York: John Wiley & Sons.

Bowers, J. W. (1970). *Designing the Communication Experiment*. New York: Random House.

Brehm, J. W., and A. R. Cohen (1962). *Explorations in Cognitive Dissonance*. New York: John Wiley & Sons.

Festinger, L. (1957). *A Theory of Cognitive Dissonance*. Stanford: Stanford University Press.

Festinger, L., and J. M. Carlsmith (1959). Cognitive Consequences of Forced Compliance. *Journal of Abnormal and Social Psychology* 58: 203–210.

Fontes, N. (1973). Structural-Functionalism: An Attempt to Delineate a Methodology for Theory Construction. Unpublished manuscript, Department of Communication, Michigan State University.

Freedman, J. L., and D. O. Sears (1965). Selective Exposure. In L. Berkowitz (ed.), *Advances in Experimental Social Psychology*, Vol. 2, pp. 57–97. New York: Academic Press.

Gergen, K. J. (1969). *The Psychology of Behavior Exchange*. Reading, Mass.: Addison-Wesley.

Greenspoon, J. (1955). The Reinforcing Effect of Two Spoken Sounds on the Frequency of Two Responses. *American Journal of Psychology* 68: 409–416.

Higbee, K. L. (1969). Fifteen Years of Fear Arousal: Research on Threat Appeals: 1953–1968. *Psychological Bulletin* 72: 426–444.

Hildum, D. C., and R. W. Brown (1956). Verbal Reinforcement and Interviewer Bias. *Journal of Abnormal and Social Psychology* 53: 108–111.

Homans, G. C. (1961). *Social Behavior: Its Elementary Forms*. New York: Harcourt, Brace & World.

Isenberg, A. I. (1948). Critical Communication. *Philosophical Review* 58: 330–344.

Janis, I. L., and S. Feshbach (1953). Effects of Fear-Arousing Communications. *Journal of Abnormal and Social Psychology* 48: 78–92.

Meehan, E. J. (1968). *Explanation in Social Science: A System Paradigm*. Homewood, Ill.: The Dorsey Press.

Miller, G. R., and M. Burgoon (1973). *New Techniques of Persuasion*. New York: Harper & Row.

Miller, G. R., and M. A. Hewgill (1966). Some Recent Research in Fear-Arousing Message Appeals. *Speech Monographs* **33:** 377–391.

Newcomb, T. M. (1953). An Approach to the Study of Communicative Acts. *Psychological Review* **60:** 393–404.

Osgood, C. E., and P. H. Tannenbaum (1955). The Principle of Congruity in the Prediction of Attitude Change. *Psychological Review* **62:** 42–55.

Popper, K. R. (1959). *The Logic of Scientific Discovery*. New York: Basic Books.

Scriven, M. (1964). Views on Human Nature. In T. W. Wann (ed.), *Behaviorism and Phenomenology*, pp. 163–190. Chicago: The University of Chicago Press.

Skinner, B. F. (1953). *Science and Human Behavior*. New York: Macmillan.

Skinner, B. F. (1971). *Beyond Freedom and Dignity*. New York: Alfred A. Knopf.

Stinchcombe, A. L. (1968). *Constructing Social Theories*. New York: Harcourt, Brace & World.

Thibaut, J. W., and H. H. Kelley (1959). *The Social Psychology of Groups*. New York: John Wiley & Sons.

Verplanck, W. S. (1955). The Control of the Content of Conversation: Reinforcement of Statements of Opinion. *Journal of Abnormal and Social Psychology* **51:** 668–676.

3
Definition

"*But 'glory' doesn't mean a 'nice knock-down argument.'*"

"*When I use a word, it means just what I choose it to mean—neither more nor less.*"

"*The question is whether you can make words mean so many different things.*"

"*The question is which is to be master—that's all.*"

—conversation between Alice and Humpty Dumpty in **LEWIS CARROLL'S** *Through the Looking Glass*

THE TROUBLE WITH WORDS: THE HUMPTY DUMPTY IN US ALL

Meaningful question-asking begins with definition. Put another way, people cannot answer any question intelligently until they understand what the words in the question mean. This latter statement may at first seem so trivial or so obvious as to merit little attention. You may think, "Who would ever ask a question using words he or she didn't understand?" or "How could you even ask a question if you didn't know the words you were using?" The key to the problem is simply that terms and phrases such as "understanding" and "knowing the meaning of" may themselves have different meanings in different situations. Everyday communication seldom forces persons to realize the frequent vagueness of their own definitions for words or the lack of congruity in the meanings that others attach to the same words. Consider the following exchange:

JACK: "I bought a new plane yesterday."

MARK: (Pondering—"How could he afford an airplane on his salary?")

JACK: "I really enjoy woodworking."

MARK: "Oh, a *plane*."

Such a conversation exemplifies one aspect of this multifaceted problem with words and their meanings, but this aspect (call it *multiple referents*) most commonly occurs in situations where the difference in meanings is so obvious that the problem is quickly resolved. A more subtle problem, and one more appropriate to our discussion of definition, underlies the following conversation:

PHIL: "Boy, is that Jack irresponsible! He told me last week he'd be 'ready to go' on our election campaign by the time of the meeting last night, and he showed up without any materials or posters—just some ideas."

SAM: "That's funny, Jack is a pretty conscientious guy. Did he know the posters were supposed to be ready?"

PHIL: "I thought he did. I mean, it's pretty difficult to be 'ready to go' on a campaign without any posters."

SAM: "Maybe he meant 'ready to go' in the sense of ready to start working on the posters."

PHIL: "Maybe so, but that's not what I assumed he meant."

Assuming that both parties were interacting sincerely, Phil's conclusion that Jack is "irresponsible" represents a misattribution of the cause of the problem. Instead, the major difficulty lies in the different meanings that Jack and Phil attach to the phrase "ready to go." Because of the subtlety of the problem, it is more difficult to discover the cause of this communicative breakdown than it was in the preceding one. The difference between Jack's and Phil's meanings for "ready to go" is much less obvious than the difference between Mark's and Jack's meanings for "plane." In fact, even at this point in their hypothetical conversation, it is unlikely that either Jack or Phil comprehend the meaning the other is attaching to the troublesome phrase, "ready to go." We will label this problem *vagueness of referent,* because the meanings involved, rather than being categorically different, are variations of a single meaning. In short, the exact meaning of the phrase is idiosyncratic to the parties involved, and their communicative problem holds potentially detrimental consequences for their relationship. When Phil thinks of Jack as "irresponsible" he confuses the problem's symptom with its cause. In this example the failure to have the same definition (or at least the failure to recognize differences in meaning) is the cause of the problem; the lack of posters is only the symptom.

Inquiry is synonymous with the pursuit of knowledge. But in order to acquire knowledge, one must be aware of exactly what he or she already knows, exactly what he or she does not know, and exactly what it is he or she desires to know. Stated differently, one must be able to state accurately the knowledge already acquired so that his or her search for new knowledge is not redundant; one must also be able to state with some exactness what it is he or she is searching for (or, in fact, discovers) so that when found it can be used with confidence and precision. The need for clear definitions in making these knowledge claims should be apparent.[1]

The intuitive or "Oh, I've heard of that before!" approach to definition does not satisfy the precise requirements of sound inquiry. Note the following three uses of the term "attitude."

1. "I don't like John's *attitude*."
2. "Well, let me say my *attitude* has always been. . . ."
3. "Karen apparently has a favorable *attitude* toward the Red Cross—she donated $100 this year."

In Speaker 1's statement the referent of the term "attitude" is apparently John's general outlook on life, or at least that portion which directly concerns the speaker. Apparently "attitude" summarizes a collection of impressions of John's character or personality, about which the speaker has passed an overall judgment. In some situations this may be an adequate use of the term, but such usage lacks precision. If asked, the speaker might be hard-pressed to be more specific about John's qualities. It is apparent that the speaker does not like something about John but exactly what that "something" is remains unknown. It is conceivable that the statement refers to John's facial expressions, mode of dress, quickness of movement, independence, sociability, or a host of other qualities or behaviors. Also, if the speaker were to add, "Those guys from New York are always that way," the relationship "observed" between home-state and personal qualities would not be very useful to "know" because anyone who overheard the remark would still be in the dark about the referent of the term "attitude."

Speaker 2's use of the word "attitude" seems different, but just how it differs is unclear. Probably most listeners would feel that Speaker 2 is somehow being more specific than Speaker 1. Obviously, Speaker 2 is talking about something inside his or her own head. Whether it is a feeling, a prejudice, or an idea remains unclear, but there is an apparent reference to some internal state. The discovery of a relationship between what Speaker 2 is calling "attitude" and some other variable would still leave others somewhat in the dark, but at least they would have focused upon some set of entities which are all internal states.

Speaker 3 takes an approach more conducive to inquiry. He or she uses the term "attitude" much more precisely than Speakers 1 and 2. First, he or she implies that "attitude" is an internal state that controls, precedes, or causes behavior. The speaker further suggests that certain dimensions of behavior (for example, amount of monetary contribution) are useful behavioral measures of this unobservable concept, "attitude." Finally, he or she implies that "attitude" is at least somewhat specifiable, i.e., that imaginary boundaries can be drawn around a set of unobservable states and that distinctions between the things that are inside and outside these boundaries can be observed. Speaker 3 does not actually define "attitude," rather, a definition can be inferred from the words used. Whether this definition actually "fits" the common way of conceiving of an attitude is another question, but at least Speaker 3 has narrowed his or her definitional focus to some finite and specifiable set of mediating and behavioral entities.

The preceding examples of definitional problems should indicate that people sometimes do ask questions and make assertions without carefully considering the meanings of key terms. Words used to construct questions need not be alien or new for definitional problems to arise, and without precise definitions of the key terms of his or her questions an inquirer can never be assured of adequate, or even relevant, answers. Without precise definitional guidelines, it is impossible to be sure if one is looking in the right place for the answers to questions. The old adage, "You only get out of something what you put into it," is particularly appropriate to the process of inquiry. An answer can never be more precise than the definitions of the terms contained in the question.

THE COMMUNICATION SCIENTIST'S RAW MATERIALS: CONCEPTS, CONSTRUCTS, AND CLASSIFICATIONS

Having noted that meanings for words vary from person to person, we should nevertheless indicate that words *can* be used relatively unambiguously. For example, a mailing address, which consists of a set of words along with a few numbers, designates exactly the place where the addressee lives. Mail may occasionally be misdelivered, but the cause of such a mistake is usually poor penmanship or carelessness rather than an inherent deficiency in the address system. Such a revelation, however, offers little reason for optimism to communication scientists because their job requires specifying classes or collections of objects for examination, not designating a specific object or a unique feature of the environment. To draw an analogy, they are not so much interested in the particular house designated by a particular address as they are in, say, all houses in its price range or all houses of its style located on the East Coast.[2] Their concern with characteristics of a class, or classes, of objects was underscored in Chapter 1, where we pointed out that communication scientists are primarily interested in empirical generalizations, not in questions dealing with specific facts. Communication scientists assume that the objects they set aside for examination are essentially similar in all respects save one: the degree to which they possess the property or properties entering into a particular hypothesis.[3] These *variables* (i.e., properties of people or things that vary in quality or magnitude from person to person or object to object) may be tangible and observable, or they may be assumed or "constructed" properties that the communication scientist theorizes control other events, though they remain directly unobservable. Such "invisible" variables are often called *constructs* to distinguish them from *concepts* (i.e., variables in general) and to point out that their existence has never been directly verified. Based upon indirect evidence of their existence and their effects, the scientist has postulated their existence, or constructed them, in order to examine empirically some theoretical model.

It may at first seem odd that communication scientists, of all people, should believe in something they have never seen; surely if anyone should require hard evidence before accepting an idea it is a scientist. The complexity of human behavior, however, often requires communication scientists to place a premium on cleverness, rather than stubbornness. For them, the best evidence of the existence of a construct usually lies in observing that its effects on some other variable are in accord with theoretically predicted outcomes. For example, if someone who has always been quiet and retiring were observed at a party enjoying animated conversations with everyone, the observers might immediately conclude that that person's attitude toward people (or perhaps that person's attitude toward his or her attitude toward people) had changed. Of course observers cannot possibly see anyone's "attitude," but they can see behavioral manifestations of its effects. Such a conclusion may be totally wrong—e.g., the party-goer may be socializing to win a bet—but in the absence of other evidence it would be a compelling inference. Any communication scientist can temporarily espouse an idea for purposes of argument or investigation; however, continued belief in the idea demands that it be consistent with research outcomes. Thus, constructs "exist" in communication inquiry, even though they have never been directly observed, because communication scientists have defined them into existence, and the results of scientific inquiry have not led the scientist to define them out.

At this point, a brief description of an empirical model of inquiry may prove helpful in underscoring the crucial role of definition in the inquiry process. The box at the bottom of Fig. 3.1 represents the theoretic model that guides the communication scientist's work. The scientist hypothesizes relationships between variables, either from observation of a number of similar occurrences or from theoretical deductions. Confirming evidence for a theoretical model, however, is gleaned from systematic observation. To test a hypothesis, or hypotheses, a scientist must transform his or her abstract intuitions about the variables into observable representations of their effects. This transformation is accomplished by a series of definitional translations: first, verbalizing the domain of the variable; second, specifying ways to measure it; and, finally, combining the measurements into a meaningful statement of relationship (often in the form of a mathematical equation). After each definitional step, the end product must be accepted as the scientist's full and total meaning for the variable. Inferences beyond the scientist's stipulations are not allowed. A scientist must constantly strive to ensure close logical connections between each step of the process. The merits of a hypothesis are judged by the outcome of the operational definitions representing it in the observational and statistical court. In a very real sense, a scientist's operational definitions and measures of the variables, the end-product of this process, *are* his or her concepts.

Although Fig. 3.1 shows the simplest scheme for a scientific test (one containing only two variables) the complexity of the process is readily apparent. Notice the difference between the theoretical scheme and the operational one. The theoretic diagram reflects the basic idea in the communication scientist's head. The operational scheme illustrates the process one must go through to test an idea. This operational process differentiates scientific communication inquiry from other types of inquiry. Recall the hypothetical speaker of a few pages ago who suggested that all people from New York have disagreeable attitudes; remember also how difficult it was understanding exactly what was meant. If a scientist suggested the same relationship, he or she would also define such key terms as "from New York" (born there or lived there once? from the state or the

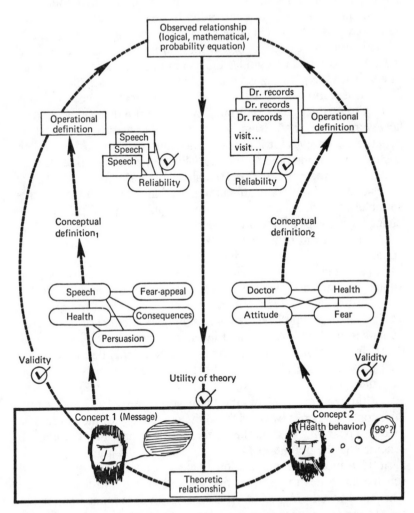

Fig. 3.1 *The Process of Definition in Scientific Communication Inquiry. The whole diagram represents the operational scientific scheme (includes the operations necessary to provide an adequate empirical test of the theoretic notion. The box at the bottom of the diagram represents that original theoretic notion.)*

city? etc.), "attitudes" (life style? sociability? etc.), and "disagreeable" (hostile? self-serving? etc.). Because the scientist's terms are defined clearly, his or her answer—i.e., the statement of the relationship between the two variables—is also more clearly defined and, therefore, more useful. Each step in the operational diagram is a logical link, a translation that takes the inquirer closer to the answer. Precision in the answer is sought not for its own sake but in order that the inquirer will not only arrive at an answer but will also know what the answer *means*. Inquirers not only want to know; they also want to know exactly *what* it is they know.[4] Because their work requires precision, communication scientists want to compare precisely defined entities, and, in many cases, they rely upon well-constructed numerical measurements of the variables.[5]

To understand the process illustrated by the diagram, we will now introduce two new terms: *validity* and *reliability*. Briefly defined, "validity" refers to the accuracy with which a representation of something reflects the thing iself. For instance, a photograph is usually accepted as a valid past representation of some person or event. A degree of distortion, or invalidity, may be present—e.g., colors are often slightly off, three dimensions are reduced to two, etc.—but for most practical purposes the accuracy of the representation is high.[6] By contrast, an impressionist or surrealist portrait of a person would constitute a less valid representation, even though artistically worthy, because of its probable lack of realism.

It is important to distinguish between *internal* and *external* validity. Basically, internal validity deals with the congruence of intent and fact within the inquiry. Did the manipulations the inquirer performed have the intended effect? Do the measures of subject response give us accurate readings of the intended variables? Internal validity deals with these kinds of questions. By contrast, external validity refers to the degree to which the observations made by the inquirer are generalizable to "real-world" situations of the type examined. Both internal and external validity are essential to sound inquiry: the former ensures that the inquirer observed and measured what he or she purported to observe and measure; the latter permits a generalization of findings to less structured and controlled situations.

CASE 1.   *Definition and the real world: The problem of external validity*

Numerous researchers have conducted experiments where they attempted to relate the kind of communication network within the group to such group process outcomes as time taken to solve a problem, number of messages required for problem solution, and the difficulty of organizing the group to solve the problem (Shaw, 1964). For example, Guetzkow and Simon (1955) used five-person groups arranged in one of the following three communication networks:

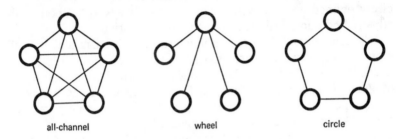

all-channel   wheel   circle

Guetzkow and Simon found that persons in the wheel network not only had the least difficulty in organizing to solve the problem, but that they solved the problem more rapidly and used fewer messages to solve it. These researchers argue that there can be too few opportunities for communication (circle) or too many opportunities (all-channel) for problem solving that depends upon pooling information. (The problem used involved giving each group member a card with five of six symbols appearing on it, and the task was to discover which symbol was common to the cards of all five members of the group.)

Our interest in these kinds of studies lies in the choices of networks used in them. Specifically, the problem with such an approach stems from the fact that the arrangement of the networks is largely unrealistic—they hardly conform with the communication structure one finds in the "real world." Also, the fact that only written messages could be passed through dividers reduced the realism of the situation. These restrictions suggest that the results obtained in the numerous studies on group communication networks may not be generalizable to actual ongoing groups, since such groups function face-to-face and are usually freer to adapt to the task situation. Through their own process of definition, then, the researchers cast doubt on the external validity of the studies.

This kind of problem is often faced in laboratory experiments and frequently stems from the need to maintain tight control over the research environment. Although we heartily endorse sound control practices, we believe that inquirers must be cautious, lest their definitions and procedures affect the study's external validity. A more extensive discussion of the group communication-network studies can be found in the following references:

Guetzkow, H., and H. E. Simon (1955). The Impact of Certain Communication Nets upon Organization and Performance in Task-Oriented Groups. *Management Science* 1: 233–250.

Leavitt, H. J. (1951). Some Effects of Certain Communication Patterns on Group Performance. *Journal of Abnormal and Social Psychology* 46: 38–50.

Shaw, M. E. (1964). Communication Networks. In L. Berkowitz (ed.), *Advances in Experimental Social Psychology*, Vol. 1, pp. 111–147. New York: Academic Press.

"Reliability," while related to validity, can be thought of as the relationship between two or more representations of the same thing. For example, two photographs of a Salvador Dali self-portrait would be highly reliable; if conditions such as lighting, distance, and film development were similar, it would be difficult to distinguish between the two photos. However, neither would be a valid representation of Dali himself because his surrealist self-portrait would have distorted reality. Two photographs taken at the same time of Dali himself would be both reliable and valid representations of his appearance. Reliability thus involves agreement between two or more observers or agreement of a single observer at two or more points in time. Observations can be reliable but not valid—consider, for example, the agreement among observers in the children's tale, "The Emperor's New Clothes."[7]

In a scientific context, reliability is the similarity of measurements of a given property; validity is the degree of similarity between the measurement and the actual amount of the property. Both are interrelated measures of observational efficiency. If a set of measurements is unreliable their validity is also suspect. But, as we have indicated, high reliability does not guarantee high validity. In other words, reliability is a *necessary* condition for validity but not a *sufficient* one.

Comparison of the two schemes in Fig. 3.1 will help to illustrate the difference between theoretical thinking, which is the genesis of factual inquiry, and experimental practice, which involves the actual conduct of inquiry. Communication scientists want to assess and specify exactly the degree of relationship existing between two or more variables, some of which may not be directly observable. Because they wish to express this knowledge exactly, they often translate the richness of the communicative behaviors or the human traits they are studying into numerical representations or mathematical measurements. Such a translation, if properly performed, frequently offers benefits in precision and exactness. Numbers are not necessary for empirical inquiry, but they are frequently used by communication scientists. The crucial process of deriving "measurements" (be they numbers or whatever) from theoretical notions about the components of human communication behavior is an important aspect of what we are calling the process of scientific definition. Before continuing the discussion about our specific model, however, let us back up and look at the definitional process in a more generalized scientific environment.

THE ROLE OF DEFINITION IN COMMUNICATION SCIENCE: GOOD IS USEFUL

If you have ever taken a course in mathematics, no doubt you quickly became aware of the exactness with which mathematical concepts are defined. At first these definitions probably sounded unusual or mysterious because they were phrased in the language of the subject, yet it soon was obvious that everything "fit together." A "circle," for example, was defined as the locus of all points equidistant from a given point in two-dimensional space. Although initially you may not have recognized this definition as a "circle," its simplicity and certainty soon became more apparent. Not only can any circle be described this way, but only circles can result from this definition.

Continued study in a course such as geometry confers heightened appreciation of the complexity of the interlocking rules, theorems, and definitions that make up the subject. Starting with a set of observations, someone constructed a body of rules (loosely translatable as "theories") which yield the formal proofs and pragmatic conclusions that make geometry both a coherent set of propositions and a means for finding answers to practical questions. Geometry, then, is a deductive system which both yields tools to find answers and produces answers themselves. Geometry also bears a valid relationship to reality, i.e., the same "theoretical" operations that can be carried out on paper can also produce useful answers when designing the frame of a building or when constructing a car engine. Thus, the definitions of geometry are "good" ones because they yield answers which have valid application to the "real world." If someone discovered that the rules of geometry were not useful in some area where they apparently should be, the beauty of geometry as a coherent, deductive system would not be diminished; rather, attempts would be made to expand or modify the system so its coherence was maintained but its applicability broadened. The new theories produced by this expansion or modification would probably necessitate new definitions or at least redefinitions of existing concepts. In other words, there is a working relationship between theories and definitions, such that a change in one usually necessitates a change in the other. Moreover, as we emphasized earlier, the assessment of a definition's quality is based upon its utility; in factual communication inquiry, this amounts to how well it fits into theory and how well the theory, using that definition, applies to reality.

A glance at the field of physics may help to clarify some of our preceding comments. Like geometry, Newtonian mechanics, the core of most elementary physics courses, is a coherent set of definitions and theories that can be applied to reality. Anyone familiar with Newtonian laws quickly realizes the interdependence of definitions and theory. For example, the formula: $F = ma$ (Force = mass times acceleration) defies detection as to which of its constituent variables was defined first or how the theory was constructed. In its present form, the formula fits reality so well that if someone should observe a discrepancy between its prediction and some actual occurrence his or her first hunch would be that the observations were faulty. This is not to say that Newtonian mechanics is a universally valid deductive system, for Einstein later showed that it is not. But this system of theories is extremely useful in numerous practical situations, and because of its utility the system is prized highly.

In each of the above systems, one's vantage point makes it difficult to assess which of the key ingredients, theory or definition, came first because they go hand-in-hand. Both systems, geometry and Newtonian mechanics, share an additional feature: they have a small set of basic, independent dimensions from which all other variables are derived. In geometry, distance (or length) and angle are the basic variables, and all geometric definitions make use of them. Recall our previous definition of a "circle" as the locus of points *equidistant* from a given point. Newtonian mechanics, while more complex, has a similar set of basic variables—distance, time, and mass—which enter into all other definitions of variables.

With these ideas in mind, you can begin to appreciate the dilemma faced by students of factual communication inquiry. Their main job is the construction of theories that accurately predict communicative behavior, yet in order to construct such theories they must stipulate definitions of the key concepts which in turn affects the applicability of the theory. Although "good" definitions are necessary for a "good" theory, they alone do not ensure theoretical success.

Let us next consider what communication inquirers have at their disposal for defining the concepts that interest them. They know that the proving ground for any definitional scheme is its theoretic utility. Until they conduct an empirical test, they cannot be sure any set of definitions they propose will be worthy of further consideration. Furthermore, their authoritative sources are limited. Everyone has "looked up a word in the dictionary" to find its "meaning." But as we emphasized in Chapter 1, the dictionary is neither a creator nor an arbiter of meaning, but rather a reporter of word use. "Meanings" so catalogued may help people understand words as they are "normally" used, but such definitions offer limited promise for the communication scientist, since communicative behavior does not necessarily conform with the ways that people talk about it.

In some research areas, however, the communication scientist may be able to gain a head start. If a sufficient body of research has been conducted in a certain area, and if the majority of the research has relied upon similar theoretical notions and similar definitions of concepts, the scientist can begin research using those definitions and reasonably expect that they will be useful. For example, much empirical research in persuasion has utilized the construct *source credibility,* which can be thought of as those perceived attributes of a message-sender which enhance the believability and/or influence of the message. This variable has been shown to have significant effects upon message receivers' behavior; it has been found to interact with message content in bringing about behavior change, and it has been analyzed into its component dimensions.[8] Moreover, much of this research has been successfully replicated. We expect that future inquiry into the persuasion process will profitably employ such a tested definitional approach for source credibility.

If communication scientists commence an inquiry from a theoretical perspective, their thinking both about conceptual definition and the actual conduct of research is greatly facilitated. Admittedly, not all communication inquiry can be based on theory, but when it can, communication scientists are aided immensely in the interpretation of results and in the stipulation and refinement of definitions. Furthermore, many models from the more exact sciences are available for theorizing. Knowing the theoretical structure of Newtonian mechanics, for example, may by analogy allow them to construct a similar theoretic system for studying communicative behavior.

Examining the way that the mathematician or the physicist has gone about the process of defining variables may also provide a valuable learning experience for the communication scientist. The mathematician's approach of defining by intersection of previously defined concepts or the physicist's method of defining "force" as a product of three basic independent variables may provide helpful clues for the communication scientist. Joseph Woelfel and John Saltiel (1974), for example, have proposed a linear force aggregation theory of communication wherein they define attitudes as movable masses in a multidimensional cognitive space. The operating theory is an analogy of Newton's Second Law ($F = ma$). Attitudes are theorized to be changed (i.e., moved within the cognitive space) when forceful messages (messages from a respected source) accelerate (move) them to a new position in relation to other cognitions. Such an adaptation of theoretical relationships from another field may greatly aid in the conduct of scientific research in communication.

Thus, things are not as hopeless as they may first seem. Communication scientists may borrow or slightly modify a theory from some other branch of science and adapt it to communication, thereby requiring them only to define or to adapt definitions for the key variables in the system. Or they may be able to specify variables using one theoretical approach and by means of close observation create another. Still, the problem of definition is always central to their work since their outcomes can be no more precise than the definitions of the concepts with which they are concerned.

THE DEFINITION PROCESS: WAS SOMETHING LOST IN TRANSLATION?

To define is to focus the attention of all upon the same thing for the purpose of common understanding: it is to establish a common ground among all participants in a transaction. If a traveler stopped someone to ask directions to a place 20 miles away, the direction-giver would begin not by describing the locale of the place the traveler wants to find, but by pointing out landmarks in the immediate vicinity and continue by describing landmarks ever closer to the traveler's goal.

Earlier we explained that communication scientists think in a world of concepts but often test their thoughts in a world of numbers. These two worlds cannot be bridged with a single leap (see Fig. 3.1); the inquirer must employ a set of steps that indicate the reasoning underlying the test and thereby lay it open to public scrutiny.

Conceptual definition, the first step in the process, is the meaning to which scientists wish to return after their testing is completed. Remember that for the most part scientists compare measurements when testing a hypothesis. If the range of their conclusions were limited to the "meaning" of their measurements, science would indeed be a sterile business. Strictly speaking, their conclusions are based only on their data, but if these measurements are carefully constructed and carefully obtained they should reflect the richness of the original verbal definition. Restating the conclusions of the test, then, in the language of the conceptual definition, should not be invalid; instead, it should serve to illustrate the total importance and meaning of their experimental observations.

The step of *operational definition* requires scientific inquirers to specify concretely the process they propose for creating and measuring variables. When defining operationally, they say: "Here are the specific observations I am going to make; based upon these and only these observations, I will conclude that variable X was present in such-and-such amount." Observations of this sort are necessarily incomplete, but communication scientists are seeking objectivity. By specifying a procedure in such a way that others can follow it, they ensure that the data they "see" are not products of their imagination.

The final step in the process involves translation of the definition into some numerical or relational statement. This step involves definition in a somewhat different sense. Here, scientists define terms in a logical statement; hence, they are restricted by their observations, their measurement techniques, and the principles of logic. Exactness is required here as elsewhere, because the conclusion they reach forms the nucleus of future generalizations and thinking about the concepts being tested.

There are many advantages to this stepwise process of definition. The primary advantage is exactness. By concentrating upon each step of the definitional process, communication scientists are forced to desert their ivory towers and to describe clearly the boundaries of the abstract concepts with which they are dealing. Exactness aids greatly in the empirical testing of abstract notions because communication scientists have before them the logical links connecting the theory to the data and vice versa. If they have defined their terms carefully, they know the limitations of their conclusions as well as their full potential. They are not forced to make "in the dark" generalizations about the applicability of their experimental results. Moreover, readers of their work are placed in the same enlightened position. They can trace the scientist's steps from theory to results and can appraise the efficiency with which the original theoretical notions have been captured and tested.

These additional sets of opinions often contribute to a valuable critique of any research report. Beyond this immediate benefit, the definitional steps taken by one communication scientist sometimes spark another scientist's insight concerning the concept and produce a new, more powerful definition. This act of redefinition, which is often accompanied by retheorizing, frequently provides the impetus for a major conceptual breakthrough. To the ancient Greeks, all matter was composed of four elements: fire, earth, air, and water. This definition of matter was certainly insightful given the observational techniques available at the time, but redefinition in terms of atomic theory and the periodic table of elements was the conceptual step that allowed chemistry to become the useful body of knowledge it is today.

Major breakthroughs aside, in developing sciences such as communication, even standardization of a definition lays the groundwork for possible theory development. Consider the semantic-differential technique for evaluating subjective meaning described in Case 2 of Chapter 1, an approach which has become common in communication inquiry. The underlying assumption in this set of conceptual and operational definitions is that the meaning of a word or a concept can be analyzed into a small number of independent, measurable dimensions—e.g., an evaluative dimension, a potency dimension, and an activity dimension. Such an analysis allows useful comparisons between the meanings of concepts and offers insight into people's thinking processes. When using this technique, the dimensions of meaning are determined by pairs of adjectives that have opposite meaning. Respondents are asked to locate on several such dimensions their own meaning for the concept in question. For example, a comparison of one person's meaning for the concepts "mother" and "father" might look like this:

MOTHER

```
Good:——:——X——:——:——:——:——:——: Bad
Strong:——:——:——:——X——:——:——:——: Weak
Passive:——:——X——:——:——:——:——:——: Active
```

FATHER

```
Good:——:——X——:——:——:——:——:——: Bad
Strong:——X——:——:——:——:——:——:——: Weak
Passive:——:——:——:——:——:——X——:——: Active
```

As we can see from the above example, such a technique allows precise specification of differences in meaning by analyzing the dimensions of meaning for one person and the differences in meaning among various people. The concept of "meaning" itself is very abstract, but such a standardized definition has utility because it allows comparison of research results among similar lines of inquiry and integration of results from different lines of inquiry. Thus, using this standardized approach, Osgood (1974) and his associates have found that the connotative dimensions of meaning identified for English-speaking Americans (Evaluation, Potency, Activity, as represented by the scales above) also exist with much the same structure and importance in a vast sampling of other languages and cultures.

Sometimes a broad redefinition of a concept changes the entire thrust of a field of inquiry. Such a reconceptualization is itself a definitional process, but instead of starting at "ground level," the process is based upon experience with a previous definition. In communication inquiry, the conceptualization of persuasion as an interaction of source, message, *and* audience represents one such redefinition. For the most part, previous conceptualizations concentrated almost exclusively upon source and message. Such conceptualizations naturally imposed severe limitations upon discovering more effective persuasion strategies, since audience composition and reaction have been shown to be important parts of the influence process. The three-part reconceptualization of persuasion strongly suggests that no universal rules of speaker preparation or message construction exist. Motivational research has capitalized upon this reconceptualization by casting a scientific eye upon potential advertising audiences to discover effective buying appeals. The later popularization of motivational research and many of its discoveries (e.g., Packard, 1957) masked the scientific impact of the new conceptualization. The discovery that a person's choice of a car may reveal subconscious urges is interesting in itself, but it also shows the power that reconceptualization can provide in pursuing knowledge.

The process of definition involves a series of abstractions and redefinitions. To define a concept scientifically, communication inquirers must abstract from the concept level-by-level, realizing that each successive abstraction actually produces something increasingly different from their original intent. The end result is a set of carefully planned measurements or observations. Suppose, for example, that a communication scientist is interested in the concept *empathic ability.* If the scientist thinks that empathic ability is related to a speaker's persuasive power, he or she may want to conduct an experiment where persons of varying empathic ability deliver the same speech to various randomly constructed audiences and then measure the relative persuasive impact of each speaker. Intuitively, *empathic ability* seems a rich, multifaceted concept. Some "speaker behaviors" which may cause one to be perceived as empathic are "warmth" of voice, use of personal examples when communicating, and nonverbal reactions similar to those of the audience, to mention but a few. To test the theoretical relationship, however, the communication scientist must boil down all this richness to several valid, reliable, and precise dimensions of the concept. The metaphor "boil down" is not chosen accidentally. The end product of the definitional process is an ultimate abstraction. In the extreme case, the communication scientist has reduced a warm, human attribute to a set of numbers with decimal points. Many people contend that such a reduction fatally damages the concept— that in the process of scientific definition the essence of the concept is also lost.

Perhaps an analogy can illustrate the error of this contention. In many societies in the world (and in America in the last century) women highly valued a "pale" complexion. Such "paleness" had social and psychic value. It was a human "behavior" which had many beneficial connotations. Still, paleness may stem from several causes: it may result from genetic and environmental circumstances among healthy people; it may result from cosmetics among healthy and unhealthy people; or it may be a signal of ill health. Obviously, it is of great importance to any woman to know from which of the three sources her "paleness" stems. The pale complexion of ill health cannot easily be distinguished from the other sources by persons who have not been specifically trained to detect the differences. These differences boil down to specific observations (sometimes of things other than skin color, e.g., blood counts) or operational definitions of specific illnesses. The trained doctor can make these distinctions by making the corresponding observations. It seems far-fetched to argue that if doctors were to make a determination of the cause of a patient's paleness they would also destroy the richness of the variable "paleness."

As we mentioned, the abstraction and transformation of the communication scientist's original theoretical scheme into concise statements of relationship can be seen as a series of translations. In any translation (as, for example, from one language to another), some of the original meaning is lost, but this loss can be minimized. The notion of minimizing loss through translation, or efficiency of translation, is important to keep in mind. The translation process inherent in scientific definition is itself a compromise necessary to the pursuit of knowledge. The sacrifice of some richness for the benefits of exactness and clarity is a tradeoff that must be made by communication scientists, since for their purposes neither richness nor precision *alone* is optimally useful. Because loss of richness always accompanies translation, some omniscient being could conceivably give each logical link in any definitional scheme (conceptual definition, operational definition, even statistical analysis) an "efficiency rating" based on the total amount of meaning surviving the translation.

Given such an omniscient judgment, the efficiency of the communication scientist's total theoretical and experimental scheme can be no greater than the smallest efficiency rating of any of its links. For example, even with a very good rating of 80 percent on each of the three translations and a probability rating of 95 percent on the statistical test, the total efficiency is: $80\% \times 80\% \times 80\% \times 95\% = 48.6\%$. It should be noted that the arbitrary figure of 80 percent chosen here is higher than many reliability coefficients, and, although validity is difficult to measure, we suspect that it exceeds many validity coefficients. The resultant figure of 48 percent shows that even with careful attention to their work, scientists can end up with an experimental result which mirrors only about one-half of the richness and meaning they envisioned in the original theoretical scheme. It is for this reason that communication scientists try to achieve precision and exactness in their definitions.[9]

CONCEPTUAL DEFINITION: TELL ME WHAT YOU MEAN

Hayakawa reports the humorous story of two Englishmen discussing politics:

> "What's all this about 'one man, one vote'?" asked the Nottingham miner.
>
> "Why, one bloody man, one bloody vote," Bill replied.
>
> "Well, why the hell can't they say so?" (1964, p. 118)

The story is humorous, of course, because in some situations and for some people, such an "explanation" is perfectly adequate. In another sense, though, the story ironically reminds us of the difficulty in making ourselves clear to others.

Conceptual definition comprises the first step in the series of translations we have labeled "the definition process." In its broadest sense, conceptual definition consists of translating the theoretical notion in the mind of the communication scientist into a meaningful verbal message.

To clarify what we mean, suppose Fred and Kate, along with a mutual acquaintance, Jim, are celebrating the end of final exams in a local bar. Jim has offered to buy drinks for Kate and Fred:

FRED: "O.K., I'll have something cool, and Kate doesn't drink much so get something sweet for her."

JIM: "Right, something cool and something sweet." (As Jim walks to the bar, he mulls over the orders.)

JIM: "Let's see now, something cool—maybe a gin and tonic for Fred—now something sweet. Something sweet—aha, a bacardi for Kate."[10]

Whether or not he is aware of it, Jim has just performed an act of conceptual definition. He has taken the abstract concepts "cool" and "sweet" and transformed them into meaningful verbal messages. Obviously, gin and tonic is not the only cool drink available, nor is a bacardi the only sweet one. Although Jim has limited the conceptual field by specifying particular drinks for his friends, he has managed to preserve the meaning of their original specifications. *Conceptual definition may be thought of as meaningfully verbalizing the abstract.* When performing this translation, there are several criteria communication scientists should employ:

1. *Clarity of delineation.* The "outline" or "boundaries" of the concept should be as clearly identified as words permit. The many intuitive notions about what "goes on in people's heads" or "what communication is" constitute a tangled ideational network. Communication scientists should carefully separate their own variables from similar or related variables so as to achieve precision and clar-

ity in their work. This is especially important when the defined concept already has popular or intuitive definitions which are at odds with the meaning stipulated for the research or when the concept has achieved a different standardized definition in prior scientific work. For example, if an inquirer is interested in the persuasive effects of communicator credibility, he or she must be careful to conceptually (and operationally) separate the components of credibility from other similar factors such as the believability of the message, the prior attitudes of the audience; and perhaps most important, personality factors of the communicator which for either logical or pragmatic reasons do not or should not contribute to his or her credibility.[11]

2. *Composition description.* The components of the concept, whether or not they are variables worthy of study in their own right, should be carefully described and their relationship to each other detailed. Many constructs which are internal or mental mediators of behavior are defined as a collection of smaller concepts. The specification of the component parts and their relationships offers scientist and critic alike a more precise grasp of the concept and a better ground for assessing its operationalization. With a clear understanding of the components of the construct, the researcher can assess more accurately the requirements for his or her operational definition and make this translation with maximal meaningfulness.[12]

3. *Proper range of meaning.* This criterion forces communication scientists to examine more concretely the parts of a theoretic relationship. For their work to be useful, their concepts must be of sufficient universality to encompass a substantial range of human activities. Conversely, if their concepts are too broad, they may not offer the kind of exactness and precision which science requires. In one direction, the scientist risks insignificant research; in the other, unfathomable generality. The first problem can be illustrated by considering a hypothetical research project designed to examine the relationship between number of eye blinks and speaking rate when a person delivers the Gettysburg Address. Although the concepts are specific, their scientific value is negligible because of their probable minimal importance to human communication behavior. The opposite extreme can be exemplified by the suggestion that a person's communicative style is related to his or her mental makeup. In the

absence of further conceptual refinement, this seemingly acceptable generality cannot be adequately tested because of extremely broad, poorly defined concepts. In short, conceptual definition should afford richness by embedding concepts in fertile theoretic soil, and should ensure that they do not crowd out the other concepts that share the scientific plot of land.

4. *Avoidance of tautology.* Tautology can be briefly described as *identity by definition.* The scientific method requires that conclusions be based upon evidence, which in turn demands that any relationship a scientist proposes must be capable of being disproved. Communication scientists should search for truth, not ego satisfaction. Thus, in each inquiry they conduct, there must exist at least one possible outcome which would falsify the original prediction. If they are careless (and perhaps also eager) they may accidentally define components of the variables that they think are related quite similarly. In such a situation, it would be small wonder that a statistical analysis would reveal a relationship.

Tautology is more common to operational than to conceptual definition. The leap from verbal definitions to operational procedures is a big one and creates a greater possibility for being off-target than does the transition between theorizing and verbalizing. The difficulties of tapping an abstract concept with a test or an instrument may result in invalid observations of the intended variable. Moreover, because of the vague and often interrelated nature of mental states, methods of observation that yield inferences about one such state often permit inferences to other states as well. This is especially true if the observation method involves a self-report, where the individual responds to written statements or questions. It would be difficult, for example, to imagine a self-report instrument to assess internalization of middle-class norms that did not also tap such mediating variables as degree of conformity, general sociability, and political conservatism. If these variables were specifically excluded from the conceptual scheme—or worse yet, if they were the other variables in the scientist's hypothetical equation—the results of any empirical test would immediately become suspect.

5. *Previous usage.* Often the concept that communication scientists seek to define has already been subjected to conceptual scrutiny by other inquirers. If it is a "popular" variable—e.g.,

source credibility—"standardized" conceptual and operational definitions may already exist. If a body of literature exists which expresses relationships between credibility and numerous other variables, and if this research has relied on a particular definition of credibility, communication scientists must determine whether the purposes of inquiry would better be served by retaining the existing definition or by redefining. If they choose the latter, the results will not "fit" the existing body of research and they cannot evaluate their findings on the same basis as previous work. This is not necessarily an argument against redefining a concept, but it does emphasize that the potential benefits of redefinition should be weighed against the value of adding to a unified, coherent body of knowledge.

CASE 2. *Some information about information: Problems of relating constructs and their definitions to human communication*

We should again make the point that the conduct of inquiry often requires the wisdom of compromise to satisfy disparate goals, rather than dogged search for an ideal solution. Dealing with the concept of information offers an example of problems that may arise. In *The Mathematical Theory of Communication,* Shannon and Weaver (1949) explored relationships among components of communication systems and derived a mathematical system for dealing with them. To give perspective to their work, we should explain that their focus was on mechanical or electronic systems which transmit, store, or receive signals (information) such as might be used in telephone or computer applications.

To Shannon and Weaver, the concept of *information* was the opposite of entropy, chaos, or randomness. Information imposed some structure, or predictability, on an environment of choices, or to put it another way, amount of information was equivalent to amount of uncertainty reduction. Thus, if many potential events were possible and all were equally probable, uncertainty as to which event would occur would be high and anything that would make the situation more predictable would contain high information. On the other hand, if the impending event were a foregone conclusion, its occurrence (or anything which made its occurrence seem more likely) would contain little information. Shannon and Weaver operation-alized *information* mathematically as:

$$H = -K \sum_{i=1}^{n} p_i \log p_i,$$ where H = amount of information contained in any event;

K = a constant, and p_i = the probability of event i.

This definition satisfies several of our criteria for operational definitions, but it is extremely difficult to apply to human communi-cation. The problem, of course, stems from our inability to attach exact probabilities to the pool of potential events (or potential mes-sages) which a person may choose to send. We certainly do this on an informal level—e.g., if we have been hospitalized, we expect a number of messages pertaining to our health—but it is impossible to attach precise probability values to these expectations.

Our point is that Shannon and Weaver's operational definition fills the bill *given* their conceptual definition of *information*. Sub-sequent attempts to apply the same operationalization to human communication tread on thin ice because the construct of *informa-tion* takes on new conceptual dimensions when applied to human beings, rather than electronic signal systems. Therefore, to apply quantification to human information transfer, new conceptual and operational definitions tailored to suit that purpose are needed. The following references discuss in greater detail some of the issues related to information:

Krippendorff, K. (1975). Information Theory. In G. J. Hanneman and W. J. McEwen, (eds.), *Communication and Behavior*, pp. 351–389. Reading, Mass.: Addison-Wesley.

Piel, G., *et al.*, eds. (1966). *Information*. San Francisco: W. H. Freeman.

Shannon, C. E., and W. Weaver (1949). *The Mathematical Theory of Communication*. Urbana, Ill.: University of Illinois Press.

We have consistently stressed that the sole determinant of a definition's quality is its utility. The preceding five criteria detail the major considerations involved in assessing the utility of a conceptual definition. Obviously, it is difficult, if not impossible, for the communication scientist to optimize all five. Tradeoffs are inevitable; to ensure clarity of delineation it may be necessary to restrict range of meaning; to guard against tautology some of the concept's richness may be lost. Nevertheless, when translating abstract concepts to verbal definitions, the communication scientist should weigh each of the criteria and attempt to strike a fruitful balance among them.

OPERATIONAL DEFINITION: TELL ME WHAT YOU REALLY MEAN

Let us return to our hypothetical big spender, Jim, who when last encountered a few pages ago was on his way to the bar to buy drinks for Kate and Fred:

JIM: (After getting the bartender's attention) "I'd like two gin and tonics and a bacardi, please."

BARTENDER: "Sure, but I wonder if you could help me out? You see, I'm just filling in for a friend tonight. The gin and tonics are no problem, but I've never mixed a bacardi. So if you tell me how, I'll be glad to mix it."

JIM: "O.K., you mix 1½ ounces of rum with a half-ounce of lime juice, add one teaspoon of sugar syrup and one teaspoon of grenadine, shake well in a shaker with cracked ice, and strain into a cocktail glass."

Again, Jim has unknowingly performed an act of scientific definition. This time, however, he has translated a verbal definition into concrete operations; he has *operationally defined* his drink order.

This leap from the verbal, conceptual world to the workaday world of observation by means of operational definition is perhaps the mightiest jump, or conversely, the weakest link in the definitional chain. This step highlights the basic paradox of communication scientists: their primary aim is to construct abstract, universal laws which explain and predict communicative behavior, but they can offer no such law for consideration without testing it in very concrete situations using limited numbers of people and making specific, concrete observations. The refining of rich components of human behavior into particular observations is often a difficult process. Fortunately, in some cases, previously constructed operationalizations exist for certain "standardized" constructs; yet, for the most part, these require adaptation or modification for particular situations. *The primary purpose of operational definition is the translation of verbal definitions to a set of observable operations.*

One could reasonably argue that any enterprise which demands exactness relies upon operational definition. To a nonscientist the notion of operational definition may sound foreign or even pretentious, yet people use it daily. Everyone has probably had the experience of buying clothes for someone not knowing the correct size. Typically, the purchaser ponders over a selection explaining to the salesperson, "She's about your size, maybe a little shorter, of average weight and has relatively long arms." The end result of such vague specifications is often *futility.* The end result of a clear operational definition is *utility.*

Fields such as law, economics, and medicine, regardless of appearances of subjectivity, make extensive use of operational definition. Although practices commonly used outside of a courtroom (e.g., polygraph examination and psychological testing) are frequently not admissible as evidence, the legal profession does make use of more traditional scientific methods of validation and evidence collection. When classifying a crime, the law (a written description of categories of behavior) specifies certain acts that must have occurred in order for a given event to be classified as, say, a burglary. Likewise, though we hear terms such as "recession," and "inflation" bandied about in the news as though they were catch-all words, economists do have standardized operational definitions for these labels and do not apply them haphazardly. For example, a *recession* is normally defined as a decline in the nation's Gross National Product for two consecutive quarters. Though such a definition can encompass a wide range of economic setbacks, it does impose some standardization upon the rather abstract concepts of economics. Similarly, the joke about the standard doctor's reply, "Take some aspirin and go to bed," does injustice to practitioners of modern medicine. In a physical examination, the doctor is "looking" for specific, observable behaviors of organs or organisms in order to classify symptoms into meaningful categories. If the doctor feels chemical therapy is in order it will be necessary to define precisely what type and amount is to be administered. The prescribed treatment is an operational definition. A doctor does not say, "Take an antibiotic until you feel better"; instead, he or she says, "Take 50 milligrams of x-penicillin four times daily at equal intervals for 10 days." With such an approach, the doctor is trying to minimize misunderstanding and to maximize compliance with the prescription.

Most persons would feel ridiculous if they pulled into a gas station and said, "Give me a moderate amount of gas." It is no less ridiculous to attempt systematic, precise statements about relationships between concepts without having a precise and concrete set of steps for creating and observing these concepts. Operational definition is at the heart of this process of creating and observing concepts.

As was true with their conceptual counterparts, operational definitions should be carefully evaluated along several criterial dimensions. Let us examine those criteria that are particularly crucial in determining the utility of an operational definition:

1. *An operational definition should tap or encompass as much of the richness of the conceptual definition as is possible.* Specifically, this means that an operational definition should flow logically from the conceptual definition that the communication scientist has posited. Stated differently, it should include a way of operationalizing every area or dimension that the scientist wishes to include in the conceptual definition. Suppose, for example, that a communication scientist becomes interested in the concept of *social status* and its potential relationships with certain communication variables. Abstractly speaking, variables such as *popular recognition, influence,* and *income* may all contribute to the concept of *social status.* Assume that the scientist's conceptual definition includes all these aspects of status. If so, operational definitions should be designed to provide measures and weights of each of the dimensions. For example, the scientist could assess the popular recognition of a person by counting the number of people who recognize the person's name, expecting, for instance, that almost everyone would identify Ted Kennedy or Helen Hayes, but that few would know Marvin Cooney of Muscatine, Iowa, or Mary Wenzlick of East Lansing, Michigan. To assess influence the scientist could examine the names of persons

appearing in an organizational chart and determine the number of individuals who were subordinate to each: the greater the number of subordinates, the higher the influence within the organization and, consequently, the higher the person's social status on the influence dimension. Finally, the scientist could measure income by asking persons how much money they make yearly, inspecting their tax records, or, in the case of extremely wealthy individuals such as Ted Kennedy, relying upon other sources of income information.[13]

Suppose, however, that our hypothetical communication scientist decides that attempts to measure all three dimensions of social status are bound to be too time-consuming and elects to settle solely for a measurement of income. Even though the income variable permits a fine measurement scale, it alone does not encompass the relevant dimensions of social status posited by the scientist in his or her own conceptual definition.[14] Two major problems arise from this operational shortchanging. First, the outcomes of any research using only income are certain to be deceptive, albeit the deception is unintentional. The scientist has not observed what he or she has professed to observe, since the observations do not take account of the variables of popular recognition and influence. For instance, there is no distinction between well-known and obscure millionaires; there is no status distinction between millionaire Howard Hughes and millionaire Joe Blow, even though the conceptual definition recognizes such a distinction. Second, our hypothetical scientist has opened the door to error or inefficiency by loosening the links between conceptual and operational definitions. According to the original conceptual definition, an unemployed person who won a million dollars in the Michigan lottery would be unlikely to gain markedly in social status, but given the scientist's operational definition, the lottery-winner's status would increase astronomically.[15] If the scientist had conceptualized social status solely on the basis of income this would not be a problem; it is the disparity between the conceptual and operational definitions that causes concern.[16] Given the original conceptualization, it would make better operational sense to construct an index of the recognition, influence, and income measures. Such an index would eliminate deception, and while error is still possible, its likelihood is reduced since it is unlikely a person would be rich, influential, and well-known and still have low social status.[17]

CASE 3. *Searching for speech anxiety: Some alternative operationalizations*

In scientific communication inquiry, selection of operational definitions for the variables of interest often involves difficult choices. Obviously, the inquirer seeks a set of observable behaviors that are highly correlated with the conceptual definition; and, at the same time, uncorrelated with irrelevant, outside influences. Given this ideal situation, the inquirer can get a direct "reading" of the relevant concepts without the reading being contaminated by other factors. Realistically, this ideal is seldom completely attainable, and most operationalizations suffer from lower than desired correlations with the conceptual definitions, excessive influence by outside factors, or both.

To illustrate differing methods of operationalizing the same concept, we will examine some of the research using the variable *speech anxiety,* and look at the problems posed by different operationalizations. Three distinct approaches have been taken by inquirers interested in *speech anxiety:* (1) the use of direct physiological measures of anxiety correlates, such as galvanic skin response, respiration, or heart rate, (2) self-reports of anxiety by speakers using questionnaire-rating scales; and, (3) observer reports, where persons watching the speaker rate apparent speech anxiety on the basis of visible or audible cues such as trembling or stammering (Dickens and Parker, 1951; Clevenger, Jr., 1959).

Each of these methods taken by itself seems a reasonable way of arriving at a quantitative measure of *speech anxiety,* yet notice how different the results could be. Although each method seems to be at least moderately correlated with the intended conceptual variable, *speech anxiety,* each probably also includes a component of general anxiety not directly related to the presentation of a speech. Specifically, the physiological measures, while affording greater precision than the other methods, may also tap general anxiety and may even cause additional anxiety by their obtrusive presence. The problem they present—i.e., some contraption must be attached to the speaker—is not easily overcome. In comparison, the self-report method offers greater potential for distinguishing between anxiety arising specifically from the speech situation and such things as general anxiety, nervous habits, or other irrelevant factors. Its accuracy, however, depends upon the speaker's awareness of his or her own emotional state and, perhaps more important, willingness to tell others how he or she feels about speaking. This last problem is extremely bothersome, for willingness to tell about one's feelings may itself vary with the amount of anxiety experienced. Finally, the method of observer reports not only poses the problem of differentiating sources of anxiety, but also depends upon unknown bases of judgment. Thus, when an observer provides a rating for the anxiety of a speaker, it must be assumed that the criteria for the rating are valid. Often these criteria are not explicitly known even by the rater.

One might argue that *speech anxiety* could have different conceptual meanings depending upon the type of inquiry undertaken. For instance, if an investigation centered upon the relationship of a speaker's emotional state to the topic of the speech, physiological measures might be best suited because they not only give a direct reading of physical measures, but also eliminate the psychological judgments of the observer listening to the message. On the other hand, if an inquirer were investigating the efficacy of several techniques for reducing the speech anxiety of public speakers, measures based upon observer reports might be more useful.

Comparison between pairs of the above measures in the same situations reveal only moderate correlations, which indicates that each is affected differently by external factors and illustrates the problem of linking observable measures to conceptual entities (Clevenger, Jr., 1959). The following references provide more information on measures of speech anxiety:

Behnke, R. R. (1970). Psychophysiological Technologies. In P. Emmert and W. D. Brooks, (eds.), *Methods of Research in Communication,* pp. 429–452. New York: Houghton Mifflin.

Clevenger, T., Jr. (1959). A Synthesis of Experimental Research in Stage Fright. *Quarterly Journal of Speech* 45: 134–145.

Dickens, M., and W. R. Parker (1951). An Experimental Study of Certain Physiological, Introspective and Rating-Scale Techniques for the Measurement of Stage Fright. *Speech Monographs* 18: 251–259.

Miller, G. R. (1972). Speech: An Approach to Human Communication. In R. W. Budd and B. D. Ruben (eds.), *Approaches to Human Communication*, pp. 383–400. New York: Spartan Books.

---

2. *An operational definition should allow for standardization of terms through concreteness.* Usually operational definitions serve to reduce the boundaries of a concept to a level where the words or terms comprising the concept have a narrower range of meanings. As Hayakawa (1964) points out, there are numerous ways of referring to a farmer's cow, "Bessie." The list of possible labels includes "Bessie," "cow," "livestock," "animals," "property," and "wealth." The difference among these terms lies in the number of other referents which could be indicated by the same label. As we have stressed, one primary purpose of definition is to eliminate from consideration all things that are not intended to be included. Thus, to use a term such as "livestock" when what is meant is "cow," or "social status" when what is meant is "income," or "credibility" when what is meant is "trustworthiness," is to define sloppily. Operational definitions should concretely specify *what* is being observed. Abstractness for its own sake is undesirable and is often counterproductive in scientific communication inquiry.

3. *An operational definition should be replicable.* Scientific inquiry is a cumulative process; communication scientists build upon the findings of their ancestors. Obviously, it is impossible to expand yesterday's findings and to correct yesterday's errors if the meanings of key terms and concepts are not communicated clearly. If our hypothetical scientist creates a three-dimensional index to measure *social status,* other scientists should be able to replicate, or reproduce, the same index. This requirement demands not only specificity of terms but a complete description of the major steps of the measurement process. Thus, while *credibility* may be more concretely defined as *competence, trustworthiness,* and *dynamism,* it still is necessary to construct a series of operational steps that permit observation of the concept. Differences in replicability can best be illustrated by contrasting two different approaches to this problem:

APPROACH 1: "Ask people how competent, trustworthy, and dynamic they perceive various communicators to be."

APPROACH 2: "Select four semantic differential-type scales that load highly on the *competence* dimension of credibility, four that load highly on the *trustworthiness* dimension, and four that load highly on the *dynamism* dimension. (Here one might possibly even specify the bipolar adjectives bounding each of the 12 scales.) Have each person place a check mark on the interval for each of the 12 scales that best indicates his or her perception of the communicator's credibility. Assign numerical values to each of the seven intervals, with a score of seven representing the interval on each scale that reflects maximally high credibility and a score of one representing the interval that reflects maximally low credibility. Sum across the four scales used to measure each of the dimensions of credibility. The resultant three scores constitute the individual's perception of the communicator's competence, trustworthiness, and dynamism.

Both Approach 1 and Approach 2 specify operational definitions of credibility. Obviously, however, it would be difficult, if not impossible, for other inquirers to replicate the operational steps embodied in Approach 1. How are the relevant questions to be put to respondents? Are the questions to be open-ended or structured? How are the respondents' answers to be coded and analyzed? Questions such as these must be answered before the operational definition can be unambiguously employed by other communication scientists.

By contrast, Approach 2 affords an opportunity for replication by numerous researchers. Armed with the clear description of procedures contained in the operational definition, any number of communication scientists could use this measurement of credibility. Thus, the operational definition detailed in Approach 2 better meets the criterion of replicability than does the vague, sketchy operationalization used in Approach 1.

4. *An operational definition should match the concept to a good numerical scale.* While we will discuss this criterion more extensively in Chapter 4, it merits brief mention here. The theory of scaling is complex and has been extensively treated by numerous writers (e.g., Guilford, 1954; Torgerson, 1958). Suffice it to say that the more mathematically useful the numbers on the scale used to measure the variables, the better. In more concrete terms, this

means the communication scientist should use higher-order measurement scales (interval or ratio) whenever possible, since such scales permit a meaningful discussion of differences or ratios between two or more measurements. Such measurement scales allow the inquirer to set the differences between responses or observations to some external numerical standard. This may not seem earthshaking because the types of measurements with which we are familiar (temperature, length, area, volume) make use of such scaling. Human behavior, though, does not always conform to criteria which allow this external numerical standard. When the logical assumptions which do allow it are met, the inquirer is usually able to extract more information from his or her investigations. Interval and ratio scaling not only permit precise measurement, they also enable the scientist to apply powerful statistical techniques to the measurements to discover existing relational patterns. Quite often, success or failure in discovering a pattern hinges on the type of statistical test applied, and, in turn, this is dependent upon the scaling technique used, since each test has certain requirements for the data it uses.

At this stage of the inquiry process, many of the operational definitions used by communication scientists do not satisfy the requirements for interval or ratio scaling. Scale construction for psychological variables is a complex business, and the scientist may be forced to settle for less precision than he or she would like. For instance, if a scientist wishes to study the influence of conformity-oriented messages on conforming behavior, it may be necessary to settle for the measurement statement, "X and Y conformed, but Z did not," when it would be preferable to be able to say, "X manifested 40 units of conformity, Y 20 units, and Z zero units." Then, too, intervality is a tricky concept when applied to mental dispositions or behaviors. Suppose a communication scientist wished to study the effect of room temperature on the type and frequency of communicative behaviors. In manipulating the variable of room temperature, the scientist can take advantage of an interval scale: he or she might, for example, vary the room temperature in ten-degree intervals from 50 to 100 degrees. Psychologically, the distance between the physically equal intervals may vary; e.g., the distance between 60 and 70 degrees may not correspond *psychologically* with the distance between 80 and 90 degrees. This is why communication scientists, as well as their colleagues from other behavioral sciences, usually speak of *equal-appearing intervals,* rather than *equal intervals.*

Although these problems pose formidable challenges, they should not deter communication scientists from operationally defining their variables as precisely and powerfully as possible. Often scientists endure gross, imprecise levels of measurement when a bit more ingenuity or hard work could yield a more powerful scale. As we have already stressed and will amplify in the next chapter, acquiescence to imprecise measurement is disadvantageous to the communication scientist. It may prevent detection of existing relationships or it may necessitate an imprecise statement of detected relationships.

One final point merits reemphasis: *conceptual and operational definition are inextricably bound together in the inquiry process.* Communication scientists' conceptual definitions of their abstract ideas dictate the priorities they bring to the task of operationally defining concepts; their skill and precision in the operational domain determine the confidence with which they can relate their observations back to their original theoretical propositions or statements of hypothesized relationships. To restate a caveat offered early in this chapter: *the answers provided for factual communication questions can be no more useful or precise than are the definitions stipulated for the key concepts contained in the questions.*

DEFINITION IN DEALING WITH VALUE QUESTIONS: SOME OBSERVATIONS

We have already stressed the distinction between questions of fact and questions of value, arguing that the former inquire about properties of objects and events external to the observer whereas the latter inquire about an observer's aesthetic or ethical judgments of such objects and events. Although there are many similarities to the process of definition used for inquiry into factual and value questions, several important differences deserve comment. To illustrate one of these differences, let us listen in on a conversation of Fred, Kate, and Jim as they are leaving a movie theater:

JIM: "That sure was a good movie."

KATE: "I'll say!"

FRED: "Yeah, it was real good; very few movies make me cry like that one did."

JIM: "That's one of the classic scenes of tragedy—the hero's tragic flaw leading to his demise."

KATE: "That's true, but I liked it because evil seemed to triumph; that reflects what often happens in real life."

In this hypothetical conversation, all three conversants have observed the same event, and all three have arrived at similar aesthetic judgments about it. The processes used in making these judgments, however, were somewhat different.

Fred concluded the movie was "good" by observing himself as he watched it. In other words, he defined "good" in terms of the movie's observable effect on him: it triggered a strong emotional reaction, therefore, it must have been "good."[18] To evaluate and define things in terms of their effects is nothing new; we all do it every day. Often we evaluate the clothes we wear in terms of what effect they have on our own moods and on others' views of us. Although such a process seems closely akin to scientific definition, there are some important differences. The focus of Fred's remark is upon his own aesthetic reaction to the movie, not upon the ways that most movie-goers are likely to respond. Consequently, his reaction may be unique rather than representative; other movie-goers may have reacted quite differently to the same film. As a result, his aesthetic judgment has validity for *him*, and even if 20 other people say the movie was "lousy" because it left them unmoved, he is not compelled to surrender his personal judgment.

Jim's conclusion, though the same as Fred's, was arrived at differently. He has defined "good" by applying established aesthetic criteria to the movie's content. His thinking is based upon a generalization, grounded in the authority of dramatic critics, which says that a movie showing the hero's demise because of a tragic flaw is "good." Of course, a seasoned critic would say that application of this single criterion constitutes oversimplification. There are many exceptions to such a rule: similar scenes may sometimes seem maudlin and in some instances (as, for example, in a cartoon) even funny. Still, Jim's conclusion embraces elements of scientific definition, for he has "operationalized" his meaning of "good" by relating it to an observable aspect of the movie.

Kate's definition of "good" raises numerous factual and value issues. Apparently, her assessment rests on the aesthetic premise that dramatic events should mirror real-life happenings. One initial difficulty arises with the term "evil," for it may be hard for persons to agree on its definition—after all, assigning meaning to terms such as "evil" requires value judgments on the part of the defining parties. Moreover, assuming definitional agreement, Kate may be wrong in her factual assertion that evil often triumphs over virtue in everyday life. If so, Kate will have a hard time defending her aesthetic judgment on the premise that drama should mirror real life. But this does not require her to alter her judgment; she may merely change her criterion and say that in this case the triumph of evil moved her emotionally—a redefinition of "good" on grounds similar to Fred's. By contrast, a scientist who argues that a given definition of "credibility" is useful because it enters into many theoretical and empirical propositions would, if proven wrong, be greeted with amusement and disdain by other scientists if he or she shifted ground and contended that the definition is useful because of its euphonious style.

Thus, each of the three conversants has defined "goodness" in movies from a different perspective. Keep in mind, though, that the goodness is not a property of the movie, but rather a characteristic reaction of three of its viewers. Fred makes this fact quite clear, for he does not mention specific observations which elicited his reaction—he alludes only to his own behavior. Kate and Jim both mention attributes of the movie which led to their evaluations, but each names a different property. Consequently, all three agree the movie was good, but "good" means something different to each of them. Furthermore, had one or more of them perceived the movie differently (e.g., had Fred not been emotionally moved by the movie) there would have been vigorous disagreement about its aesthetic merit. One can imagine the following exchange:

FRED: "Boy, that movie was a real loser!"

JIM: "What do you mean; it's the best one I've seen in a long time!"

FRED: "I didn't feel one emotion. I was unmoved by the whole thing."

JIM: "That says a lot more about your emotions than it does about the quality of the movie. Man, that flick captured the classic sense of tragedy, a hero's tragic flaw leading to his demise."

FRED: "Well, I wish his demise would have occurred in the first reel."

Of particular note in this dialogue is Jim's inconsistent thinking. On the one hand, he is dead right in asserting that Fred's judgment tells us more about Fred than about the movie. On the other, he is far off-base in assuming that his position focuses on the movie rather than himself. Nevertheless, it must be granted that Jim's approach lends itself more readily to reasoned argument. When compared with statements concerning emotional arousal, it is easier to argue rationally about: (1) what forms and content distinguish a good movie from a poor one, or (2) assuming agreement on (1), the extent to which a particular movie embodies these preferred forms and content. Indeed, one's emotional response to a work of art is a psychological fact; in this case, it would be absurd to argue that Fred does not feel this way.

Consider the distinction from this perspective. In factual communication inquiry, the assertion, "*X* is a *good* communicator," demands agreement on a definition for the factual sense of the term "good." Usually, communication scientists agree to equate "good" with "effective;" i.e., a "good" communicator is one who elicits his or her desired responses from others. In value inquiry, however, the judgment, "*X* is a *good* communicator," does not require common assent on a definition for the value sense of the term "good." Some may feel a communicator is ethical because he or she supports commendable causes, others because he or she is always truthful and honest, and still others because he or she belongs to the proper political party.

To a large extent, this disparity in the need for definitional agreement stems from the fundamental difference between factual and value questions. When inquirers are concerned with properties of objects, acts, and situations, they must have rules for determining whether such properties do or do not exist. At a minimum, they must be able to agree on whether or not they observe the property. Consequently, their observations must be related to a shared definition or else they will not be looking for the same thing. By contrast, when inquirers are interested in their own ethical or aesthetic states of mind, they can legitimately define terms idiosyncratically. While as old as the hills, the cliche, "Beauty (and, consequently, its definition) is in the eye of the beholder," accurately describes the situation. It is entirely possible to defend rationally a broad range of definitions for crucial ethical and aesthetic terms.

Such definitional freedom carries with it potential problems. For example, an inquirer may unwittingly become trapped in a totally symbolic universe. Abstract value symbols such as "justice," "beauty," and "truth," are usually defined by recourse to other symbols. Whether the various verbal definitions generated have any relationship to physical or social reality sometimes seems questionable. Thus, in many of his dialogues, Plato offers elegant verbal definitions of numerous value constructs. The critical reader, however, may reasonably ask how some of these definitions can be translated into referential language.

Sometimes, too, a term used in a value sense may appear to be defined factually. Consider the statement, "It isn't *natural* for people to swear." The assertion appears to confer a property of "unnaturalness" on situations where profane language is used. Actually, of course, the term "natural" captures the speaker's ethical posture in regard to profanity. By any criterion of quantitative frequency, swearing is a common, everyday communicative activity. To deny its naturalness is to say that it is ethically repugnant, not to assert that it is alien to people's daily experience.[19]

Value inquiry in communication seeks to arrive at reasoned judgments about the ethical and aesthetic dimensions of communication events. The value inquirer may employ any of the definitional approaches discussed in this chapter. He or she may judge a specific communication event to be "good" because it has particular effects, because it possesses certain properties which have been described as desirable, or because it conforms to widely accepted social or cultural norms. Each of these three bases for definition, as well as others, may support the answer that the value inquirer provides. However, there always is a point where a subjective judgment must be made. The value judgment of the inquirer is not directly amenable to empirical testing and validation. Since the inquiry is not focused upon properties of some object, act, or situation, no definitive empirical checks are possible.

NOTES

1. It may seem that we are overstating our case, in that knowledge can be accidentally discovered. Our apparent overstatement derives from our talking about planned inquiry into specific questions. Even accidentally discovered knowledge would not be discovered if the inquirer could not differentiate what he or she observes from previous observations.

2. Even here the scientist would have to define more specifically. Particularly, the terms "price range," "style," and "East Coast" would need to be defined more precisely.

3. Scientists, of course, realize that each person, object, or event is unique in many ways. For the purposes of scientific inquiry, however, these unique features are irrelevant if they do not enter into the theoretic scheme being tested and if they do not systematically influence the scientist's observations. The reasoning behind this approach is discussed at more length in Chapter 4.

4. We should clarify what may at first glance seem to be an essentially trivial distinction. It is one thing to know that stepping on the accelerator pedal will make a car go faster—an empirical generalization. It is another thing to know *why* the generalization is true—more fuel/air mixture is fed to the engine—and *under what conditions* the generalization will not hold—e.g., the car is not started or it is out of gas. Knowledge of these facts makes the initial knowledge more applicable and puts it into better perspective.

5. Although universally applicable mathematical equations are a desirable, albeit an ambitious, goal for scientific inquiry, communication scientists fall far short of this objective on most occasions. Nonetheless, they do make use of probability equations and logical deductions in arriving at answers, both of which are close cousins to mathematical equations.

6. Obviously, scientific inquirers are not usually interested in true representations of *all* aspects of people or events, but only in true representations of certain specified properties thereof. Similarly, a photograph is obviously *not* the scene pictured; most people accept it as a valid representation of the salient or memorable features of the scene.

7. To a certain extent, the philosophical school called *pragmatism* equates reliability with validity by arguing that the factual status of a statement is determined by whether or not people agree with it. We prefer an approach that is closely akin to naive or commonsense realism; i.e., we hold that the features of our external environment *do or do not* have certain properties, and the fact that people may consistently err in their statements about these properties does not make the statements true. Thus, if later investigation shows that 500 people mistakenly labeled the object *weather balloon* as "flying saucer," this does not imply that the statement, "There is a flying saucer in the sky," was true until later investigation disconfirmed it. In a similar vein, we assume the planet Earth had a property of roundness both before and after 1492, even though before that date people consistently attributed a property of flatness to it.

8. Numerous investigations of this construct suggest that it has three principal, relatively independent dimensions: the *expertness, trustworthiness,* and *dynamism* of the source as perceived by the audience.

9. To say that the efficiency of an empirical test is 50% is *not* the same as saying that the proposition thereby tested is 50% true, or true 50% of the time. The proposition might well be totally and irrevocably true (or false) but the testing scheme has 50% distortion resulting from a variety of errors, giving the conclusion an appearance of truth (or falsity) which is sometimes indistinguishable from the real situation. Such discrepancies can be easily and graphically observed by empirically testing any of several laws of physics in the typical classroom laboratory. The distinction between the efficiency, or "trueness," of the testing scheme and the truth of a proposition might be thought of as being loosely similar to the difference between the validity of an argument and the truth of its conclusion.

10. In the interest of brevity and realism, we are skipping an important and perhaps largely unconscious step in Jim's thinking. Before thinking, "gin and tonic," Jim probably defined the general class "cool drinks"; e.g., "Cool drinks are tall, iced drinks that often contain citrus fruit and a minimum of sugar." Likewise, he may have defined "sweet drinks" as "Drinks relatively low in liquor content that contain sugar and are often creamy." Note that the two classes mentioned in the dialogue are not mutually exclusive; some drinks may be both "cool" and "sweet."

11. The first situation illustrates one of the major problems faced by communication scientists, as well as other behavioral scientists. Since many of their concepts are taken from ordinary language—e.g., "attitude," "credibility," and "communication" itself—people will have diverse meanings for them. By contrast, terms such as "specific gravity," "friction coefficient," and "deoxyribonucleic acid" are not usually part of the layman's vocabulary, and thus it is easier to establish shared meaning for them. In general, the second situation should be avoided. If a term has achieved standardized meaning in scientific inquiry, little, save confusion, is added by redefining it. The exception occurs when redefinition contributes to an entire reconceptualization of a problem area, a situation discussed earlier in this chapter.

12. Consider the following example of this rather abstract point: "attitude" is often defined conceptually as "a predisposition to respond in a positive or negative manner." Only recently have some writers (e.g., Rokeach, 1968), pointed out that there are *attitude-object* and *attitude-situation* components involved in one's attitude. Thus, for instance, it may not be useful to talk of a generalized attitude toward the attitude-object, *a male homosexual*. Instead, one may have a very different attitude about *a male homosexual working on my research team* (Attitude-situation[1]) and *a male homosexual marrying my sister* (Attitude-situation[2]).

13. We suggest inspection of tax records merely to illustrate the point that indirect observation of some variables provides more accurate observations. Naturally we would have both ethical

qualms and legal problems with this procedure even though we would expect it to serve our goals of precision and accuracy.

14. The broad subject of evaluating measurement scales will be discussed more extensively in Chapter 4.

15. Under certain circumstances, of course, a lottery-winner might demonstrate at least temporary increases on the other two measures of social status. Thus, a great deal of interest was generated in Michigan's first million-dollar drawing, and the winner, Hermus Millsaps, became a temporary celebrity. Mr. Millsaps, while considerably richer, has now faded to obscurity and the drawing has become so commonplace that it receives relatively little publicity.

16. The concept *social status* could be operationally defined solely on grounds of income, but such a step does not seem very useful. If income is the only measure taken, the concept might better be labeled *income,* rather than the more complex *social status.*

17. One might argue that a Syndicate member who possesses all three characteristics still has low social status. Although a rare exception, this kind of case could be handled by adding a fourth dimension, *source of income.*

18. The notion of inferring one's disposition or attitude from self-observations has been studied extensively, particularly by Bem (1965) and his colleagues.

19. Our selection of this particular example is not capricious. The phrase "natural law" has been used cleverly by political theorists for centuries to imply factual claims. We would argue that it reflects a value judgment about the ideal moral state of affairs, not a description of any property of "naturalness" in the external world.

QUESTIONS AND EXERCISES

1. For several days, count the number of discussions you overhear or participate in where the issue could be settled or agreement could be reached by stipulating operational definitions for certain terms. Can you identify certain types of terms for which

operational definitions are particularly crucial? (For starters, consider terms that describe personal dispositions; e.g., "Miller is *inconsiderate*," or "Nicholson is *thoughtful*.")

2. Read an automobile insurance policy, concentrating on the section headed, "Definitions." Are the definitions conceptual or operational? Do they leave room for interpretation? Can you produce less ambiguous definitions for any of the terms?

3. Watch some television commercials with a critical eye toward definition. Note how frequently words and phrases are used ambiguously and left undefined; e.g., "a recent medical survey," or "the leading pain reliever recommended by doctors." Watch also for definitions by decree; i.e., assertions of a particular definition by persons in the commercial. Rewrite a short commercial redefining terms in a more concise, crisp manner.

4. Suppose three researchers wished to study the influence of amount of *communication anxiety* on persuasive effectiveness. Researcher 1 operationally defines *communication anxiety* as the communicator's self-report of how fearful he or she feels about communicating with an audience; Researcher 2 defines it as measures of physiological response (e.g., heart rate or palm sweating) of the communicator while communicating with an audience; and Researcher 3 defines it as ratings of the communicator's anxiety obtained from members of an audience. Would you expect all three definitions to relate in the same way to persuasive effectiveness? Would you expect all three to be positively related for a particular communicator? What reasons can you give for your answers?

5. Take a crack at conceptually and operationally defining the following communication terms: *information, nonverbal communication,* and *language intensity*. Exchange definitions with a classmate for advice and criticism. Can you identify exceptions that should have been included or parts of your original definitions that you now wish to exclude?

REFERENCES

Bem, D. J. (1965). An Experimental Analysis of Self-Persuasion. *Journal of Experimental Social Psychology* 1: 199-218.

Guilford, J. P. (1954). *Psychometric Methods,* 2d ed. New York: McGraw-Hill.

Hayakawa, S. I. (1964). *Language in Thought and Action,* 2d ed. New York: Harcourt, Brace, and World.

Osgood, C. E. (1974). Probing Subjective Culture. Parts I and II. *Journal of Communication* 1 (21-35) and 2 (82-100).

Osgood, C. E., G. Suci, and P. H. Tannenbaum (1957). *The Measurement of Meaning.* Urbana: University of Illinois Press.

Packard, V. (1957). *The Hidden Persuaders.* New York: David McKay.

Rokeach, M. (1968). *Beliefs, Attitudes, and Values,* pp. 109-132. San Francisco: Jossey-Bass.

Torgerson, W. (1958). *Theory and Method of Scaling.* New York: John Wiley & Sons.

Woelfel, J., and J. Saltiel (1974). Cognitive Processes as Motions in a Multidimensional Space: A General Linear Model. Unpublished manuscript, Department of Communication, Michigan State University.

4
Observation

Father: "Look, son, aren't the emperor's new clothes beautiful!"

Son: "But, Father, the emperor isn't wearing any clothes!"

Father: "Never have I seen such a beautiful suit of clothes!"

—paraphrased excerpt from the **HANS CHRISTIAN ANDERSEN** tale, "The Emperor's New Clothes."

If asked, most persons would probably say that they assume some sort of observation is the initial basis for all knowledge. Yet in the pursuit of knowledge people often fail to remind themselves of this assumption. Observations come in many kinds and qualities and often determine the kind and quality of knowledge obtained. In this chapter we will explore the process of observation and the requirements and limitations of various observational methods, and we will consider how communication inquirers cope with these restrictions.

OBSERVATION IN SCIENTIFIC COMMUNICATION INQUIRY

In previous chapters we have discussed theory and definition in scientific inquiry. If viable theory can be thought of as the goal of science and definition as the bridge between this goal and reality, then observation can be thought of as the foundation of the bridge: supporting it, fundamental to reaching the goal, and firmly grounded in both the theoretical and the real sides of the chasm. If theory is the intended end-product of our observations, how could it be needed initially? The answer to this question is simple, but requires some discussion. The construction of theories which explain and predict human communicative behavior is the goal of communication science. But the construction (and the destruction) of a theory is accomplished by empirically testing the theory's predictions. Now in order to conduct any empirical test inquirers must make observations—but what observations do they make? The observations suggested by the theory, of course. Thus, if they were testing a theory which predicted different political behavior by men than by women following exposure to a speech criticizing the state of American politics, observations of the dress styles or the heights of audience members would be irrelevant. Such observations might provide intuitive insights into other conceptual relationships, but to test the theory at hand inquirers must observe some of the variables which clearly relate to it.

The above discussion is not meant to diminish the role of inspiration and insight in scientific inquiry. Obviously, people like Newton, Freud. and others made numerous unguided observations before arriving at their theoretical propositions.[1] The genius involved in seeing simple regularity in seemingly random patterns is a faculty few possess. Yet these individuals, too, tested their theories through careful observation.

Scientific observation can be thought of as systematic examination of the properties of people, objects, or events for the purpose of determining regularity and relationships among these properties. To say that scientific observation is systematic is to say that it is not performed haphazardly; it is guided by theoretical predictions and accepted "rules" of objectivity. Scientific observation is also concerned with properties of objects and events themselves, not with evaluations of these properties. The scientist's concern with relationships between properties is an attempt to determine regularity and order in what at first glance may seem a disordered world. The discovery of order allows prediction, which may in turn allow control, and certainly produces knowledge and understanding.

If communication scientists make observations to check the fit of a theory to the real world, then they must be sure that the real world is, in fact, what they are observing. They must take care that their observations are *unbiased,* not colored by the "inside world" of hopes, prejudices, and expectations which all persons carry in their heads, and that they are not distorted beyond recognition by careless observational techniques. As we mentioned in the preceding chapter, the process of definition is a potential distorter of concepts; the process of scientific observation also has this potential for distortion, but the scientist consciously tries to minimize it. Later in this chapter we shall discuss how various parts of the observation process itself can contribute bias to the observations a communication scientist makes and consider how the scientist can deal with these problems.

The By-Words of Scientific Observation: Accuracy and Precision

In the last chapter we presented two concepts central to the scientific process: validity and reliability. Before proceeding, we should introduce two parallel concepts which are pertinent to matters of observation. These concepts are *accuracy* and *precision.*

In scientific contexts, the terms "accuracy" and "precision" have quite different meanings. Accuracy in observation involves the degree of relationship between an observation made and the thing observed. For instance, someone's observation that a typical piano has 88 keys would be accurate. If anyone counted 39 or 106 keys or claimed they were red with green stripes, these observations would be inaccurate. If one were to measure the width of a piece of standard typing paper, a measurement of 8.50 inches would be reasonably accurate because in fact that is exactly how wide it is according to all available measuring instruments.[2] If a measurement of 8.692543700 inches were reported, this observation would be precise but not accurate. A measurement of 8.5000000 inches would be both very precise and very accurate.

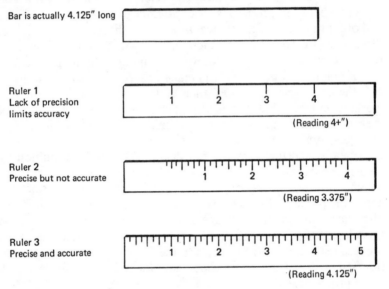

Fig. 4.1 *Accuracy and Precision of Measures.*

As you may have deduced by now, precision has to do with the fineness of observation, accuracy has to do with the correspondence of the observation with the thing observed. A ruler which is marked to 1/100 of an inch can give more precise measures than one which can only be read to the nearest 1/10 inch, but accuracy depends upon its construction and use. Precision is a prerequisite for high accuracy, but it is not sufficient to produce accuracy. Inspection of Fig. 4.1 may help to clarify these concepts.

There are many misconceptions about precision and accuracy which may blur the distinction between them. One such misconception results from the common tendency to accept very precise observations as also being very accurate. The writing of the novelist, the painting of the artist, even the measurements of the scientist, as precisely detailed and fine as they may be, are not necessarily blessed with accuracy. Confusion between these two concepts may sometimes lead to *false precision*. If a professor reported that there are exactly 32.00000 students in a communication class, this count (regardless of its accuracy) would be falsely precise because such a precise measure implies that the enrollment could change by as little as .00001 student—which, of course, it could not. Nothing is gained by using observations which imply that we can make finer distinctions than the atomic unit of the event we observe. False precision becomes doubly troublesome when falsely precise measurements are employed in combination with other measures in mathematical operations. Results of such chicanery are always misleading.

Initial Problems: Looking at the Invisible

As we have said, the goal of the communication scientist is the construction of theories which explain and predict human communication behavior. The correspondence between the theories and the events they describe is gauged by observation of those events and comparison of actual outcomes with predicted outcomes. Such empirical tests depend upon accurate translation of the theoretical variables into potential "real-world" observations (definition), and accurate translation of those potential observations into data. This latter process is the focus of our attention when discussing scientific observation. Communication scientists constantly try to observe "real" properties of people and events. They make every effort to eliminate judgments from their observations. To allow subjective evaluation to color their data would not contribute to their goals of theory testing.

For the most part, the study of human communication involves concepts or constructs which are intangible and which transcend any number of people and situations. A brief checklist of common constructs used in communication research reinforces the intangibility of the work. How does the scientist observe such things as "communicator credibility," "sociability," "attitudes toward health care," "cognitive complexity," or "self-disclosure potential?" The vast majority of constructs used in scientific communication inquiry refer to internal states or qualities ascribed to a person by a theory which explains some communication process.

In the last chapter we discussed the process of operational definition whereby the scientific inquirer specifies observable behaviors or properties which, according to his or her reasoning, are end-products or by-products of the intangible constructs he or she wishes to measure. A very simple example of this process would be to say that the length of a man's beard (which is directly observable and easily measured assuming the subject is cooperative) could be an operational indicant of length of time since his last shave (which is not so directly observable).Although the example is not perfectly analogous, note some problems inherent in this operationalization. There is certainly "theory" to suggest that if a man does not shave, his beard will grow; thus, the operational scheme is grounded in logic. Yet, close observation has shown that every man's beard grows at a slightly different rate, and also that beards grow at different rates at different times of day. Therefore, if an observer were interested in small amounts of time (say, less than a day) considerable error might accrue to the equation made in the operational definition. Comparing measurements for two or more men could also lead to erroneous comparative assessments of time because of differential rates of beard growth. Also, it is rumored that hair stops growing or radically slows its rate of growth after it reaches a certain length. If this is true, comparisons over long periods of time would be inaccurate because of a "ceiling effect" in our measuring process. Similarly, the possibility of a "basement effect" can be imagined since no razor shaves completely down to the skin. Therefore, even immediately after shaving, the beard has some small length greater than zero.

Obviously, beard growth is not a consuming interest of most communication inquirers, but similar operational problems are often encountered in relationships more common to communication research. For example, several inquirers (e.g., Miller, Zavos, Vlandis, and Rosenbaum, 1961; Miller, 1964; Vlandis, 1964), have observed speaking nonfluencies in order to make inferences about the anxiety or mental stress of the speaker. While this relationship has some theoretical validity, there are numerous factors which could distort it. Persons giving a speech may stumble over certain words or lose their place, which while causing nonfluencies would not necessarily denote anxiety. Extremely anxious persons may sometimes be aware of their inner state and may exert careful control over their speech in such a situation, giving a falsely underrated appearance to their anxiety. The problem of exactly defining what is to be called a "nonfluency" is also potentially distorting. If pauses are counted as nonfluencies, then hesitations for dramatic effect or to take a breath might falsely indicate anxiety.

These examples serve to illustrate the problems associated with operationalization. The translation process employed to gain observability necessarily demands some sacrifice in accuracy. The goal of the communication scientist is to choose those observable aspects of the underlying process of interest which are highly and functionally related to the process. The degree of the relationship, or the correlation, between the unobservable and the observable will determine the validity of the measures taken. Beard length and elapsed time since last shave, even though functionally related and highly correlated, are not a totally valid operationalization. Nor, for that matter, is number of nonfluencies likely to provide a perfectly valid index of communicator anxiety.

The complexity and vagueness of most scientific communication constructs creates numerous observational problems. Choosing, or even finding, observable behaviors which accompany and are highly associated with internal constructs is often a speculative business. The two tools the communication scientist has available in this endeavor are theory and common sense. Theories which have withstood empirical testing and which relate a number of communication variables may be used to specify observational procedures. However, many theories employed in scientific communication inquiry are situationally limited; thus, their applicability to this purpose may likewise be limited. In the absence of applicable theory, scientists must rely upon their own reasoning to concoct an observational procedure. Rudolph Flesch (1946), for example, invented what he called a readability formula that he suggested could be applied to written material to test its suitability for particular audiences. The essence of the formula was to operationally define *readability* (a rather vague label) in terms of the number of affixes per word and the sentence lengths of the written material. The precise formula can be applied to any copy and a comparative measure derived. Such an operationalization is less dependent upon coherent, empirically tested theory than upon the simple notion that longer words and longer sentences are more difficult to read and understand than are shorter ones.

ERROR: CUTTING THE BIAS (AND THE UNBIASED)

The biggest obstruction to the work of the communication scientist is error. Regardless of its source, error is either *biased* or *unbiased*. Biased error is characterized by reliable but inaccurate observations. Unbiased error is characterized by observations which exhibit individual variation (unreliability) but which in the aggregate prove valid. In any scientific endeavor error may result from the nature of the variables being observed, the testing scheme used by the scientist, the instruments the scientist employs in making observations, the characteristics and behaviors of the people being observed, or the actions of the individual scientist. In each case, however, the error produced can be characterized as either biased or unbiased.

An example may help to clarify this distinction. Assume someone is interested in observing (measuring) the speed of a car. Naturally the handiest instrument for making observations is the car's speedometer. But suppose that the speedometer needle constantly fluctuates, no matter what speed the car is moving. For example, when the car is traveling at a constant 50 miles per hour, the needle waves back and forth between 40 and 60. Since the speedometer is supposed to provide measurements of the car's speed at any instant in time, most of the observations made on this particular speedometer will be inaccurate. Furthermore, because of its fluctuations, if numerous speedometer observations were made at a constant speed, these observations would be different, or unreliable. However, if an average (mean) of these observations were to be computed, this average would probably be a reasonably accurate report of the true speed of the car. In this case, we would characterize the error in the observations as *unbiased,* because, *in the long run,* the average of the observations reflects no tendency to be invalid, even though any particular observation may have been. An analogous situation occurs when people take tests aimed at measuring their ability at some task. Supposedly, a test is a valid operational measure of some trait or ability. Yet even though many of an individual's abilities remain relatively constant, on any particular day, performance may be better or worse on a particular test than the individual's ability would normally dictate. Such a "good day" or a "bad day" may result from a multitude of factors that affect the person's outlook, health, alertness, or ability to concentrate. In the long run, the ways these factors combine will probably be such that the average of a number of attempts at the test will accurately reflect the person's ability. On any particular occasion, however, a given test result may drastically differ from a person's "true" ability.

As a contrasting example, suppose someone owned a car whose speedometer showed a reading of 10 miles per hour when the car was standing still. When the person started driving the car, the speedometer began to move upward, so that when the car was going 50 miles per hour the speedometer showed 60. It is apparent that no matter how reliable the observations made on such a speedometer, no single observation nor any combination of them will give an *accurate* indication of the car's speed. Such a situation characterizes biased error.

In the preceding example, the erroneous speedometer readings are a surmountable problem because an observer could easily be aware that the readings were in error. Persons riding in either car would have an independent comparison (their own sensations of movement) of the car's speed. A person in the first car would know, for example, that the car was not accelerating and decelerating between 40 and 60 miles an hour as the needle indicated, and would thus realize the speedometer reading was in error. In conducting scientific communication inquiry such independent comparisons of variable measurements are not always attainable.[3] Thus, communication scientists are placed in a difficult position. It is sometimes impossible for them to know whether or not their measurements or observations are in error, let alone to estimate the degree of error. This is somewhat the same problem one faces in "knowing" what the surface of the planet Venus looks like. One has only descriptions offered by the government agency which sent a spacecraft there, and, in the absence of an independent comparison, one cannot know for certain what degree of distortion or error exists in the available description.

Scientific inquirers are therefore interested in the potential sources of error in their work. By identifying these sources they can take steps to *control* the error—i.e., to reduce its likelihood and magnitude—even though they cannot detect its presence. Painting a cut with antiseptic represents a similar precaution. The bacteria which may be trying to enter the cut are invisible; in fact, none may be present, but application of the antiseptic will reduce the possibility of infection if they are present.

In most scientific communication inquiry there are three major potential sources of error: variations in the make-up of the people being observed, the varying conditions under which the inquiry is made, and the process and instruments used in making the observations or measurements. We shall examine each of these sources and discuss the type of error, its implications, and the methods of control applicable in each case.

To help illustrate the problem of error, let us trace each of these types of error through hypothetical experiments. Suppose an inquirer wants to investigate the effect of messages containing high and low fear-arousing appeals upon the subsequent health behavior of an audience. Specifically, the inquirer decides to present a persuasive speech to each of two audiences exhorting them to make more extensive use of preventive health services. The inquirer predicts that the message with high fear-arousing appeals—i.e., the one containing descriptions of potential aversive consequences for not following its suggestion—will cause listeners to seek more preventive health care than will the low fear-appeal message. Suppose, further, that high and low fear-appeal messages are operationally defined by stipulating that the two stimuli will be identical speeches on the benefits of preventive medicine with the single difference that the high fear-appeal message will contain five short stories about people who suffered long or painful illnesses following the detection of symptoms for which they did not seek medical advice. If the inquirer were to perform this experiment on college students he or she could check their subsequent health behavior by observing their later visits to the health center on the campus or by asking the students themselves how many times they had visited doctors in some specified period of time.

Error Source 1: People and Their Differences

The first problem that comes to mind is how the inquirer is going to compare the behavior of the two audiences. If members of the audience who heard the high fear-appeal (HFA) message visited doctors between zero (least) and six (most) times in the year following the speech and members of the audience who heard the low fear-appeal (LFA) message visited doctors between one (least) and five (most) times in that year, the inquirer might well wonder what the experiment showed. Even assuming that he or she was working within a theoretical framework, the results at first seem to be ambiguous or uninterpretable. The problem, of course, is random, or unbiased error. Although HFA audience members are expected, as a group, to seek more health care than LFA audience members, this does not mean that this difference will hold for each and every audience member. The degree to which the messages affect each listener will differ according to the individual's views on health care, relative persuasibility, past health, and numerous other factors. Such unreliability among observed effects is to be expected and does not necessarily negate the truth of the original prediction. If the inquirer assumes that in any group people differ in persuasibility, physical health, and a host of other factors, he or she is forced to conclude that what will demonstrate the accuracy of a prediction is not the measure for any individual but rather the averages for the two groups.[4] In the absence of any reason to believe otherwise, one must assume that the differences in the behavior among subjects in any group are the result of *unbiased* error and, therefore, the average performance of the group more nearly and accurately describes the true effect of the variable under investigation—in this case, level of fear arousal.

Note carefully what this assumption implies. While, *in general,* the inquirer thinks he or she knows the relationship between fear arousal and doctor visits, it is impossible to make an exact prediction of the relationship in any one case; consequently, the inquirer controls for the error, or unreliability owing to differences in people, by averaging a number of people's responses to the stimulus. This is exactly the strategy a life insurance company follows in calculating its premium charges. While *on the average* an American male is expected to live to age 68, there is no certainty that any particular male will live exactly this long. The premiums the insurance company passes on to its policyholders reflect an *average* cost and will allow the company to stay in business only if it can attract a number of customers so as to average out the differences in individual life spans.

Consider again the hypothetical experiment on fear-arousing messages. Suppose that the HFA audience *on the average* made 4.2 doctor visits per year after hearing the speech as compared to 2.5 doctor visits for the LFA audience. Should the inquirer rush to conclude that the hypothesis was dramatically supported by empirical evidence? Given an awareness of differences in people and some careful thought, one might reasonably conclude that such a disparity, though sizable, reflects differences that existed initially between the two audiences. In other words, how does one know that the HFA group were not fanatic hypochondriacs and/or the LFA group abnormally healthy people *before the experiment began?* If either or both of these possibilities were true, obviously the speech might have had little bearing on audience behavior and the counts of doctor visits might merely reflect long-standing habits about health care.[5]

How can the inquirer enhance the likelihood that the observed differences can be attributed to the speeches, rather than premessage differences between the two groups? There are two general methods available, each of which has its own limitations and advantages. The first way is to observe the health behavior of audience members before the experiment takes place. Such a control procedure implies that potential audiences must be chosen long before the experiment is conducted and must be followed closely to learn their health habits. Such a procedure enables an inquirer to specify *exactly* the *change* in habits that the experimental message produces because relevant observations that were taken before its presentation are available.

This control procedure can be accomplished in a number of ways. One way is pure mathematical manipulation, a method that entails comparing *changes* in doctor visits for the two experimental groups. Having found the number of times the group members visit doctors before the experiment, the inquirer subtracts this number from their postexperimental visit count. Averaging these differences for the two groups provides a reasonably exact accounting of the differences in the effects of the messages. Such premeasures, if taken in phase with other variable measures, permit considerable *statistical* control over the outcome of the experiment. This approach to control consists merely of taking out of the final outcome known effects of other variables which are not central to the study at hand. Thus, for example, if the members of one group happen to be older than the other group and if the inquirer knows that age affects number of yearly doctor visits (and also to what extent) he or she can equalize the effect on the outcome by making adjustments to one, or both, groups. The comparison of results would then be *as if* both groups were of the same average age. Finally, the inquirer could *match* the experimental groups on the basis of preexperimental observations. In this situation, the actual experimental group members would be chosen in pairs who exhibited similar characteristics on whatever variables were being observed, and one member of each pair would be assigned to each group. This process is actually beforehand statistical control, since the same ends are met but the control is carried out before the actual experiment, rather than after the final observations are made.

A problem exists when using such control procedures. When making many of the necessary preexperimental observations, such close observation may be necessary that some of the audience members become aware of the observation and thus become "sensitized" to the experiment. Unfortunately, there is usually no way of knowing how an audience member's knowledge of the inquirer's purpose or presence influences the theoretical relationship under study. Consequently, the inquirer can only conclude that if an audience member has such knowledge then his or her behavior in the experimental situation will be affected in an unknown way, thereby rendering observations of this individual uninterpretable. This is a commonsense principle. One would hardly expect a police officer giving a speeding ticket to treat the violator "normally" if the violator "sensitized" the officer by giving him or her a 20-dollar bill—the officer might tear up the ticket or cite the violator for bribery.[6]

The second method of controlling for differences in experimental audiences is to *randomize* the selection of audience members. The principle of randomization pervades research design. Essentially, it holds that if selections are made in an unbiased manner—i.e., so that every potential selection has the *same probability* of being selected—then, *on the average*, differences between groups of selections can be expected to cancel out. This approach to control precludes the necessity of observing people for long periods before an experiment and thus avoids some of the danger of sensitization. Randomization works best as a control method when large groups are chosen and does not necessarily negate all differences between groups.[7]

Randomization allows control for factors which even the scientific inquirer cannot anticipate or specify. There are literally hundreds of individual factors that could affect the way a person would react to a speech on health care. By randomly selecting the subjects for the experiment and randomly assigning them to experimental audiences, the inquirer theoretically gives each of these factors (and their combinations) its rightful chance to appear in the experimental groups. The effects of any factor will thus theoretically have the same probability of being observed in the experiment as the probability of observing that factor in the population at large. Again, randomization will not ensure reliability among individual observations, but, in principle, it should allow accurate group observations.

The two general types of control we have discussed exert different effects upon the outcome of scientific observations. Control through matching, statistics, or mathematics maximizes precision and exactness because it reduces unbiased variation in observations stemming from numerous sources. It often gives the scientific inquirer a very clear picture of the effect of manipulations. However, the inquirer pays a price for this selectivity in subjects. That price is generalizability. Using these procedures, the inquirer can legitimately assume any experimental outcome is true only of people like those in the experimental groups. If people of homogeneous characteristics are subjects in the experiment, the findings may be of very limited applicability.

When randomization is employed the situation is quite different. Randomization generally allows more variance in observation (more unbiased error) to creep into the final experimental result. But theorems of probability indicate that findings for subjects *randomly selected* from some larger group are also true for that larger group.[8] And the fewer the variables controlled for by matching or statistical adjustment, the larger the parent group, or population. Thus, randomization normally decreases precision but increases generalizability. It is obvious, therefore, that whatever decision the inquirer reaches about control techniques reflects a compromise between precision and generalizability. Usually, of course, one's preference is somewhere in the middle, in an attempt to produce easily interpretable outcomes which have wide application.

Error Source 2: The Conditions Surrounding the Inquiry

The second major source of error in scientific inquiry derives from the conditions under which the inquiry—and, of course, the observations—are made. The most pernicious error arising from this source is bias resulting from unintended systematic differences in experimental conditions or questionable experimental practices. In most cases, an experiment may be thought of as a situation that allows controlled and therefore bias-free observation of specified variables. The scientific communication inquirer is interested in what is observed in the "laboratory" only if it accurately reflects what goes on outside. The purpose of conducting an experiment is not to distort the relation of the variables, but to better permit their observation. By empirically testing communication hypotheses, the inquirer hopes to better understand real people and how communication affects them. Nothing would be gained by biasing the outcome of the experiments, since no real knowledge would result.

But there may be any number of variables that affect the behavior of experimental audiences. Even though inquirers conduct themselves and their observations judiciously, inadvertent bias may influence experimental outcomes. Consider the following "experiment" conducted by Fred and Jim:

FRED: "Jim, you remember the idea you had about advertising our fraternity's weekly Friday night parties with colored posters instead of black-and-white ones?"

JIM: "Yeah, I remember."

FRED: "Well, we experimented with it for two weeks and finally gave it up because of the cost. I can't figure out whether it did any good or not, but it sure doesn't seem that way."

JIM: "Well, what happened?"

FRED: "Well, as you know, we always attracted more guys than girls, so three weeks ago we decided to put the new posters up in the girls' dorms—result, that Friday night hardly any girls showed up and even fewer guys than usual. So the next week we went all out, put them up all over campus—result, more girls than ever before at the party and about the same number of guys as usual. Last week we went back to our old black-and-white posters, and on Friday the place was packed, more people of both sexes than we've ever had. So you tell me what the answer is."

This example of informal experimentation illustrates many of the points made earlier in this book, specifically those relating to the uses of theory in science, the uses of hypotheses, and particularly, several issues relating to observation and control.

The apparent hypothesis in this "experiment" was that colored posters would attract more attention and, therefore, more attendance to the fraternity parties.[9] The test of this hypothesis is, of course, the attendance count. Assume that the first week the colored posters were used coincided with midterm examinations. Given this assumption, one might expect that even if the hypothesis were true attendance at the party *that week* would be limited to regulars and compulsive party-goers. In other words, attendance would be low regardless of advertising medium. If the hypothesis were true, though, an increase in female attendance would be expected as soon as other factors such as midterm exams did not interfere. This is exactly what happened the next week. The effect of the second week's posters is unknown because it had by that time become mixed with the influence of the first week's posters. The third week's attendance can be explained by the fact that word had probably gotten around to campus males about the increase in female attendance. Such news presumably made the party seem more attractive, and resulted in more men attending. Such an explanation is reasonable, explains the total set of results, and further upholds the original hypothesis. Still, it is not verifiable because no direct and unambiguous observations were made at the time to either confirm or disconfirm it.

Why were the results of the whole "experiment" so confusing? The reason, of course, is that the experimental conditions—i.e., the conditions under which the observations and comparisons were made—were not controlled; consequently, other factors could have influenced the outcome. During the first week, for example, exams influenced the attendance at the party. In other words, the time relative to the school term was different for the two conditions being compared. Factors other than the variable of interest—in this case, the type of posters—differed between the two conditions, and so the influence of the experimental variable is unknown. The second week of the experiment is probably a more "normal" week to check attendance, but by this time the inquirer, Fred, has mixed two experimental stimuli (colored posters in girls' dorms alone versus colored posters all over campus) so the effect of either stimulus by itself is unknown. The large female attendance may have resulted from the mixture of both strategies. The third week's attendance does not reflect merely the impact of black-and-white posters, as Fred seems to assume, but also mirrors the indirect results of two weeks of colored-poster advertising. This bumper third-week attendance is probably the best support for Jim's idea, but because of improper control in the experiment, it is questionable to say that the hypothesis was substantiated.

Note carefully a distinguishing difference between this type of error (error arising from differences in experimental conditions) and the type of error discussed earlier (error arising from individual differences). When error arises from differences in experimental conditions, the factors that affect the outcome are *the same* for all members of a group, which normally produces *biased* error. In the case of individual differences, the factors affecting the variables in question are *different* for each individual, a circumstance normally producing *unbiased* error. Consider, also, that if the poster experiment were to be repeated many times using no other control than random selection of time and campus, the average of all such outcomes would probably give an *unbiased* indication of the relative effect of colored and black-and-white posters on party attendance.

Thus, we return to our original contention that an experiment should facilitate valid observations of the way that variables are related. To eliminate the confusion caused by the presence of situational differences other than the experimental stimuli, the scientific inquirer attempts to control these other conditions. The type of control used is qualitatively different from control through randomization; it is direct intervention by the inquirer. In randomization the inquirer is, in effect, letting nature take its course. When using intervention the inquirer is controlling nature. Randomization worked in the situations described earlier because a large number of people or observations were used, thereby averaging out the error in any one observation. Since in both the fear-appeal and the poster experiments the inquirers are making only *one* comparison, they do not have a number of randomly selected comparisons to average. How could this situation be remedied? In the hypothetical experiment concerning fear appeals the inquirer could make both conditions as similar as possible on such factors as the credibility of the speaker, the length and wording of the speech,[10] the amount of distraction, the listening conditions (room temperature, color, size, volume of speech), the time of day, and the time of week. We should reiterate that inquirers usually do not know in advance the effects of any of the variables mentioned, but they do know that by equalizing them their effect should be the same for both groups, and, therefore, they should cause no differences to appear other than those produced by the stimuli.[11] Naturally one cannot possibly exert direct control over all the possible variables present in any experimental situation. But communication scientists first attempt to directly control those variables which they expect, either because of empirical knowledge or relevant theory, to have potentially the greatest effect upon their observations. Others which they know or expect to have less influence they may ignore or may control if the effort and/or expense required is small. If they have some empirical knowledge of the effects of certain variables they may also control them statistically. This procedure allows them to let these factors function freely and extract their effects later. Given preexperimental measurements and knowledge of how these previously measured variables react with the ones in the hypothesis, they can later adjust their observations mathematically to account for these influences.

Error Source 3:   Procedures and Instruments of Observation

The third major source of error in scientific communication inquiry arises from the observation or measuring procedures themselves. Since these procedures (the operational definitions of experimental variables) are for all practical purposes the only assessment that the communication scientist has of the variables of interest, they will reflect not only the values of those variables but also all types of error, including those types already discussed in this chapter. The type of error we are now concerned with is *inherent* in the observations or procedures *per se,* not error arising from other sources. The only way to identify such error is to exert control over the other sources of error. Assuming that these controls have been effective, any error remaining is due to observation or measurement procedures. But even though scientists know that if their controls are perfect all errors must arise from their procedures, they can have no idea of the degree that such error is present without making certain independent observations. In most inquiry no such comparisons are made because of the expense or because of the impossibility of identifying better methods than those being used. Thus, in many situations, the error arising from observations or procedures must be accepted. Let us examine this troublesome type of error more closely.

If you recall the earlier discussion of the two faulty speedometers, it will help you understand how the scientist can deal at least partially with this type of error. Procedural error can be either biased or unbiased. In general, the unbiased type is easier to detect and to combat. When unbiased (random) error is present in observation techniques, it will manifest itself as variations in measurements of the same thing at different times using the same procedures. In other words, the occurrence of such error is analogous to the wavering speedometer. For example, suppose a communication scientist wants to measure the persuasibility of a number of people prior to an experiment. Suppose also that the measuring instrument is a written test that purports to measure a person's persuasibility from zero (least) to 100 (greatest). If the scientist administered this same test to one person on three different occasions and observed scores of 25, 89, and 53, he or she would probably conclude that the variation is largely due to the instrument. This reasoning assumes that the test respondent was equally honest and alert on all three administrations. But central to the conclusion is the assumption that persuasibility is a relatively stable trait. Not that it will never change (say with age, or experience), but over short periods of time changes of the observed magnitude are viewed as theoretically unrealistic. Such a conclusion is even more justified if extreme changes are observed for many subjects with no apparent pattern to the group changes. The causes of such variability may be ambiguous wording in the test, poorly outlined scoring procedures, or numerous combinations of factors, but close scrutiny of the test is clearly in order.

Suppose now, that the only error inherent in this test is biased error. In this case, a particular subject's three scores might be 84,

84, and 84. The problem of biased instrument error is perhaps obvious. Short of an independent comparison, there is no way to detect whether these scores contain bias or whether they perfectly reflect the subject's persuasibility. Because of their consistency, their bias, if any, is hidden.

Control of observational and procedural errors (both biased and unbiased) is a somewhat more troublesome process than control of the types of error discussed earlier. There are two major reasons for this fact. First, independent comparisons (which are necessary to eliminate biased error) are often troublesome, expensive, and sometimes no more accurate than the original procedure. Thus, even if inquirers take the trouble to check their observations, and assuming they find some differences, they may be in the dark as to which actually is the best measure. Second, with respect to unbiased error, variation in the observations could indicate any number of things including imperfect control of other sources of error. But even if imperfect control were not the problem, to assume that the observed variables have constant values for any particular person may be a faulty assumption. Many human traits do vary from day to day and from situation to situation. Lacking very good evidence to the contrary, the inquirer may actually be detecting true changes in the variables of interest.

Thus, to gain "control" of this type of error inquirers must institute procedures which are probable rather than certain, and indirect rather than direct. This is much the same type of procedure as having one's car checked and maintained at regular intervals. Such preventive maintenance does not guarantee that problems will not arise at a later date, but it does reduce this possibility.

The preventive procedures that help ensure error-free observations consist essentially of those criteria for assessing operational definitions set forth in Chapter 3. We will restate them here briefly. First, an operational definition should tap as much as possible of the original concept. When observation procedures adhere to this dictum there is less chance of one or two components of the concept over-contributing to the total picture. If this were to happen the observations would likely contain biased error. By actually observing all of the intended dimensions of the construct, these biases are minimized. Additionally, if possible, the communication scientist should attempt some kind of external validity check (an independent comparison) to detect other biases which may be inherent in his or her procedures.

When procedures are concrete, replicable, and attached to a good numerical scale, the inquirer has taken giant steps toward eliminating unbiased error. The more specificity that is built into the procedures, the less the observations will vary in and of themselves from observation to observation.

CASE 1.   *Real versus reel: Some problems in controlling error*

In order to amplify the preceding comments on sources of error, we will examine some actual research: first, to illustrate the methods used in combatting the various sources of error; second, to describe the tradeoffs made in order to maximize the outcomes of research objectives. Under the auspices of a National Science Foundation grant (Miller and Siebert, 1974, 1975), we have been investigating the effects of videotaped trial materials on juror information processing and juror decision making. One phase of the project involved a relatively simple field experiment in which one group of jurors saw a live trial and a comparable group saw the same trial on videotape (Miller, 1974; Miller, Bender, Florence and Nicholson, 1974). We wanted to compare the following responses of jurors in the two conditions: their verdicts, their retention of trial-related information, their perceptions of the credibility of the opposing attorneys, and their interest and motivation in serving as jurors.

In terms of error sources, we first dealt with the problem of differences in subjects. Typically, of course, a jury consists of 12 persons. If we assume that jurors differ individually and if we want an accurate comparison of the two jury groups, 12 jurors in each condition might not permit us to detect differences between responses to the two trials because of variations in individual juror responses within the groups (error source 1). One solution to this problem is to increase the size of the groups. Naturally, we also wanted to maximize external validity, to make the conditions surrounding the inquiry (error source 2) as real as possible. We chose to use groups of approximately 50 jurors randomly assigned to each condition so as to minimize source 1 error and to deal with source 2 error by having the judge tell the jurors that the litigants had agreed to a larger jury as part of a study dealing with the influence of jury size on verdicts. In addition, the rest of the conditions were quite realistic: the jurors were actual impaneled jurors who thought they were hearing a real case, and the case was tried in an actual courtroom with a presiding judge. All these steps were taken to preserve an appearance of realism and thus to reduce source 2 error.

The third source of error related to measurement of juror responses. The variables we intended to measure were generally attitudes toward trial participants or retention of information associated with the trial. Two methods of obtaining this information are the interview and the questionnaire. We opted for the questionnaire for several reasons.

First, considering that 100 people were involved, the questionnaire provided a more standardized procedure for gathering data. Every juror responded to the same questions and their responses could not be differentially influenced by the tone of voice or the wording of questions by the interviewers. The questionnaire was explained thoroughly and sample items were used to reduce error that might result from misunderstanding of the questions or of the appropriate style of response.

Second, the questionnaire approach permitted the use of equal-appearing interval scales. Since each juror answered about 150 questions, the use of such scaling would have been clumsy and time-consuming in an interview situation. Moreover, the time consideration was not based entirely on convenience or expedience. The interview could have been accomplished in three ways: individual interviews by the same interviewer, individual sessions with several interviewers, or group interviews. The first approach controls for differences among interviewers but permits differences in juror responses due to the varying amounts of time between trial viewing and responding to the questions. This varying time lag could particularly produce error in retention of trial-related information. The second approach eliminates this problem, but substitutes possible error resulting from differences in the interviewers. Finally, the third approach involves a public setting which confounds the measures because one juror's responses might be affected by his or her knowledge of the responses of other jurors. All of the preceding issues are relevant to the controlling of error, and all are discussed more extensively in the following references:

Miller, G. R. (1974). Televised Trials: How Do Jurors React? *Judicature* 58: 242–246.

Miller, G. R., and F. S. Siebert (March 1974). Effects of Videotaped Testimony on Information Processing and Decision-Making in Jury Trials: Progress Report 1. NSF-RANN Grant #GI 38398, Department of Communication, Michigan State University.

Miller, G. R., and F. S. Siebert (February 1975). Effects of Videotaped Testimony on Information Processing and Decision-Making in Jury Trials: Progress Report 2. NSF-RANN Grant #GI 38398, Department of Communication, Michigan State University.

Miller, G. R., D. C. Bender, B. T. Florence, and H. E. Nicholson (1974). Real versus Reel: What's the Verdict? *Journal of Communication* 24: 99–111.

MEASUREMENT AND NUMBERS: A FEW WORDS

The words "numbers" or "scaling" may bring negative associations to mind. Few people find numbers inherently interesting, but for purposes of scientific inquiry, numbers in the form of carefully calculated measurements are an important objective. Such measurements are of interest to scientists not because they give their work an air of complexity, but because they allow concise and exact comparisons of their observations.

We shall talk about some of the advantages and drawbacks of various measuring techniques to impart a better understanding of what constitutes a good observation. The everyday use of various measuring techniques can be illustrated by the following conversation between Fred and Jim:

FRED: "Hi, Jim."

JIM: "Hi, Fred, what's new?"

FRED: "I don't know if you should come near me. Two of my roommates are sick in bed with the flu."

JIM: "No kidding, which ones?"

FRED: "Tom and Bill. You remember Tom—he's the heavy guy, about six feet five; he's got a temperature of 100°."

JIM: "Oh yeah. I met Tom at that party you guys had last month."

FRED: "Right. And Bill—he's about medium weight, maybe five feet ten. He's running a temperature of 102°."

JIM: "Wasn't Bill the guy that helped you fix your bike?"

FRED: "He's the one."

This abbreviated exchange illustrates each of the four types of scaling used by scientific inquirers. The first and simplest type of scaling is called *nominal* and is illustrated (believe it or not) by Fred's use of his roommates' names, i.e., by calling them "Tom" and "Bill." Although calling someone by name may seem to have little to do with measurement, if "measurement" is defined as a *standardized way of classifying and comparing,* it is easier to see what has happened. By naming his friends, Fred has classified each into categories of one, labeled by the names "Tom" and "Bill." This measurement system seems extremely simple: first, because we are dealing only with two people; second, because thinking of names as measurements seems quite strange. There are literally hundreds of common nominal scales that possess more readily apparent utility. The numbers athletes wear on their uniforms, for example, while having no mathematical meaning, help to distinguish one player from another. Likewise, the names of positions on a baseball team help to differentiate the location and actions of each player from those of the others.

The common thread in all these examples is that the things observed are classified into categories on the basis of whether or not they are alike. *To apply a nominal scale of measurement is to say that observed differences in the variable have no discernible, inherent mathematical relationship, while at the same time recognizing that these differences may produce varying effects.* The variable *sex,* for example, is normally treated as a nominal variable with two possible values or measurements: *male* and *female.* To classify subjects in an experiment this way is to say that while there are observable differences among people with respect to their sex, no mathematical relationships about the variable "sex" are inherent in the classification scheme. Such classification in terms of quality rather than quantity bothers certain researchers, and some do not consider nominal scaling as true measurement. Such an outlook is valid in the sense that the classification is not an arithmetic one, yet it overlooks the fact that nominal classification serves a useful purpose in inquiry.

All measurement scales available to the communication scientist build upon the classifying, categorizing principle of the nominal scale. Thus, the next, more complex type—the *ordinal* scale—also categorizes according to similarity, but underlying its classifications is a quantitative dimension. In his conversation with Jim, Fred referred to one of his friends as "heavy" and the other as "medium" weight. These terms constitute an ordinal scale. While everyone could presumably be classified into such categories on the basis of similarities and differences in their weights, there is a weight dimension underlying these labels which confers mathematical sense on their differences. People know, for example, that a person in the "heavy" category weighs more than a person in the "medium" category, *even though no numbers have been used.* This is not to say that numbers are impossible in ordinal measurement. For instance, a listener may rank four speakers talking on the same subject on perceived dynamism, giving the most dynamic speaker the rank "1," and so on, with the least dynamic speaker being given the rank "4." This type of measurement is *quantitative* because it orders observations in terms of the *amount* of some conceptual quality. The numbers assigned designate a mathematical relation: 1 is representative of a greater amount of this quality than 2, 2 represents a greater amount than 3, and so on. Any ranking scheme (e.g., hockey teams or entrants in beauty contests) comprises an ordinal scale. One limitation of this type of measurement is that though the numbers represent differences in quantity, the difference in terms of amount of the variable between any two measurements is unknown because the measured objects are being compared only with each other and not to an external standard. Thus, to say that a speech which was ranked fourth is twice as good as one ranked eighth is to misunderstand the logic behind the scale.

The next more precise and more mathematically useful scale is the *interval* scale, so named because it provides not only the information that ordinal and nominal scales do, but, in addition, provides information about the *intervals,* or separations, between sets of observations by establishing a fixed relationship between increments on the measuring scale and increments in the amount of the property measured. Consequently, equal numerical differences in measurements denote equal differences in the variable measured. When Fred mentions that his friends have temperatures of 100 and 102 degrees (temperature being an intervally scaled variable) we know: (1) that his friends have different temperatures, (2) that Tom's temperature is higher than Bill's, and (3) that the difference between the two temperatures is two degrees.[12] When used for comparative purposes, such mathematically exact differences can give the scientific inquirer valuable insight into the workings of communication phenomena. An examination of Fig. 4.2 will quickly show the difference between knowing the ranking and the actual amount of fear arousal in a hypothetical experiment involving high-fear, medium-fear, and low-fear messages. Note that in one case the difference (on an interval scale) is almost zero, while in another case it seems substantial. Such a difference in differences is lost with an ordinal scale.

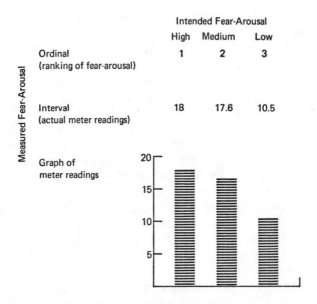

Fig. 4.2 *Fear-Arousal Caused by Three Different Speeches as Indicated by Galvanic Skin Response (GSR) Mechanism Reported on Ordinal and Interval Scales.*

The fourth, and most mathematically useful, of the scales used in scientific inquiry is the *ratio* scale. Ratio scaling has all of the qualities of the preceding three types of scaling and, in addition, establishes a correspondence between zero on the measuring scale and zero amount (none) of the property being measured. In other words, a ratio scale is an interval scale with a *true* zero point.

When talking about body temperature, our psychological "zero-point" is "normal"; but we do not call it zero degrees but rather 98.6 degrees. Nor does "normal" temperature indicate absence of temperature—only absence of fever. Zero degrees Fahrenheit on a thermometer does not indicate total absence of temperature since obviously temperatures have been experienced which were below zero. In fact, while temperature has an absolute zero, the only way it can conceivably be produced is with extremely expensive laboratory equipment. Similarly, there is no reason to believe that zero on an I.Q. scale actually represents a measurement of zero intelligence, or that a grade of zero on an examination indicates no grasp of the material covered in the course. Such scales are usually treated as interval scales.

Ratio scales do have this zero-zero correspondence. In Fred's and Jim's conversation, the height of Fred's friends is expressed on a ratio scale. Zero on the height scale truly represents no height. Thus, it would be justifiable to say that Tom is 10 percent taller than Bill or that Tom is 1.1 times as tall as Bill, but it would be incorrect to say that Bill's temperature was two percent greater than Tom's, since it is inappropriate to draw any ratio relationships between the temperature measurements. Ratio scaling allows not only different intervals to be compared, but because of this zero-zero correspondence, it allows direct comparison of quantities of the measured variable.

These four scales, in the order we have presented them, impose increasingly stringent requirements upon the relationship between the measurement and the object measured (See Fig. 4.3). Each imposes all the requirements of lesser scaling techniques plus an additional "identifying" characteristic. Obviously, then, an inquirer must be able to observe more clearly and more precisely to apply a ratio scale to some concept than to apply an ordinal scale. Because of the requirements imposed upon the relationship between scale and object, those scales with more requirements also allow communication scientists to better understand and describe the relationships they observe.

Throughout this discussion we have stressed the greater information and measurement potential inherent in interval and ratio scales. Perhaps we have created the false impressions that lesser scales are to be shunned or that each variable known to communication scientists is inextricably linked to one and only one scale type. In practice, the matter is not so cut-and-dried. Often what is of upmost importance to the inquirer is not what the variable is called, but instead its effects. Researchers in children's language acquisition, for example, may find that "age" behaves like a nominal variable rather than a ratio variable because, in general, children under eight years do not use adverbs while children eight and older do. Likewise, researchers studying the nonverbal communication of chauvinistic attitudes may find among a group of men a graded con-

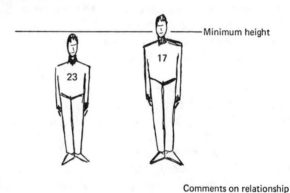

Two football team candidates
(minimum height 5'6")

Minimum height

17

23

Comments on relationship

Nominal scale	Jack (23)	Bill (17)	They are different
Ordinal scale	Too short	Tall (enough)	17 is taller (has more height)
Interval scale	2" less than required	4" more than minimum	He is 6" taller (true height unknown)
Ratio scale	5'4"	5'10"	He is 1.09 times as tall (9% taller)

Fig. 4.3 *Comparison of Scale Types. Measurements on each of the four scales. Note that in this two-subject situation the measurements (regardless of scale type) apply uniquely to the individuals. Note also that regardless of which scale we associate with a measurement, the requirements of all lower level scales will be met by the measurement as well.*

tinuum of "typically male" behaviors. Thus, they may interpret as an ordinal variable what at first was assumed to be nominal—namely, the variable of *sex*. Decisions about the proper scaling technique cannot always be made before inquirers have reflected on the expected relationships among variables and the effects of the variables they are observing.

The attempt to describe concepts with sophisticated quantitative measures is often frustrating, particularly for the kinds of concepts communication researchers typically employ. High and low fear-appeal messages, formality of group structure, morale, and interpersonal control, for example, do not initially seem to lend themselves to precise quantification. Communication scientists, however, attempt to employ the method of analysis; they break concepts down into component parts. The method of analysis suggests that each object, concept, or event is made up of a specific combination of smaller, more easily quantifiable components, and this combination of components is a close translation of the whole, stated in quantitative terms. For example, an apple and an orange are *qualitatively* different, but this difference can be explained in terms of the differing types and amounts of chemicals which comprise each fruit. The method of analysis has allowed the physical scientist to quantify such apparently unfathomable concepts as color and sound by analyzing each as a combination of waves of specific lengths. This is not to say that the variables studied by communication scientists have component structures as simple as many of the variables of physics, but rather to suggest that the method of analysis often pays dividends by clarifying just what is meant (and measured) by the definition of some construct. The concept of "source credibility" has been explored by communication researchers employing a technique known as factor analysis (which is a breakdown by statistical methods) and has been found to contain three important dimensions: competence, trustworthiness, and dynamism. Knowledge of this underlying dimensional structure aids in analyzing the effect of certain speakers on certain audience behaviors. Moreover, two persons judged to be of similar overall credibility may possess varying amounts of the components of credibility and therefore differ in their ability to elicit certain responses from others. Such a possibility would not be suggested by a one-dimensional view of credibility.

CASE 2.   *In quest of power: Determining levels of measurement*

In the last two chapters we have stressed that the use of higher levels of measurement (interval and ratio scales) offers dividends in information gained. Unfortunately, considerations of scaling and statistical analysis often seem to be matters solved by habit or availability, rather than issues which merit careful attention. We will discuss this problem briefly against the background of a recent study taken from a communication journal.

Knapp, Hart, and Dennis (1974) conducted an exploratory inquiry into the verbal and nonverbal behaviors associated with lying. The behaviors of interest included types of references in speaking, stylistic patterns, and nonverbal behaviors. For example, among the variables studied were duration of eye contact, frequency of nodding, number of disparaging remarks about others, and repetition of words and phrases. Note that each of these variables could have been measured by having observers categorize the subject's speech as disparaging or not disparaging, or as manifesting high, medium, or low word repetition. What the researchers did, however, was use actual counts of occurrences of the target events or time the occurrence of the event so that, at least potentially, ratio measurement scales were produced. This point seems simple, yet many instances of research exist where ratio variables—e.g., age or years of education—have been reduced to dichotomies.

Interestingly, Knapp, Hart, and Dennis treated the frequency counts of various behaviors as if they were lower level scales—i.e., they applied less powerful statistical tests appropriate to rank order measures—but treated the time measures as ratio-scaled variables. This is a relatively conservative procedure, perhaps predicated upon the idea that to qualify as a ratio scale, each occurrence in the frequency count must be logically and conceptually equal; e.g., one head nod must mean no more nor no less than another. We suspect the authors felt that this assumption might not be met in certain cases and chose the more tenable set of assumptions required for nonparametric analysis. In this case, the chosen method is about 95 percent as powerful in detecting differences as the method normally employed for ratio-scaled variables.

Obviously, other things being equal, powerful techniques for testing for differences are preferable to weaker methods. In the case of exploratory inquiry power seems particularly important, since an initial finding of no difference may seal off a potentially fruitful area of research from further investigation. In studies such as this one, which include examination of numerous variables, differences in the power of various statistical procedures may cause several actual relationships to be dismissed out of hand as being unworthy of further attention. The following references discuss the issue of levels of scaling and measurement more comprehensively:

Kerlinger, F. N. (1973). *Foundations of Behavioral Research*. 2d ed. New York: Holt, Rinehart and Winston.

Klugh, H. E. (1970) *Statistics: The Essentials for Research*. New York: John Wiley and Sons.

Knapp, M. L., R. P. Hart, and H. S. Dennis (1974). An Exploration of Deception as a Communication Construct. *Human Communication Research* 1: 15–29.

Roscoe, J. T. (1969). *Fundamental Research Statistics for the Behavioral Sciences*. New York: Holt, Rinehart and Winston.

Analyzing concepts and choosing or designing methods for measuring their relationship are important first steps for communication scientists. The outcomes of their work depend upon the sophistication of their preexperimental insights regarding the component structures and relationships of key variables. Quickly conceived and executed research using measuring instruments, subjects, and techniques that are "handy" is often not worth doing. Careful analysis and planning of scientific communication research pays dividends in knowledge gained.

INDIRECT OBSERVATION: SEEING THE INVISIBLE AROUND CORNERS

Not all communication inquiry can be conducted by direct, first-person observation. The conclusions of inquirers attempting to trace the development of Abraham Lincoln's speaking style or Martin Luther King's political impact must necessarily rest upon the observations of others. Indirect observational methods pose an additional set of problems. Inquirers must not only be able to evaluate the variables that will assist them in their search for answers, they must also be able to evaluate accurately the observational acuity of the sources upon whose reports they must rely. To be sure, no two accounts of Lincoln's Gettysburg Address will coincide in every detail. What method, then, can be used to evaluate several conflicting reports of the same event? Unlike first-hand empirical research, where inquirers can control a great number of external factors that may adversely affect their observations, the only control available in secondary observational situations is what might be called *logical control*.

Logical control is analogous to statistical control in first-hand empirical situations. For although inquirers cannot physically control the environment in which the event of interest took place, they can attempt to understand the frame of reference of the primary observer in order to find clues as to what biases may have been operating and to interpret the observations accordingly. For example, since we know that the Gettysburg Address was given during the Civil War and that many people disliked Lincoln and blamed him for the war, reports which refer to the "warmonger" Lincoln or which suggest that the Address was an empty political gesture may cause the inquirer to conclude that these statements reveal more about the biases of the primary observer than about the actual events. This is not to say that such a report is necessarily invalid, only that the inquirer attempts to increase the validity of any report by excluding what logically appear to be reports of the internal states of the primary observer.

Indirect observational methods serve several functions in scientific inquiry. Since science is about the business of discovering universal laws that apply to all people at all times, accounts of the past or of other cultures may well provide a good testing ground for what seems to be applicable theory. Also, for some theoretical ideas, it may be impossible to answer the central questions by experimentation either because time is too limited, controls impossible, or the scope of the question too great. In such cases, second-person accounts of acceptable real-life situations may provide the needed data.[13]

There are many analogies between the methods employed by scientific and historical inquirers. When seeking answers to questions of fact, each is interested in finding valid evidence to support some conclusion, evidence pertaining to the behavior of persons engaged in communicative acts. In assessing this evidence, the historian must remember the distinction between *primary* and *secondary* sources—first-hand accounts of events as opposed to second-hand accounts. The primary source, having directly observed the event, is presumed to provide a more valid account than secondary sources can give. Of course, primary sources are not always available, and the historical inquirer must study extant secondary accounts to evaluate their relative validity. As indicated earlier, this process principally involves comparing different accounts to find themes of agreement (evidence for validity) and to attribute differences to sources in a reasoned manner—i.e., to find factors that explain the differences. In some cases, of course, there is direct evidence (tape recordings, photographs, etc.) which can be used not only as unimpeachable sources of information but which can also serve as a criterion for comparison of other sources to gain insight into the factors that affect them.

The scientific inquirer faces similar choices and problems. The historian's distinction between primary and secondary sources is analogous to the scientist's choice of measuring tools. In some cases, the scientist is fortunate to have available a tested and reliable measuring instrument for measuring subjects' responses. Such a situation is similar to the historian discovering a primary source. In other cases, however, the scientist must rely upon observer reports of subject behavior or other more indirect, unobtrusive measures. Since they leave more room for interpretation and judgment, such methods are usually less desirable and less valid; they are the equivalent of the historian's secondary sources. When the scientist can make observation of rather gross differences between subjects— e.g., whether the subject does or does not join a discussion—he or she is in approximately the same position as the historian with direct primary evidence. In conducting factual inquiry, both the scientist and the historian are in the position of evaluating the effect of the event of interest upon their report of it and of evaluating the influence of outside, irrelevant factors upon the same measure.

In certain cases the historian is investigating events that are recent enough so that the principal participants can be personally interviewed. For example, if a historian were studying the intent and effects of George Wallace's speeches, one good primary source would obviously be Mr. Wallace himself. Availability of such a source does not, however, magically solve all the problems of inquiry; on the contrary, the source may be in a poor position to evaluate not only the effects of his or her speeches but also his or her intent at the time they were presented. Factors which cause distortion include changes in attitude since the event in question, forgetting or confusion, and improper interview techniques. In other words, the historical figure's self-perceptions are constantly molded by the environment; consequently, direct questioning may not necessarily produce valid answers.

One way that scientific inquirers deal with this problem is by use of indirect observation. Indirect observation can be used in experiments or surveys when it is expected that direct observation of the central variables will result in an intolerable amount of error. The following brief everyday conversations should illustrate the role of indirect observation in certain studies:

JOHN: "Hi, Phil, how are you?"

PHIL: "Fine." (Thinking, "I'm not really sure just how I feel.")

PROFESSOR: "Well, what do you think of this course?"

STUDENT: "Oh, it's great." (Thinking. "Yeah, a great bore!")

PAMPHLETEER ON STREET: "Pardon me, are you a registered Republican?"

PASSERBY: "None of your business!"

Our point, of course, is that for such reasons as social convention, status differences, and sense of propriety, people are often less than candid about their feelings and attitudes. Rather than accepting such information, communication scientists sometimes employ observational techniques which are less direct but also potentially more accurate. Such techniques are often considered when the subject of inquiry includes areas of thought or behavior that have strong connections to emotionally charged topics or accepted social conventions.

Indirect observation, as used here, does not necessarily mean devious techniques. Most techniques of indirect observation are rather pedestrian, though some incorporate cleverness in their design. Although we will not attempt a complete cataloging of specific methods of indirect observation, we shall briefly mention three general approaches: (1) those in which a third person(s) make(s) an assessment of the subject, (2) those in which a self-assessment is indirectly obtained from the subject, and (3) those which rely upon records or artifacts of the subject's behavior.

When a third person is asked for an assessment, he or she may have personal knowledge of the subject or may merely observe certain of the subject's actions. In either case, the reason this third person renders an assessment, rather than the subject, is to avoid, or at least to minimize, inaccurate reporting. Thus, this indirect observational method is primarily used when the subjects are expected to be poor estimators of their own attributes, as in the first short conservation above.

Indirect self-assessments are often carried out by means of written "tests" which include decoy items and psychologically revealing questions to disguise the test's true purpose. This procedure is most valuable when more direct methods of inquiry would lead to intentional inaccuracy on the part of the respondent, as in the second short conversation above.

Because accurate records of people's behavior are often inaccessible, the third indirect method is usually resorted to only when other approaches seem impractical or when conducting large, anonymous group surveys. Actually, this method has considerable potential for accuracy and for producing interesting insights. Many cleverly conceived and interesting studies have incorporated such techniques.[14] Under some circumstances, it may be possible to obtain answers to the kinds of questions raised in the third short conversation above, i.e., questions that the respondents are unwilling to answer. As we will indicate in Chapter 5, however, inquirers must be sensitive to the ethical constraints of the situation; in particular, they should avoid actions that smack of invasion of privacy.

DATA REDUCTION AND STATISTICS: MAKING SENSE OUT OF WHAT IS SEEN

Thus far, we have examined some of the problems involved in making individual observations of communication behaviors. Although individual observations provide the bedrock scientific data for studying communication relationships, they must be aggregated, or reduced, before the scientist can make much sense out of them. As you may know, a newspaper picture is composed of many dots, but it would be impossible to interpret the picture by looking closely at each one individually. Rather, the picture can be interpreted only by observing the pattern in which the dots are arranged. By the same token, the scientist cannot interpret the outcomes of 50 or 100 individual observations of some communication variable; instead, he or she must group the observations and study the emergent patterns.

Techniques for aggregating, grouping, and interpreting observations are usually assigned the general label *statistics*.[15] "Statistics" are a collection of mathematical methods or algebraic rules for dealing with measurements for two types of purposes: *descriptive* and *inferential*. Descriptive statistics are those methods which yield meaningful and mathematically useful summary profiles of a large number of individual observations. Suppose, for instance, that a communication researcher wants to determine how much time students at a particular college spend watching commercial television. To gain this information, the researcher asks 100 students the single question: How many hours do you spend in an average day watching national network and local commercial television programs? The data thus consist of 100 individual student self-reports of the amount of time they spend daily watching commercial television.[16]

Obviously, without combining them, it is extremely difficult for the researcher to interpret these 100 individual observations or to communicate effectively with others about them *even though such individual measures provide a maximum amount of information*. So to *reduce* the observations, the researcher calculates a common descriptive statistic, the *mean*. This statistic shows the average amount of time that these 100 students spend daily watching commercial television. The researcher may conclude that *as a group* they average one hour daily of television viewing.

Now assume for a moment that an exceedingly unlikely event occurs: each of the 100 students reports that he or she watches television one hour daily. If this happened, there would be no variance in the observations, and the mean would describe the situation quite accurately—in fact, under these unlikely circumstances, the researcher would have no trouble interpreting the individual observations or communicating about them. Under normal conditions, however, one would bet one's last dollar against such an outcome; there is almost certain to be a *range*, or *distribution*, of viewing times reported by the students. The nature of that distribution determines the relative utility of the mean as a descriptive statistic. If the observations group closely around one hour, the mean describes the situation fairly well; if they depart radically from one hour—e.g., 50 students report that they watch television two hours daily and 50 report that they do not watch it at all—the mean provides sketchy information. In the unlikely event that the observations do split evenly between zero and two hours, the researcher would probably report that the mean of one hour is based upon a perfect bimodal distribution of zero and two, the *mode* being that point (or those points) on the scale where the greatest number of observations lie.

Descriptive statistics such as the mean, mode, and *median* (the point on the scale above and below which 50 percent of the measurements lie) are sometimes referred to as *measures of central tendency,* because they describe the central point of a distribution. For each such measure, "central" has a somewhat different definition: the mode is central because it is the most typical observation or measurement in a group; the median because it divides the measures in two equal parts; and the mean because it is the balance point if all observations had equal weight and were actually placed on their proper point on the measurement scale. These differences in defining "centrality" arise from the properties of the scales with which each measure is normally associated.

A second set of descriptive statistics are those called *measures of variability.* We have already mentioned an important member of this set, namely, variance. The variance of a collection of measurements indicates how compactly those measurements are clustered around the mean, or conversely, to what degree they are scattered about the mean. Thus, if all 100 reports were exactly one hour, no variance would exist in the group of measurements; if each of the 100 students reported a different viewing time, the variance, or scatter, of the measurements might well be substantial.[17]

The arithmetic operations of descriptive statistics represent only one way of describing the overall pattern in a set of observations. Figures, graphs, and narratives can be used to supplement, or even supplant them. The beauty of descriptive statistics lies in their conciseness; their importance stems from the fact that they are used in the calculation of inferential statistics, an area we shall turn to momentarily.

It should be stressed that even so-called descriptive statistics are usually employed inferentially by the communication scientist. *A case of pure description occurs only when observations are obtained from each member of the relevant population.* Thus, if our hypothetical researcher were interested in *only* the 100 students who reported their viewing times, he or she would have made all of the observations necessary to describe the extent of their daily television watching. But if he or she wishes to generalize to other unobserved students—i.e., to argue that the sample mean rather closely reflects the mean of some larger population of college students—it is necessary to make an inference. Since scientists are interested in empirical generalizations, rather than statements about singular facts or limited samples of people, their descriptive *sample* facts are useful only as they permit generalizations about probable population facts.[18]

Our emphasis on the importance of generalization to scientific inquiry leads us to the area of inferential statistics: *mathematical methods that are applied to the shorthand descriptions of the obtained observations to make reasonable inferences about observations not yet made.* As we suggested in the previous paragraph, the communication scientist sometimes wants to make inferences from a single sample to a single population; e.g., to infer the average daily television-viewing time of undergraduate students in a particular college from the reports of a sample of 100 of that college's students. More frequently, however, the scientist is interested in making inferences about possible differences in some behavior of members of two or more samples. We shall return to our convenient example of television viewing to illustrate how this approach works.

Suppose our hypothetical researcher wants to explore this question: Do upper division students and lower division students at a particular college differ in the amount of time they spend daily watching commercial television?[19] To investigate this question, a sample of 60 freshmen and sophomores (the lower division group) and a sample of 60 juniors and seniors (the upper division group) are asked the same question used in our earlier hypothetical study. Having collected their responses, the researcher can now reduce the observations in each sample by calculating means and variances for both.

Assume that the mean for the upper division group is 51.33 minutes per day while the mean for the lower division group is 50.50 minutes. Does this prove, as all lower division students have always suspected, that juniors and seniors have more idle time to spend in front of the tube? Not necessarily, for the differences in the two means may have resulted from chance factors, rather than systematic differences in viewing times between the two populations from which the samples were drawn. After all, it is extremely unlikely that the two means would turn out to be identical. The researcher must now determine the probability that the observed difference reflects an actual difference between the two groups in viewing time; or, stated more accurately, that a difference of this magnitude in the sample means reflects a difference in the means of the two populations from which the samples were drawn.

In making this probability assessment, the variance of the scores within each of the two sample distributions plays a key role, for it provides an estimate of sample-to-sample differences that could be expected due to random error alone. This estimate can then be compared to the observed deviation in average viewing time between the two samples to determine the probability that they were drawn from populations that differ in amount of daily television watching. The inferential statistic used by the researcher is thus based on the following ratio:

$$\text{Statistic} = \frac{\text{observed difference between groups}}{\begin{array}{c}\text{expected difference between groups}\\\text{due to random error alone}\end{array}}$$

Most formulas for inferential statistics take this general form, though the exact components depend upon the type of scaling, the controls exercised, the number of conditions studied, and other design considerations.

The researcher's next step is to divide the observed deviation by the expected deviation: the larger the resultant quotient, the greater the probability that the samples were drawn from two populations that differ in amount of daily television watching.[20] Since most commonly used statistics are "standardized" measures, the researcher can determine the exact probability by referring the result of the division to standard probability tables.

After completing this entire process, the researcher draws one of two inferences: (1) the two populations (lower division students and upper division students) differ in the amount of time spent daily in television watching, or (2) the two populations do not differ. More accurately, the researcher tests the hypothesis that there is no difference between the two population means (the null hypothesis) and then either rejects or fails to reject this hypothesis. Logically speaking, there exist two opportunities to be right and two to be wrong— though probabilistically, of course, each of the four outcomes is not equally likely. The four outcomes are as follows:

Situation	Populations "Really" Are:	Researcher Says:
1.	Not Different	"Not Different"
2.	Not Different	"Different" (wrong-error 1)
3.	Different	"Different"
4.	Different	"Not Different" (wrong-error 2)

Suppose the researcher considers it very important to avoid error 1 in the above listing, i.e., to avoid concluding that there is a difference in daily television viewing time between lower division students and upper division students when in fact there is not. He or she can minimize (though never totally eliminate) this error by setting a stringent *level of significance*. Loosely speaking, the level of significance chosen dictates the exact probability that an observed difference could have occurred because of chance, rather than because of systematic differences between the populations from which the samples were drawn. For example, if the researcher chooses the .05 (5%) level of significance, this means that an inference will be made that the two populations are different if the observed differences in television viewing time for the two samples would occur no more than five times out of 100 by chance. By comparison, selection of the .01 (1%) level decreases the likelihood of an erroneous inference of population difference, since for the two populations to be deemed different in time spent watching television by this criterion, the observed differences would occur only one time out of 100 by chance.

How can the researcher reduce the likelihood of the second mentioned error found in the above listing, i.e., concluding that the two populations do not differ in time spent viewing television when in fact they do? Many factors influence such an erroneous inference. All of the kinds of unbiased error discussed earlier contribute to the probability of this mistake, for as the magnitude of random error increases, the variance of the scores within the sample also increases. Sample size is another important consideration (primarily because it influences the expected random error); all other things equal, the larger the sample size the less the likelihood of failing to discover an actual difference between the populations. Thus, given differences in television viewing time of the magnitude observed between the lower division students and the upper division students in our hypothetical study, observing two samples of five would almost certainly result in the inference that the two populations do not differ; with a sample of 60 from each population, the same observed differences are likely to result in the opposite inference by the researcher.

The many complexities of the inferential process transcend the scope of our remarks. A final point merits emphasis: if you have followed the basic logic underlying the drawing of inferences from samples to populations, it should be apparent that the two types of mistaken inferences are closely related. *More specifically, attempts to reduce the likelihood of one erroneous inference usually increase the probability of making the other.* Thus, by setting a stringent significance level, the probability of inferring a population difference when none exists is reduced *but* the likelihood of inferring no population difference when one actually exists is increased. Scientific communication inquiry necessarily demands a calculated tradeoff between the two types of inferential mistakes.

This brief discussion of the process involved in reducing individual observations to aggregated data and of the steps required to interpret these data has been, of necessity, oversimplified. Literally hundreds of books have been written about data analysis and statistics. What we have sought to provide is a brief explanation of how the communication scientist makes sense out of the individual observations he or she collects. As a final illustration, Fig. 4.4 contains descriptive statistics for the hypothetical study we have just discussed. The solid curve depicts the distribution of times for the 60 upper division students, while the broken curve shows the times for the 60 lower division students.

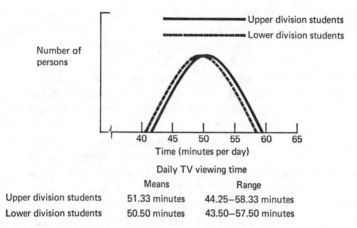

Daily TV viewing time

	Means	Range
Upper division students	51.33 minutes	44.25–58.33 minutes
Lower division students	50.50 minutes	43.50–57.50 minutes

Fig. 4.4 *Daily Television Viewing Among College Students.*

Actual computation of an inferential statistic called a *t* test reveals that if the researcher chose the .05 level of significance, he or she would infer that the two samples are drawn from populations that differ in amount of daily television watching. Notice that the difference in mean daily viewing time of the two groups is relatively small when compared to differences in viewing time from student to student. Note also that because of the large individual variations, a few changes in subjects selected or in research conditions might have resulted in the measurements being quite different. Nevertheless, even with this seemingly frail evidence, the communication scientist can make an exact and useful probability statement about yet unobserved persons; i.e., formulate an empirical generalization about differences in the daily television viewing habits of upper division students and lower division students at the particular college investigated.

OBSERVATION: A CONCLUDING THOUGHT

In its fullest sense, observation is one of the most complex topics in communication inquiry and, as we have indicated, one of the most thoroughly studied and developed areas of the field. We have attempted to introduce you to some basic concepts and considerations of observation in order to increase your understanding of, and appreciation for, this crucial dimension of inquiry.

NOTES

1. The word "unguided" as used here means without theoretical guidance rather than random or haphazard. Certainly previous observations and probably educated intuition gave direction to their observations.

2. In all scientific honesty, we would be forced to admit that some inaccuracy exists in this measurement because of the limitations of conventional yardsticks and the rather hasty measurement procedures employed.

3. Because observational techniques in communication inquiry are often difficult to design and carry out and because even the most carefully planned technique can allow considerable error, an independent comparison (i.e., observation by means of a second technique—perhaps in error itself) may be of little value as a comparison.

4. This situation is analogous to that in the example of the first speedometer (p. 160).

5. This situation would be analogous to that in the example of the second speedometer (p. 161).

6. Such sensitization effects have been the object of extensive research. Rosenthal and his associates (1966) have shown that the researcher can influence observations by very subtle behavioral cues stemming from his or her expectations about observational outcomes. Orne (1959, 1962) found that subjects who can guess the inquirer's hypothesis behave differently than those who cannot. Combs and Miller (1968) reported that subjects who were asked (in the guise of research confederates) to give a speaker negative feedback rated his or her speaking significantly less favorably than subjects who gave the same speaker positive feedback. These kinds of effects are closely related to the philosophical problem of *reflexive prediction;* i.e., "a prediction comes true because it comes to the attention of actors on the social scene whose actions will determine its truth-value" (Buck, 1969, p. 153).

7. Randomization, too, may be understood more clearly in relation to the example of the first speedometer (p. 160). Obviously, if we recorded a million different readings of the wavering needle in a five-minute interval, the average of these readings would be 50 miles per hour. But if we recorded readings at 30 randomly selected instants in that five-minute interval, we would also expect the average of these observations to be very close to 50 miles per hour. This is because we are making an *unbiased selection* of observations containing *unbiased error*. The greater the number of such randomly selected observations we include in our average, the more likely it will approach the true value of 50 miles per hour, though no average must necessarily be exactly this value. In this situation, though, we would expect that our sample of 30 observations is representative of, though not necessarily equal to, the millions of observations we might have made, in all mathematically meaningful ways. The fact that randomization does not *necessarily* assume mathematically exact equality of selected groups in any particular case does not prevent the application of statistical tests which produce precise probability statements from single experiments in order to test hypotheses. Finally, since randomization is based on a probability model grounded in an infinite number of observations, the scientist cannot prove that it "works" in any given instance. We might say that randomization is to the communication scientist as God is to the theologian: its validity is accepted and arguments then flow from its acceptance.

8. Actually, the reasoning is not quite this simple. The statistical procedures used in generalizing from an experiment amount to translation of the magnitude of the effects of a stimulus on a *sample* into the probability of a stimulus-effect relationship in the *population,* a process discussed later in this chapter.

9. Here we are speaking a bit loosely for convenience' sake. Actually, the hypothesis would probably be stated: when compared with use of black-and-white posters, use of colored posters will result in significantly greater attendance at fraternity parties. Reasons *why* this should happen—e.g., colored posters are more attention-getting—move the researcher into theoretical considerations relating to inferences about the cognitive states of potential party-goers. Whether a significant finding in this

study will *generalize* to other social events—e.g., circuses—rests on evaluation of the kinds of sampling and control procedures used, topics discussed in the preceding section of this chapter.

10. The wording of the speech is, of course, the independent variable we are manipulating. We want all aspects of the speech to be as similar as possible *except* for the absence or presence of the fear-arousing stories.

11. Even though inquirers have equalized the "environments" in their experimental groups, the possibility still exists that these equalized variables will *interact* with the experimental variable to produce different effects. Such an interaction would probably occur, for example, in an experiment comparing information retention under two conditions—live lecture and film. If lighting is equal for both conditions and normal for the lecture condition, the film will probably be difficult to see. Thus retention in the film condition will show effects not only of that method of presentation but also of the effect of the lighting on subjects' ability to see.

12. By itself this two-degree difference is trivial and meaningless, but if we can compare it to other such differences—e.g., the difference between Bill's temperature and 98.6 degrees—its mathematical usefulness becomes more apparent.

13. For example, medical researchers investigating effects of treatments on life-span or preconditions of rare diseases may find accurate answers more quickly by referring to historical records than by observing living persons.

14. Interested readers are referred to the discussion of a variety of such techniques in *Unobtrusive Measures* (Webb *et al.*, 1972). Further understanding (and fun) can be gained by reading nearly any Sherlock Holmes adventure, or articles such as "The Art of Garbage Analysis: With Photographs of Garbage of Four Celebrities" (Weberman, 1971).

15. Like several other terms used in this volume, the term "statistics" stimulates a variety of meanings. In everyday conversation, it is often used to describe any use of, or resort to, numbers. In the discipline of statistics, a statistic refers to a sample fact while a population fact is called a parameter. Our use of the term is not totally congruent with either of these meanings.

16. It would be instructive for you to attempt to identify some of the types of error, both biased and unbiased, that may occur with such single-item self-reports.

17. More specifically, variance is calculated by summing the squared deviation of each observation from the mean and dividing by the number of observations. The square root of the variance is the *standard deviation,* a statistic with which you are probably familiar.

18. If observations are made of the entire population there is no need to use any inferential statistic. If observations are made of two or more entire populations for comparative purposes the same thing holds because any differences observed *are* population differences.

19. For simplicity, we have focused on a particular college. The communication scientist would probably be interested in generalizing beyond one school.

20. Actually, we have oversimplified this situation, since the probability depends not only on the magnitude of the quotient but also on the number of subjects in the sample.

QUESTIONS AND EXERCISES

1. Return to the cooperative exercise in Chapter 1 which involved comparing your count of statements of definition, fact, and value contained in a political speech with that of a classmate. Can you see how your extent of agreement or disagreement affects the *reliability* of this measure? Are you satisfied with your initial reliability? (There are numerous techniques for estimating reliability, but a simple percentage of statements agreed upon will give you a reasonable estimate.) What things could the two of you do to increase reliability? What statements, if any, can you make about the *validity* of your measure?

2. Consider each of the following situations and specify several sources of possible error for the observation(s) that is (are) made:
   a. A professor gives you a "D" in a course. (The "D" supposedly represents his or her best observation of the concept "your ability.")

b. After watching a single game, a professional football scout rates a quarterback's overall professional potential "4" on a scale where "5" is maximally positive.

c. Following your address to a group of student leaders, Friend 1 tells you it was one of the best speeches you've ever given, while Friend 2 tells you that you weren't at your best. (Obviously, there is unreliability in these two assessments of the concept "your level of communication performance on this occasion." While there is no way of determining the relative validity of each observation without gathering more data, what sources of error may have produced the discrepancy?)

3. Identify the level of measurement (scaling) implied in each of the following statements. In some cases, you may wish to suggest more than one possibility:

a. "Every week that course seems more boring than the week before!"

b. "Smith's class was required to attend the play but Jones's wasn't."

c. "My raise this year amounted to a 6.5 percent increase."

d. "On a scale of '4', I'd rate that joke a '2'."

4. Suppose you wished to assess the effectiveness of General MacArthur's famous resignation speech. What sources of indirect observation would you use? What criteria would be important in determining the probable validity of each of these sources?

5. Suppose you had a hunch that upper division students (juniors and seniors) talk more in class than lower division students (freshmen and sophomores). Decide on a sampling procedure and make observations to test your hunch. Using only descriptive statistics, arrange your data to show what you observed with minimum confusion and to answer the question. Finally, indicate how the following sampling procedures might introduce *biased error* into your findings:

a. You take your lower division sample from large, introductory courses (mean size, 150 students) and your upper division sample from smaller, single-section courses (mean size, 35 students).

b. You draw your upper division sample from 8 AM classes and your lower division sample from 10 AM classes.

   c. You pull your lower division sample from social science courses and your upper division sample from engineering courses.

   d. You are an upper division student registered for one of the courses you are observing.

   e. Two of the lower division classes have only female students.

REFERENCES

Buck, R. C. (1969). Do Reflexive Predictions Pose Special Problems for the Social Scientist? In Leonard I. Krimerman (ed.), *The Nature and Scope of Social Science: A Critical Anthology*, pp. 153–162. New York: Appleton-Century-Crofts.

Combs, W., and G. R. Miller (1968). The Effect of Audience Feedback on the Beginning Public Speaker: A Counterview. *The Speech Teacher* **17**: 229–231.

Flesch, R. (1946). *The Art of Plain Talk*. New York: Harper & Row.

Miller, G. R. (1964). Variations in the Verbal Behavior of a Second Speaker as a Function of Varying Audience Responses. *Speech Monographs* **31**: 109–115.

Miller, G. R., H. Zavos, J. W. Vlandis, and M. E. Rosenbaum (1961). The Effects of Differential Reward on Speech Patterns. *Speech Monographs* **28**: 9–16.

Orne, M. (1959). The Nature of Hypnosis: Artifact and Essence. *Journal of Abnormal and Social Psychology* **58**: 277–299.

Orne, M. (1962). On the Social Psychology of the Psychological Experiment: With Particular Reference to Demand Characteristics and Their Implications. *The American Psychologist* **17**: 776–783.

Rosenthal, R. (1966). *Experimental Effects in Behavioral Research*. New York: Appleton-Century-Crofts.

Vlandis, J. W. (1964). Variations in the Verbal Behavior of a Speaker as a Function of Varied Reinforcing Conditions. *Speech Monographs* **31**: 116–119.

Webb, E. J., D. T. Campbell, R. D. Schwartz, and L. Sechrest (1972). *Unobtrusive Measures: Nonreactive Research in the Social Sciences*. Chicago: Rand McNally and Co.

Weberman, A. J. (1971). The Art of Garbage Analysis with Photographs of Garbage of Four Celebrities. *Esquire* **76**: 113–117.

5
Evaluation

The fact that a piece of social research may contribute to scientific knowledge—and even to human welfare—does not make it unambiguously good, as some social scientists would like to believe. Conversely, the fact that a piece of social research may, in its purpose, method, or style, treat man as an object, shorn of his individuality, does not automatically damn it, as some humanists are prone to assume.

—HERBERT KELMAN

A third important dimension of the process of communication inquiry is evaluation. Like many of the other terms we have used, the word "evaluation" stimulates a variety of meanings. In one sense, you evaluate this book as you read it; you form judgments on the quality of its ideas and the clarity of its style. When you decide whether to spend your limited recreation funds on a ticket to the hockey match or a dinner at the student union, you evaluate; you weigh the relative outcomes of two or more alternatives and choose one. In yet another sense, any ethical or aesthetic judgment entails evaluation; whenever you assert that an act was just or unjust or that a play was pleasing or disappointing you render an evaluation.

If people yield to their Humpty Dumpty impulses and use "evaluation" to mean whatever they want it to mean, confusion is an almost certain consequence. Therefore, we want to sort out some of the ways that evaluation enters into communication inquiry and consider some of the issues associated with the evaluative process. Hopefully, our remarks will clarify just when and how the communication inquirer evaluates and increase your understanding of the multiple roles played by evaluation in the process of inquiry.

EVALUATION IN SELECTING QUESTIONS FOR INQUIRY

Sometimes it is asserted that all acts of inquiry are inherently evaluative *because the inquirer must choose to pursue one question rather than another.* Stated specifically, this argument goes as follows: Miller and Nicholson have only limited time and energy to conduct inquiry. Since there are numerous questions they might conceivably pursue, they must allocate their resources to a small subset of these questions; in other words, they must choose to do some things— e.g., write a book about communication inquiry—and not to do others—e.g., write a book about mass communication.[1] *These very choice behaviors represent an evaluative act.*

In an extremely broad sense this assertion is true; as we indicated at the chapter's outset, whenever a person makes a choice an element of evaluation is inherent in the decision. Most of the time, however, this evaluation hinges on a factual assessment of means and ends or on a matter of personal taste, not on ethical or aesthetic considerations. Thus, we did not choose to write a communication inquiry book because it seemed more ethically defensible or aesthetically pleasing than a volume about mass communication. Instead, we wrote this particular book because we felt better qualified to write it (a means-ends assessment) and because it struck us as a more interesting challenge (a manifestation of personal taste). In a similar vein, a diner's choice of top sirloin rather than filet mignon entails an evaluation, but it would usually be far-fetched to argue that the evaluation is grounded in ethical or aesthetic considerations.[2]

In Chapter 1 we identified three criteria which determine the significance of a question for communication inquiry: personal interest, social importance, and theoretical significance. Consider for a moment the latter two criteria; very often an inquirer's perceptions of the best way to advance his or her field will determine the relative importance assigned to each criterion. This short, hypothetical dialogue captures the different evaluative stances of two scientific inquirers:

INQUIRER A: "The reason communication research advances like a scientific turtle, rather than a hare, lies in our preoccupation with applied problems. We ought to concentrate more on the development of basic theory and less on dealing with a plethora of practical questions. Had Einstein started out to build an atomic reactor rather than to develop relativity theory, I doubt we'd be anywhere today."

INQUIRER B: "I don't buy that argument. First of all, I think we make a basic mistake when we compare sciences like communication with an area like physics. What we need to do is bring our knowledge and research skills to bear on practical communication problems. Out of our research endeavors we may be able to develop some theories inductively. The trouble with our field is that we've got too many ivory tower theorists and not enough people out where the action is."

INQUIRER A: "Nonsense! The journals are crammed with little one-shot communication studies, but they don't add up to very much theoretically."

INQUIRER B: "But even these studies are sterile undertakings modeled after a physical or natural science laboratory. If we'd go out and deal with some actual communication problems . . . ."

Here the two hypothetical inquirers disagree sharply about a factual question: what is the best way to advance the field of communication inquiry? Although their disagreement is grounded in different evaluative premises, the dispute does not center on ethical or aesthetic concerns. By now it may have occurred to you that the question can best be resolved empirically; inquirers can pursue both strategies and see what happens. In fact, both imaginary participants seem a bit dogmatic in their argumentative postures, for it should be possible to combine elements of both positions, i.e., to conduct theoretically significant communication studies about socially important communication problems. Still, we do not believe we have exaggerated the dialogue; disputes such as this one are commonplace to the contemporary scene in scientific communication inquiry.

By modifying this hypothetical debate the thrust of disagreement can also be changed, thus illustrating the complexity of the evaluative process when selecting questions for inquiry. Suppose the conversation had followed this course:

INQUIRER A: "Sometimes I think communication scientists are a bunch of scientific boy scouts. They always seem more concerned with helping people solve their communication problems than with developing theories of human communication."

INQUIRER B: "What's so bad about that? I think we have a moral responsibility to seek answers to some of the communication problems that plague us. While we're running around seeking elusive 'communication theories,' people are becoming more frustrated and alienated. There are very few quality relationships in the world today."

INQUIRER A: "Let's not mix our ethics with our science. I think I'm as concerned about the human communicative condition as anyone. But once I let my values get mixed with my work as a scientist, I'm in for trouble. My job is to develop some theories that help us explain and predict human communication theory, not to solve all of the world's problems.

INQUIRER B: "I'm never able to understand how people can divide their lives up so neatly. I see my roles as scientist and concerned citizen overlapping . . . ."

Once more the dispute between the two inquirers centers on the evaluation of questions for inquiry. Now, however, the protagonists differ on a value question: to what extent, if any, is the communication scientist ethically obligated to investigate questions that may aid in the solution of immediate pressing communication problems? Inquirer A apparently believes that the communication scientist should shun concern for the human condition in pursuing scientific research, while Inquirer B argues that the scientist has a moral obligation to devote at least some research activity to questions bearing directly upon society's urgent communication problems.

This argument, or some closely allied derivative, is a perennial bone of contention among members of the scientific community. Again, the positions taken by Inquirers A and B are extreme; probably communication scientists can satisfy their ethical obligations to relate their work to important social problems without sacrificing their scientific integrity. As we shall emphasize later in this chapter, however, acceptance of funds from agencies to do research and subsequent assumption of a role as policy expert create some thorny problems for the communication scientist.

Finally, the decision of whether or not to pursue questions of a particular kind often hinges on ethical considerations. For example, a communication inquirer may refuse to investigate any questions pertaining to persuasion on the grounds that persuasion is a manipulative, irrational, immoral process. Or one may balk at accepting grant monies from certain governmental agencies in the belief that these agencies will dictate the promulgation of particular values in the research undertaken. In both cases, the potential bone of contention does not lie in whether or not one should investigate a particular question; rather, it relates to the ethical judgments underlying a refusal to deal with a whole class of researchable questions. Perhaps this latter distinction can best be illustrated by eavesdropping yet again on a brief conversation between two imaginary inquirers:

INQUIRER A: "Yes, I admit it's kind of interesting to ask whether women are more susceptible to emotional appeals than men. Still, I don't want to collaborate with you on the study. I don't like to study persuasion questions because I think persuasion is inherently manipulative and antithetical to democratic values. To me it's just another form of thought control."

INQUIRER B: "But look here, we've got the opportunity for a really neat, tightly controlled design. Not only can we manipulate type of message content, we can also vary the sex of the speaker. Moreover, we could develop an instrument to measure the extent to which our female subjects accept or reject traditional female role prescriptions."

INQUIRER A: "I don't think you get my point. I'm not opposed to your particular study *per se*. What I'm saying is that all persuasion studies are unethical because they just add to the power elite's fund of information on how to control people."

INQUIRER B: "Surely you're not arguing that this group doesn't know a lot about controlling already. Furthermore, when we know more about the variables that foster control we're also in a better position to educate people on ways of resisting persuasion. Surely that kind of understanding is consistent with democratic values."

INQUIRER A: "That's fine in principle, but as a matter of fact the means of communication are largely controlled by this power elite we've been talking about and . . . ."

Obviously, a good debate is in the offing. But the grounds for dispute were not defined until Inquirer B grasped the futility of arguing about the specific study he had proposed as a collaborative venture to Inquirer A. If Inquirer A is to be induced to collaborate on this study (or any similar undertaking), she must be persuaded to modify her position concerning the ethics of persuasion research. Until she tempers her ethical stance on this issue, Inquirer A may be expected to scorn any inquiry that focuses on the persuasion process.

EVALUATION IN DEALING WITH QUESTIONS OF FACT

Let us now consider some aspects of evaluation as they relate to inquiry concerning factual communication questions.

Sometimes it is argued that all acts of factual inquiry are inherently evaluative *because the inquirer must make choices concerning the actual conduct of the research*. To illustrate, consider the problem of setting a significance level for interpreting the results of a particular scientific investigation. Recall from our discussion in the last chapter that the level of significance chosen determines the likelihood of committing a certain type of inferential error: specifically, the error of inferring that two or more samples were not drawn from the same population when in fact they were. Suppose two inquirers independently embark on the identical mission of determining whether strong fear-arousing messages are more persuasive than mild fear-arousing messages. In establishing a significance level, however, they arrive at different decisions; specifically, one opts for the .05 level while the other chooses .01. Further assume that the two obtain identical results: the strong fear-arousing message results in more attitude change than the mild fear message and the observed difference is significant at the .02 level. These identical results dictate two diametrically opposed conclusions; the inquirer who decided on the .05 level concludes that the two values of the variable differ significantly in their persuasive impact, while the inquirer who chose the .01 level concludes that they do not. Moreover, since the two values of the variable either differ or they do not, one of the two inquirers must be wrong. Unfortunately, as indicated earlier, it is impossible to know for certain which one is in error, but it is apparent that the disparity in their conclusions results from the differing choices they initially made about the conduct of the research and the interpretation of the research outcomes.

Again, however, we would argue that these kinds of choices are usually based on factual means-ends assessments, not on ethical or aesthetic considerations. Stated differently, we doubt that the two inquirers disagree about the ethics of a particular level of significance, i.e., that one would contend that the .05 level is morally superior while the other would champion the moral supremacy of .01. Instead, both are committed to a common end: the orderly, functional advance of scientific knowledge about human communication. Their selection of differing significance levels reflects disagreement about the best means for furthering this end; whereas one seems to feel that the current state of theory and research methodology warrants a relatively liberal five-percent error margin, the second seems to believe that if differences cannot be observed at the .01 level of significance, the field will best be served by reporting nonsignificant findings. Each error entails certain consequences: if a relationship between level of fear arousal and persuasive impact is reported when in fact one does not exist, researchers may be led down blind investigatory alleys and practitioners may rely upon a message strategy that is actually ineffective; if a lack of relationship is reported when in fact one does exist, researchers may overlook promising avenues for inquiry and practitioners may fail to avail themselves of a promising persuasive technique. But evaluation of the relative import of each type of error usually does not hinge on an ethical question; rather, it involves a factual judgment about the best means for advancing the study of human communication.

CASE 1. *All I know is what I read in the journals: An illustration of the problem of decisions concerning error*

The extent to which a predominant bias regarding preference for one type of error over another may affect the research posture of an area is illustrated by the prevailing policy of most communication journals. Seldom is a study published reporting no significant differences; if inquirers fail to reject the null hypothesis, they usually put their data in the file cabinet (or the wastebasket) and head back to the drawing board. Journal editors are much more willing to err in reporting a difference when none exists than they are to report a lack of differences when differences do exist. In short, the field of communication—and, for that matter, most social sciences—is loath to be caught with its Type II error showing.

In some cases, there are good reasons for this bias. Poor research procedures or inadequate sample sizes sometimes virtually guarantee that an inquirer will be unable to reject the null (Katzer and Sodt, 1973). Moreover, some inquirers seem to feel that nonsignificant differences are analogous to no scientific progress. This position, of course, rests on the assumption that being "right"— providing confirming evidence for one's theories, hypotheses, or hunches—equals progress, while being "wrong"—providing disconfirming evidence for one's theories, hypotheses, or hunches—does not.

There are, however, some dangers in focusing exclusively on research which yields significant differences. Bakan (1967) points out one of the most troublesome potential pitfalls. He argues that since there are a limited number of problems which readily suggest themselves for investigation, numerous inquirers may be simultaneously and independently pursuing tests of essentially the same hypothesis. Although the number is probably extreme, let us assume that 100 inquirers set out to test a research hypothesis. Suppose 95 of them fail to reject the statistical null hypothesis and 5 do. Given the prevailing publication climate, the 5 who reject the null will shepard their results safely into print and the 95 who do not reject the null will ponder what went wrong. But given the .05 level of significance commonly used, the results of the 100 studies conform exactly to chance expectations. Thus, what appears to be a well-replicated finding may be nothing more than a fortuitous happening. Furthermore, this possibility is enhanced by the fact that many findings do not have the benefit of even one reported replication, let alone four.

Recently, Greenwald (1975) has contended that inquirers should reassess their attitudes about the dangers of failing to reject the null hypothesis. Perhaps when there are no obvious reasons for questioning the soundness of the research procedures or the adequacy of sample sizes, studies yielding nonsignificant differences should be reported. To proceed on the belief that relationships exist when in fact they do not can create a literature replete with Type I errors and can provide unsound advice for those who wish to use the results of scientific communication inquiry to improve their communicative skills. The following references provide greater detail on the issues sketched in this case:

Bakan, D. (1967). *On Method: Toward a Reconstruction of Psychological Investigation*. San Francisco: Jossey-Bass.

Greenwald, A.G. (1975). Consequences of Prejudice Against the Null Hypothesis. *Psychological Bulletin* 82: 1–20.

Katzer, J., and J. Sodt (1973). An Analysis of the Use of Statistical Testing in Communication Research. *Journal of Communication* 23: 251-265.

Morrison, D.E., and R.E. Henkel, eds. (1970). *The Significance Test Controversy*. Chicago: Aldine.

Value Judgments in Choosing Research Strategies

Under certain circumstances, of course, a decision about the conduct of scientific research may demand the resolution of an ethical question. Consider once again the significance-level issue. Suppose a medical researcher has developed a vaccine to protect against lymphoma, or cancer of the lymph system. Although there is no question about the vaccine's effectiveness, a possibility exists that it may have the undesirable side effect of increasing the number of children born with birth defects. How certain should the researcher be that these side effects are minimal or nonexistent before advocating widespread inoculation with the vaccine? In other words, how much margin of error should one be willing to accept in reaching the conclusion that the vaccine does not produce the harmful side effect of increased birth defects?

Obviously, numerous factual and value questions are potentially relevant to the researcher's decision on this matter. What is the probability of contracting lymphoma even if the vaccine is not used? What is the maximal extent of possible harmful side effects; i.e., how great will the increase in percentage of birth-defective children born to vaccinated mothers be *assuming* that the vaccine does increase the likelihood of such births? Does the mother's primary ethical responsibility lie in the maintenance of her own health or in her maternal commitment to as yet unborn children? Do the same ethical priorities apply to childless married women and to mothers with six children? Once researchers begin to unravel the complexities of the significance-level decision, they are forced to face up to many knotty factual and value questions.

Readers of Sinclair Lewis' *Arrowsmith* will recall an ethical dilemma involving a conflict between sound research practice and concern for immediate human suffering. Faced with an impending epidemic of plague on a Caribbean island, Arrowsmith must choose between injecting half of the inhabitants with his newly developed serum while leaving the other half uninjected—a procedure resulting in sound control practices that will enable him to assess the effects of the serum precisely—or injecting everyone with the serum—a course of action that would possibly produce maximum immediate gains in saving human life but would make it impossible to assess precisely the effectiveness of the serum. Torn between his innate humanitarianism and his scientific training, Arrowsmith endures constant conflict, torn between his rational, longterm perspective as a scientist and his emotional, immediate concern for human suffering and death. Although the dilemma is never fully resolved, it graphically illustrates the ethical implications of certain research choices. The fundamental issue of whether "to give up the possible saving of millions for the immediate saving of thousands" (Lewis, 1925, p. 387) persists as Arrowsmith's personal ethical plague, a plague as damaging in its own way as the one he seeks to conquer.

Fortunately or unfortunately, as the case may be, the ethical issues faced by the communication scientist usually lack such stark drama. Still, in the course of making research decisions, the communication scientist cannot shun certain ethical questions. Two persistent concerns center on the use of deception in research undertakings and on the effects of certain operational manipulations on the well-being of research participants.

Deception is a common commodity in scientific communication research. At the most elementary level, its use is justified by the assumption that knowledge of the researcher's purpose would influence the outcome of the study. For instance, if participants were told that the researcher wished to determine whether a strong or a mild fear message results in greater persuasive impact, their knowledge of this fact might influence the way they would respond to the messages.[3] Thus, subjects are seldom apprised of the actual reason for the research. Typically, the purpose is misrepresented to them, or it is couched in such vague, general terms that little real information is divulged.

Simple misrepresentation of a study's purpose is but one form of deception commonly employed by the communication scientist. Miller (1970) outlines three other deceptive strategies that are often part and parcel of the research environment: (1) misrepresentation to facilitate the manipulation of variables, (2) misrepresentation of the relationship between researcher and subject, and (3) misrepresentation of the rewards the subject will receive for participating in the study. All three of these latter forms of deception, along with simple misrepresentation of the study's purpose, are found in a study conducted by Festinger and Carlsmith (1959), which sought to determine the persuasive effects of engaging in counterattitudinal advocacy under conditions of high and low justification. To illustrate the various ways that deception is used in scientific inquiry, we will describe this study briefly.

Each subject was told that the study's purpose was to assess performance ability on several tasks (simple misrepresentation of the study). The subject then worked for an hour on two dull, mundane activities that involved placing spools onto a tray and turning pegs in a clockwise direction. After an hour, the experimenter told the subject that the experiment was being conducted in two groups: a group where subjects received no introduction to the tasks and a group where a hired student discussed the tasks with subjects prior to their performance of them (misrepresentation of the study to manipulate a variable). Unfortunately, said the experimenter, the hired student was unable to report today and a subject is waiting in the next room to be "introduced" to the tasks. If the present subject would agree to take over the job of the paid student—a job that required telling the waiting subject that the tasks were interesting and enjoyable—the experimenter would pay the present subject one dollar (low justification condition) or 20 dollars (high justification condition).

Actually, the waiting "subject" was the real confederate of the experimenter; the person who was led to believe he was assisting the experimenter was still functioning in the role of subject (misrepresentation of the relationship between researcher and subject). When told that the experiment was interesting and enjoyable, the waiting "subject" (actually the confederate) responded that she had been told by a friend that the tasks were dull and boring. This placed the "confederate" (actually the subject) in the position of arguing counterattitudinally; he found it necessary to contend that the dull, mundane tasks were interesting and enjoyable.

After "introducing" the tasks to the supposed subject, the actual subject was taken to another room and his own rating of the attractiveness of the original tasks was obtained by the experimenter. The real purpose of the study was then divulged to the subject, and he was asked to return the money (one dollar or 20 dollars) he had been "paid" by the experimenter (misrepresentation of the rewards to be obtained for participating in the study).[4]

If you are totally confused by now it is hardly surprising. The methods used by Festinger and Carlsmith weave such an intricate web of related deceptions that it is difficult to identify the cast without a program. Moreover, the ethical issues associated with such ventures are painfully obvious. Should people be told that they are assisting the experimenter when in fact they are still cast in the role of subjects? Should payment for participation be tendered and then reclaimed when the subject has completed the task? Underlying these specific issues is the more general ethical question: *under what conditions, if any, is a researcher justified in deceiving subjects in a study?*[5]

This question assumes heightened significance when the deception employed involves manipulations that may have damaging effects on an individual's psychological well-being. Consider the moral implications of the following deceptive manipulations which, while not necessarily typical of most studies, have actually been used in scientific inquiry concerning human behavior:

1. Subjects are led to believe that they are administering dangerous electrical shocks to a fellow subject (actually a confederate) who suffers from a heart condition (Milgram, 1963, 1965).

2. After viewing slides of nude males, subjects are told their reactions to the slides indicate strong homosexual tendencies (Bramel, 1962, 1963).

3. Following completion of a test ostensibly used to measure social sensitivity, subjects are told their scores show that they are socially insensitive and inept at dealing with other people (Walster, Berscheid, Abrahams, and Aronson, 1967).

4. To examine the effects of frustration on language intensity, subjects are told their performances on a recently completed classroom assignment are incompetent and among the worst that the instructor has ever read (Carmichael and Cronkhite, 1965).

When confronted regarding the ethical defensibility of deceptive, psychologically painful manipulations, scientific inquirers typically fall back on two lines of defense: first, that the potential benefits of the knowledge gained outweigh the discomfort visited upon subjects; second, that postexperimental debriefing of subjects erases any adverse psychological effects of research manipulations. Although the first argument has merit on some occasions, its potential self-serving characteristics should be recognized. Naturally, the inquirers' ego-involvement in their research virtually ensures that they will perceive the outcomes as vitally important. One solution to such selective perception lies in removing this judgment from the province of the researcher and placing it in the hands of a group or committee charged with assessing the ethical implications of the proposed research. Certainly such a move increases objectivity. Nevertheless, the inherent difficulty of weighing the relative value of research outcomes against the extent of possible psychological harm to subjects assures wide disagreement on the ethical merits of many research practices.

The extent to which postexperimental debriefing can erase the harmful psychological effects of certain manipulations remains an open question. Walster *et al.* (1967) suggest that debriefing has definite limitations.[6] They provide the following summary of their findings:

> it is disturbing that . . . even after a very lengthy and thorough debriefing (probably atypical in thoroughness) subjects still behaved to some extent as though the debriefing had not taken place. Subjects behaved in this manner even though they had voiced . . . their understanding that the manipulation was false, their understanding of the true purpose of the experiment, and even though . . . the experimenter had been satisfied that they did indeed understand the nature of the deception.
>
> Even more disturbing is the evidence that the after effects of debriefing might be complex, unpredictable, and may depend in part on the personality traits of the subjects. (p. 380)

Moreover, common sense dictates that debriefing can have little impact on the negative psychological consequences of certain kinds of manipulations. Consider the Milgram studies, where subjects were led to believe they were administering dangerous shocks to another subject suffering from a heart condition. Assuming they really believed that they had engaged in such destructive behaviors, being told after-the-fact that no actual shocks had been administered would do little to reduce their guilt and anxiety, for they would still have to live with the knowledge of their willingness to shock the subject.[7]

We would argue that the moral implications of each deception and manipulation must be weighed carefully by the inquirer. Probably simple misrepresentation of a study's purpose is the most ethically benign form of deceit. Even here, however, alternatives to deception should be sought. As Miller has asserted elsewhere:

What is ethically worrisome is the possibility that communication researchers will make no effort to find alternatives to deception, that they will come to accept deception as an intrinsic feature of laboratory research methodology. Such an unqualified endorsement of deceit has profound ethical implications for the relationship between researcher and subject. Not only is the element of trust removed from the interaction, but in addition, the subject is likely to perceive the researcher in particular, and communication research in general, as ethically repugnant. (1970, p. 100)

Beyond simple misrepresentation of the purpose of a study, other forms of research deception should be used sparingly. Seldom, if ever, should the rewards for participating in a study be misrepresented; if researchers cannot afford to give subjects money or other material commodities, they should avoid the promise of such rewards in their manipulations. Furthermore, the practice of leading subjects to believe they are confederates of the experimenter should be discouraged; researchers should be able to devise ways of manipulating variables without resort to such trickery. In fact, it is easy to agree with Ring (1967), who argues that much behavioral research suffers from an exhibitionistic flavor with researchers striving to outdo each other in developing "contrived, flamboyant, and mirth-producing experiments" (p. 117).

Aside from deceptive practices and potentially harmful manipulations, ethical issues sometimes arise concerning invasion of privacy. Much communication inquiry, as well as other behavioral science research, relies on interviews, questionnaires, and other methods of eliciting verbal responses from subjects. Issues concerning invasion of privacy can arise from either the means used to obtain information from people or from the content of the particular questions they are asked.

Consider a common interrogative technique, the telephone interview. On the surface, a phone call does not seem to pose much of a moral problem. Still, one can legitimately ask if people should not be spared the inconvenience (and in some cases, the indignities) of unwanted callers. In the case of obscene calls, of course, this question is clearly answered by the law; such calls are illegal and apprehended offenders can be criminally prosecuted. Fortunately (at least to our knowledge) legitimate communication scientists do not occupy their phone time with such activities. But suppose you have just sat down to relax after a hard day with the books and the telephone rings. Reluctantly you vacate your chair to answer, only to discover that it is an interviewer seeking your reactions to President Ford's latest speech. Since you are in no mood to be bothered by a string of questions, you abruptly terminate the conversation and return to your chair, in a much more disgruntled frame of mind than you were before the phone rang.

Do such instances constitute an invasion of privacy? This question is not simply answered. Since we are in sympathy with the motives and objectives of most communication scientists, we would not advocate cutting them off from valuable sources of data. Still, it does seem to us that a great deal of interviewing and questionnaire distribution is carried out in a thoughtless manner. It becomes easy for inquirers to assume that respondents should be available at their beck-and-call, that they should eagerly drop whatever they are doing to toil laboriously over yet another interview or questionnaire. To minimize such intrusions, researchers should place their calls at times which are not maximally inconvenient for the respondents; meal time and late evening calls should be assiduously avoided. Questionnaires should generally be brief and concise. Most important, the inquirer should be firmly convinced that the potential knowledge returns are sufficient to warrant the time and energy demands placed on subjects. Given the easy availability of the telephone and the mimeograph machine, it is certainly tempting to deluge individuals with calls and questionnaires about a host of relatively trivial questions.

There is another way in which the means used to obtain information may constitute a subtle invasion of subjects' privacy. Most communication scientists are college professors, and the vast majority of the data they gather are provided by college students, oftentimes students who are in the classes of the scientist conducting the study. Although there is usually a facade of voluntary participation associated with these ventures, there are obviously strong pressures on students to conform with requests for research participation. Naturally, they wish to be regarded positively by their professors, particularly when the latter have such means-control devices as grades at their disposal. Then, too, some form of "extra credit" is usually granted for partaking in research projects. Small wonder communication scientists often refer jokingly to their classroom subjects as "captive audiences."

In short, we are suggesting that there is sometimes an element of coercion present when student subjects are used in studies. Almost by definition, coercion implies invasion of privacy; if subjects do not feel free to decline, their right to privacy has been violated. Again, the dilemma posed by this state of affairs is not easily resolved. Lest we alarm our scientific colleagues, we are not advocating a total moratorium on the use of student subjects. The answer seems to lie largely in sensitizing scientific inquirers to the problem, in developing their capabilities to structure research environments which minimize coercive aspects of participation. To some extent, this problem is closely linked to the deception issue; if subjects honestly understand *what* is expected of them and *why* it is expected, they are in a better position to decide if they wish to participate. It is as important for communication scientists to develop sensitivity in subject recruitment as it is for them to master operational definition or the use of statistical analysis.

Upon turning to the topic of question content, it is perhaps easier to see how a subject's privacy can be invaded. Recently we became acquainted with a study which sought to determine the kinds of things individuals are embarrassed to talk about. Although we have no reason to question the motives of the researchers, several of the questions would give us cause for thought if directed at us. Consider the following examples:

1. What parts of your body do you consider to be most unattractive? Are you embarrassed to talk with others about your body?
2. What do you consider to be the worst thing you have ever done? Are you embarrassed to talk with others about it?
3. Did you ever feel ashamed of your parents or your family? Are you embarrassed to talk with others about these feelings?

Of course, these kinds of questions are the exception, rather than the rule, in scientific communication inquiry. Still, a number of personality inventories and other measuring instruments commonly used in communication research contain similar types of personally sensitive items.[8] Even though responses to such items are usually treated confidentially, it can be strongly argued that they violate the respondent's privacy; in fact, within the broader confines of the social scientific community, considerable concern has been voiced about the ethics of certain assessment instruments. Certainly such questions should not be asked of captive respondents; to do so only compounds the moral felony. And even when participation is voluntary, the inquirer should strive to develop items which do not infringe blatantly on the personal lives and private thoughts of respondents.

No doubt you have noticed a tentativeness in our treatment of these issues which was largely absent in earlier chapters. This cautious demeanor stems from the questions we are addressing; like most others, we do not pretend to have definitive answers to the ethical dilemmas facing scientific communication inquirers as they evaluate alternative research strategies. If asked how to calculate a mean, we could respond assertively and confidently; if asked whether a particular instance of deception is morally justifiable, we could only weigh the circumstances and reply accordingly. What does concern us is awareness heightening, for we believe students of communication inquiry should be conscious of the many ethical ramifications of their research decisions. Perhaps the words of Kelman (1968) best summarize our feelings about this problem:

> In a very real sense, we have brought this situation [the imposition of external controls on the conduct of research] upon ourselves, by our failure to give attention *within* the profession to the problems of informed consent, invasion of privacy, and the human treatment of our research subjects. We have tended to act as if there were no other values to consider but those of carrying out good research (and sometimes not even that, but merely the values of carrying out publishable research). The rights and welfare of our subjects were often forgotten and treated in cavalier fashion. . . . I do not feel that social and psychological research has caused much damage to individuals, but I feel that we have been remiss in our failure to concern ourselves with the possibilities of such damage and, moreover, with the kinds of broader social values that our treatment of human subjects is fostering. (p. 205)

VALUE JUDGMENTS IN THE AREA OF SOCIAL POLICY

Communication science is social science, and by its very name, social science implies a concern with questions that have an impact on the collective and individual welfare of our society's citizens. Stated differently, the knowledge accumulated by social scientists, including the communication scientist, can be used by others to enhance or degrade the human condition. If knowledge is indeed power, the ability to explain and predict the outcomes of communication transactions confers enormous power on the possessors of that knowledge.

Since the preceding statements may sound like high-flown abstractions, consider an area such as persuasion where the implications for social power and social policy are transparently clear. Effective persuasion relies on limiting and focusing people's choice behaviors; the persuader seeks to induce others to choose a particular alternative from their available options. To use a mundane example, a network deodorant commercial is not concerned with enhancing your social attractiveness, nor, for that matter, persuading you to purchase just any deodorant; it aims at limiting your perceived choices so that you will buy a particular brand.

Once one accepts the twin premises that: (1) effective persuasion increases an individual's or a group's ability to exercise social control, and (2) the findings of communication inquiry have the potential to heighten persuasive effectiveness, the ethical questions confronting the persuasion researcher are patently obvious. Consider but one of these questions. Like most other enterprises, research costs money. Those best equipped to provide the needed financial support are the established institutions of our society, e.g., government or large private industry. Not surprisingly, the concerns of these institutions are largely source-oriented; they are interested in ways of enhancing their own persuasive effectiveness. By contrast, less financially fortunate groups and individuals within the society do not have the benefit of a large research arm to add to their informative storehouses of persuasive strategies. Thus, some writers (e.g., Simons, 1972) have leveled the charge that persuasion research serves to perpetuate the favored position of the "haves" within our society and to ensure that the "have-nots" will remain in a subordinate position.

We have deliberately oversimplified and overstated the preceding example to dramatize our point. Certainly 1984 has not yet arrived; while research has made contributions to people's understanding of the variables influencing persuasive effectiveness, the advice available falls far short of a foolproof plan for success. Moreover, a great deal of the information is within the public domain; nothing prevents almost any group or individual from reading research findings and heeding the advice found therein. Finally, as Kelman stresses, there are numerous positive effects that can result from persuasion research:

> First, one can argue that extending our general knowledge about processes of attitude change and increasing our understanding of the nature of influence are in themselves liberating forces whose value outweighs the possibility that this knowledge will be used for undesirable ends. Second, such research may not only increase the knowledge of the potential manipulator, but also help in finding ways to counteract manipulative forces, by providing the information needed for effective resistance to manipulation, or by developing knowledge about forms of influence that enhance freedom of choice. Third, one might argue that information about attitude change, despite its potential for manipulative uses, is important for the achievement of certain socially desirable goals, such as racial integration or international understanding. (1968, p. 24)

Miller and Burgoon (1973) reinforce Kelman's second point, asserting *"If knowledge can be used to exert control, it can also be used to resist control"* (p. 106, italics theirs).

All of the preceding considerations allude to arguments that can be offered to refute the charge that persuasion research serves the interests of the socially powerful elements of our society. Still, communication scientists must constantly evaluate their ethical responsibilities concerning the uses to which their findings are put. In addition, they must assess their own role as potential shapers of social policy and define the ethical boundaries of their participation in policymaking.

Perhaps a personal example will best illustrate the issues raised for communication scientists when they participate in policy-oriented research. As indicated in Case 1 of Chapter 4, both of us have been involved in an ongoing program of research designed to determine some of the effects of using videotape in courtroom trial situations. This research has been funded by the Research Applied to National Needs Program (RANN) of the National Science Foundation, a program that encourages the development of projects designed to provide information about pressing social and economic problems.[9]

Fortunately, RANN has not demonstrated a high level of ego-involvement in the research outcomes; in plain English, members of RANN do not seem to have strong preferences about the way the research *should* come out. Sometimes, of course, researchers are not this lucky; it quickly becomes apparent that the funding agency would prefer certain outcomes. To say that this may influence the conduct and interpretation of research in no way sullies the reputation of social scientists nor does it imply that they would be deliberately dishonest to please their clients. As we have tried to stress throughout this book, the conduct of inquiry is a complex logical and psychological process. When developing measures of variables and interpreting research findings (to mention but two aspects of the process of inquiry) judgments must be made. Suppose, for example, we wished to determine people's attitudes about the relative merits of live and videotaped trials. To do so, we ask the following question: If you were a litigant in a trial, would you prefer to have the case tried live or on videotape? Assume our sample provided the following observations:

> Favor Live Trial-15%
> Undecided-70%
> Favor Videotaped Trial-15%

Now consider three possible interpretations of this finding:

VERSION 1.   Results indicate that there is relatively little opposition to the use of videotaped material in courtroom trials. Of those surveyed, only 15% indicated that they would prefer a live trial to one conducted via videotape. By contrast, 15% stated that they would prefer a videotaped trial and 70% indicated that it would make little difference to them.

VERSION 2.   Results indicate that people are not very receptive to the use of videotaped material in courtroom trials. Of those surveyed, only 15% indicated that they would prefer a videotaped trial to a live one. By contrast, 15% expressed preference for a live trial and 70% indicated that they were still undecided about the matter.

VERSION 3. Results indicate that people are generally uncertain about the relative advantages of live and videotaped trials. Whereas only 30% expressed a preference for one medium or the other (15% favoring live and 15% videotaped), 70% indicated that.they were undecided as to which one they would prefer.

Perhaps a relatively impartial observer would contend that Version 3 best captures the import of the data. Still, neither Versions 1 nor 2 are totally indefensible; both report the percentages accurately and then interpret their meaning differently. If a communication scientist were conducting research funded by an advocate of the use of videotape, he or she might end up with an interpretation close to that found in Version 1; conversely, if the study were funded by an opponent of videotaped courtroom trials, Version 2 might express his or her interpretation. The different interpretations underscore the judgmental nature of the process, and these judgments can be subtly influenced by a variety of social and personal factors. Again, there is no simple answer to the problem; to a large extent, the scientist's evaluative sensitivity determines his or her susceptibility to influence.

Other ethical pitfalls can trap the communication scientist engaged in policy-oriented research. In our own research on videotaped courtroom trials, we are constantly asked for our opinions about this possible courtroom innovation. When responding, we are probably perceived as communication scientists *who are making scientific judgments about the merits of using videotape in the courts.* As long as we speak within the confines of our data and findings no problems are posed. But like other human beings, our opinions are a product of multiple influences. No doubt we had an opinion about the use of videotape in the legal system before we began our research. Since that time, we have talked with many persuasive individuals who have definite attitudes about the pluses and minuses of videotape. Thus, though we may be perceived as communication scientists, much of what we say may conceivably result from influences other than our research findings. Here the ethical problem is clear-cut: if people are persuaded by what they believe to be our scientific judgments, when in fact those judgments mirror other influences, we have in a sense deceived them, even though the deceit may have been unintentional.

A thorough analysis of the role of the communication scientist in shaping social policy, and of the ethical issues raised by such participation, far transcends the purpose of this book—and for that matter, our own philosophical expertise. We do believe it important that communication scientists understand the impossibility of the scientist operating in a moral vacuum. As long as science (rightly or wrongly) is accorded high esteem by most segments of our society, its practitioners will have an impact on social policy. Inherent in this interplay between scientific and social forces are a myriad of ethical questions, and these questions cannot be ignored by scientific inquirers. Rather, they must accept the personal responsibility for the knowledge they generate and for its use by various sectors of our society.

THE EXTRINSIC NATURE OF EVALUATION IN FACTUAL INQUIRY

In the area of factual inquiry, the process of evaluation is *extrinsic* rather than *intrinsic* to the actual questions pursued by the inquirer. Stated differently, evaluation affects the research decisions made by the inquirer, but it is not an inherent dimension of the questions themselves. This point is important, for it illustrates why one may grant that extrinsic matters of evaluation can and do intrude on the scientific inquirer while at the same time arguing that the activity of scientific question-answering is itself value free. Similarly, to say that scientific communication inquiry is value free does not imply that the individual inquirer is an automaton with no ethical or aesthetic commitments. As we pointed out in Chapter 1, *when dealing with factual questions what a person says and his or her reasons for saying it constitute separate issues.* The conclusions of a scientific study are evaluated in terms of the *reasons* for reaching them, not in terms of their ideological implications or the ideological preferences of the inquirer. To be sure, as we demonstrated in the previous section of this chapter, subtle ideological pressures may influence data interpretation, *but as long as the data and procedures are adequately and accurately reported,* the scientific soundness of the conclusions can be assessed regardless of the value system of the inquirer.

Of course, we would not argue that the ideal of segregating value questions from the process of scientific inquiry—i.e., of maintaining a strictly extrinsic posture—is always achieved. Scientists are, after all, human beings, and at times their ideological commitments or personal interests may intrude directly upon their inquiry. Occasionally it even comes to light that researchers have deliberately falsified data to arrive at findings congruent with their own value system. But it is also encouraging to note that it is the objective, value-free process of scientific inquiry which permits discovery of such shady conduct. Given a large enough cadre of concerned, competent practitioners, science is, indeed, self-correcting.[10]

CASE 2.   *The democratic group leader: Are the value judgments extrinsic?*

One of the most brilliant, creative founders of small group research was a social psychologist named Kurt Lewin. Of Jewish faith and European birth, Lewin endured the horrors of prejudice and oppression during the early years of Hitler's rise to power in Germany. As a result of these experiences, Lewin left no doubt about his personal aversion for autocratic leaders and his strong commitment to a democratic leadership climate.

In 1939 and 1940, Lewin, along with his colleagues Ronald Lippitt and Ralph White, conducted a classic research dealing with the effects of authoritarian, democratic, and laissez-faire leadership on group productivity, morale, and aggressive tendencies (Lewin, Lippitt and White, 1939). In general, the findings were interpreted as supporting the superiority of democratic leadership for creating a positive, effective group climate.

"As might be expected from the fact that this research was both original and concerned with emotionally loaded matters of political ideology, it was immediately subjected to criticism, both justified and unjustified" (Cartwright and Zander, 1960, p. 28). Of particular concern is the extent to which the observed differences in behaviors of members of the three groups warrant the conclusions drawn by Lewin and his associates. Records of the meetings exist on grainy, black-and-white movie films, and a host of social psychology students at the University of Iowa have viewed them. Numerous viewers have indicated that they have difficulty observing some of the sharp differences in behavior and behavioral outcomes noted by Lewin, Lippitt, and White. On the other hand, some observers swear that the differences are apparent to them. Consequently, a problem of reliability arises: observers disagree on what they are observing, or perhaps more precisely, on how to categorize and interpret the observations.

We have deliberately selected research that clouds the issue of extrinsicality of value judgments in scientific inquiry. Note, however, that we have emphasized the researchers' reasons for drawing certain conclusions, not their ideological predilections. The fact that all three may have been strongly committed to the ethical superiority of democratic leadership is not of paramount importance; in fact, most people in this society, ourselves included, share this value. What needs to be stressed is that no matter how much communication scientists believe that something is true, their procedures for verifying their beliefs should be public and reliable so as to permit others to assess them and to agree with them—to say it once again, values should be extrinsic to scientific inquiry, not intrinsic. Further information on the studies discussed in this case is available in the following references:

Cartwright, D., and A. Zander (1960). *Group Dynamics.* 2d ed. Evanston, Ill.: Row, Peterson.

Lewin, K., R. Lippitt, and R.K. White (1939). Patterns of Aggressive Behavior in Experimentally Created "Social Climates." *Journal of Social Psychology* **10:** 271–299.

Lippitt, R., and R.K. White (1958). An Experimental Study of Leadership and Group Life. In E.E. Maccoby, T.M. Newcomb, and E.L. Hartley (eds.), *Readings in Social Psychology.* 3rd ed., pp. 496–511. New York: Holt.

White, R.K., and R. Lippitt (1960). *Autocracy and Democracy: An Experimental Inquiry.* New York: Harper & Row.

EVALUATION IN DEALING WITH QUESTIONS OF VALUE

Ethical issues have a timeless relevance to communication transactions. From a casual, brief encounter between two friends or acquaintances to a startling, stunning national political or social crisis, "Virtually every act of speech [communication] . . . involves an ethical obligation" (Nilsen, 1966, p. 12).

We begin our discussion of evaluation in value inquiry by recourse to an admittedly rare event: the resignation of former President Richard Nixon. Certainly the events culminating in this action forcefully underscore the importance of numerous moral issues to public communication transactions: issues bearing on access to information, invasion of privacy, standards for truthful communication, and the role of the mass media in a democratic society—to mention but a few. Consequently, we believe that the Watergate episode provides a useful backdrop for considering some important aspects of ethical inquiry in communication.

The Complexity of Ethical Questions

Like almost everyone, Kate and Fred have been engrossed in the political drama they have witnessed. Let us listen in on one of their conversations:

KATE: "Well, if there's anything we can learn from all these events, it's that lying doesn't pay. If the President would have made a clean breast of his involvement in the coverup from the start, he might be better off today."

FRED: "Maybe it isn't that simple. After all, your argument implies that whenever someone is guilty of criminal charges he should immediately confess and plead guilty. Perhaps in the best of all possible worlds that's true. But I think we know that there are many guilty people who plead innocent and who suppress and conceal information that would damage them. I'm sure no lawyer is naive enough to believe that only innocent men plead not guilty. Why shouldn't a President be allowed the same options as any other citizen?"

KATE: "For one thing, the President isn't 'any other citizen.' Not only does he take an oath to uphold the Constitution, but in addition, we have a right to expect a standard of conduct from our leaders that exceeds the behavior of 'any other citizen.' If deceit and lying are the standard that leaders set for the country, it's not surprising that we have so many dire social problems."

FRED: "O.K., why do we have the Fifth Amendment? Had the President divulged his complicity in the coverup he would have been testifying against himself. Now as to our leaders being subject to a different standard of conduct, I think you're raising a pretty complex issue. If we look around we see that a lot of the actions for which the President is now being criticized seem to be condoned in most sections of our society. People lie and cheat every day; people take marriage oaths and violate them indiscriminately; political campaigns are Madison Avenue productions that emphasize image rather than substance and truth. Why wouldn't we expect our leaders to mirror their environments the same as everyone else?"

KATE: "Your Fifth Amendment point doesn't make any sense at all. First of all, no actual legal proceedings were ever involved. Moreover, if I buy your analogy, it still doesn't hold. The Fifth Amendment provides for the right of silence by the defendant, but in this case, the defendant wasn't silent, he perjured himself with his testimony. Now I want to get back to your point about our leaders reflecting the values of the society, which I'll call 'the great leveling argument.' I can't buy . . . ."

We take leave of Kate's and Fred's conversation with the knowledge that most persons have been involved in similar arguments about moral aspects of such pressing questions as the Watergate episode. Furthermore, everyone has probably experienced similar frustrations when attempting to nail down an ethical issue and arrive at a conclusion concerning it. Note that Kate and Fred disagree on the moral implications of certain communicative behaviors of the former President. More specifically, they are at odds on the justification for certain untruthful statements: Fred seems to believe that these falsehoods are defensible while Kate does not. But in attempting to support their positions, they introduce numerous factual, value, and definitional questions, each of which contains the seeds for disagreement and each of which bears upon (but does not resolve) the initial bone of contention. A brief analysis of the conversation's flow should illustrate this state of affairs more specifically:

KATE:　Introduced the universal normative generalization that lying is unethical. (Note that our analysis involves an inference about Kate's intent, since the wording of the statement, "lying doesn't pay" can be interpreted factually if it is intended to mean only that whenever people lie they will be discovered and undesirable consequences will befall them.)

FRED:　Accepted the value intent of Kate's statement and specified a set of conditions which he perceived as germane to this situation and which he felt provided justification for falsehood. (In line with our previous comment regarding the ambiguity of Kate's initial statement, Fred might have proceeded more cautiously and asked Kate for clarification of her assertion.)

KATE:　Denied the applicability of Fred's justifying conditions, and in the course of her denial offered the claim that a leader's standards of conduct should be superior to those of a rank-and-file citizen. (This latter value judgment is, of course, an old saw that is constantly disputed when discussing the behavior of clergy, teachers, and other groups within our society.)

FRED:　Introduced additional claims intended to support his original justification of lying and took issue with Kate's contention that a leader's conduct should transcend the conduct of others in the environment. (Here the grounds for dispute become even more fuzzy and complex. Fred seems to be arguing from the factual assumption that it would be impossible for an individual to transcend his or her environmental conditioning, whereas Kate is contending that leaders *ought* to rise above this common ethical denominator.)

KATE:　Attacked the validity of Fred's additional claims: first, by questioning his assumption that the events can be likened to a legal proceeding (a potential question of definition); second, by granting his assumption and then pointing out inaccuracies in his assessment of it. (Rhetorically, this is perhaps the most persuasive argument in the dialogue since it points up two potential shortcomings in Fred's argument.)

Fred's and Kate's hypothetical conversation underlines the complexity of most ethical questions. This complexity, in turn, stems from the impossibility of providing definitive answers to value questions, or, stated more precisely, the inability to verify a value statement as true or false. If Kate and Fred disagreed only on whether one of the major participants in the Watergate drama *did* or *did not* say or do something, they could probably agree on a set of procedures that would resolve the issue. But since they are at odds on the moral implications of particular actions, no such resolution is likely to occur.

This fact suggests a crucial consideration regarding ethical questions: *there exists no universally accepted set of procedures for resolving moral disputes.* Such circumstances are not found in scientific inquiry; while scientists may differ about theoretical matters or about the interpretation of findings, they share a common commitment to a set of procedures for verifying factual knowledge claims. This set of procedures, sometimes labeled *scientific method,* is itself rooted in empiricism. Scientific knowledge claims rely on sense data, or observation, for their validity. To "know" something scientifically is to agree publicly that certain events have been observed; scientific laws are descriptive, as we pointed out in Chapter 1.

It is not nearly so clear what it means when one says he or she "knows" something is right or wrong, just or unjust, or good or bad. In fact, we have taken the position that it is impossible to know the truth or falsity of value judgments. Still, everyone makes such assertions, the present authors not excluded. If Nicholson wrote all six chapters of this book and Miller claimed first authorship, Nicholson would "know" that Miller had behaved unjustly. By the same token, Miller would probably "know" that he had acted justly. And both would probably argue the merits of their conflicting "knowledge" claims to their last breath.

Suppose Nicholson based his claim on the ethical generalization: you should always treat others fairly. Note that this generalization is *prescriptive,* not descriptive; it states a rule about the way people *ought* to behave rather than describing a regularity in the way they *do* behave. Miller might attempt to refute Nicholson's claim in one or more of several ways:

1. *By denying the validity of the ethical generalization.* Such an argument could, for example, contend that people do not have the responsibility of treating others fairly, that each person's primary concern should be with his or her own self-interest. Thus, if Nicholson was short-changed in his bookwriting dealings with Miller, the fault lies with his own carelessness or naivete. Although many find

this kind of value system repugnant, it does provide a basis for numerous commercial communication transactions. Witness the classic injunction *caveat emptor*—let the buyer beware.

2. *By arguing that Nicholson was treated fairly in a factual sense.* This strategy would be particularly appropriate if Miller believed clear understanding had been reached concerning the division of labor and order of authorship. It could then be asserted that since both parties entered freely into an agreed-upon relationship, and since the conditions of the agreement were honored, neither party was treated unfairly.

3. *By arguing that Nicholson was treated fairly in a definitional sense.* This approach might be effective if no specific prior agreements were negotiated. Such an argument would contend that in light of the differences in professional status and prior publications brought to the situation by the two parties, Nicholson was treated fairly—i.e., he did the lion's share of the work in return for a second authorship that would not even have been possible without the status of his collaborator.[11]

Our extended personal example shows that much of the complexity of ethical questions stems from the lack of any standardized procedures for dealing with them. Within the broad confines of reasoned argument, ethical inquiry can be attacked from a variety of perspectives. Usually, however, inquirers will choose a set of general ethical premises, or a normative ethical generalization from which to launch their argument. We will next consider two of the most common approaches to ethical evaluation.

Utilitarian Approaches to Ethical Evaluation

One principle often used to evaluate a particular course of action—in this case, a communication transaction—is to assess its effects on others. If the effects are beneficial, the action is deemed ethical; if the effects are harmful, it is judged unethical. The rub, however, often comes when trying to reach this overall assessment. To return to our Watergate example, the members of the Nixon Administration and certain elements of the press were diametrically opposed in their assessments of the consequences of certain communication policies and behaviors of the Administration.

We will label such an effects, or consequences, orientation toward ethics as a *utilitarian approach*. Originally, of course, *utilitarianism* represented an attempt to formulate principles for a collective social ethic, as witnessed by the emphasis on the phrase, "the greatest good for the greatest number." We will take some liberties with this initial preoccupation of the Benthamites and use the phrase "utilitarian approach" to refer to any act of ethical inquiry which places primary moral emphasis on the effects that actions have upon others. Thus, both the communicative transactions of the mass media and the message exchanges of two persons can be evaluated from a utilitarian perspective.

As we have already implied, a utilitarian approach stresses the consequences of actions, rather than the actions themselves. This is not to say that certain communication behaviors do not have a greater potential for harmful effects than others. For instance, the consequences of lying and deceit are usually harmful; under most circumstances, communicators can best serve the interests of their fellow men by being truthful. Still, there is recognition that a limited category of messages can be labeled "white lies." White lies are intended to spare others' feelings and/or to avoid useless quarrels; the harmful effects of telling a gracious host that an unpalatable meal *was* unpalatable justify an untruthful, "That was a wonderful dinner!"

We see two major problems with utilitarian approaches to communicative evaluation. The first has already been mentioned: *it is often difficult, if not impossible, to weigh the beneficial and harmful consequences of a communication transaction.* Even the simplest events have multiple consequences, both *immediate* and *long-range*. To continue with our dinner example, suppose that in an unguarded moment the white liar remarks to an acquaintance about the poor quality of the meal. Eventually this negative assessment reaches the ear of the host.[12] Might not the subsequent harmful effects be more pronounced than an honest judgment at the time the meal was consumed—e.g., "I guess I can't trust him to tell me the truth," or "Does she value our friendship so little that she finds it impossible to be frank?"

A second problem lies in determining *how much relative concern should be directed at anticipated as opposed to actual effects.* Stated differently, people can never be certain how others will re-

spond to their messages; they can only arrive at probability esti-
mates of the effects of their communicative behaviors. For one
thing, communicators often are uncertain about other people; they
do not know them well enough to predict all the emotional nuances
that may be stimulated by their messages. For another, it is impossible to anticipate all of the events that may occur after having communicated with someone. Imagine, for instance, that a person *supposedly* consoles a recently divorced friend and, 15 minutes after the
conversation, the friend goes berserk, obtains a pistol, and kills
several people. Although the example is far-fetched, it underscores
the inquirer's evaluative dilemma: should the anticipated consequences of the communication—*perhaps* instilling a feeling of emotional support and friendship—or the *possible* actual consequences—the taking of other human lives—constitute the primary
grounds for moral assessment?

Our emphasis of the terms "perhaps" and "possible" underscores the complexity of the problem. Obviously, if people were
certain that the motives of the consoler were altruistic, they would
not accuse the consoler of unethical actions, though they might conclude that the actions had been unwise. But how can anyone ever be
certain of another's motives? Perhaps the consoler actually hated
this supposed friend and believed that reminding the individual of his
or her marital difficulties would trigger an emotional explosion. In a
similar vein, how can others ever be *sure* that the communicative
event in question had anything to do with subsequent events.
Perhaps the shooting rampage would have occurred even if the conversation had not taken place. Consequently, to establish ethical
obligation for the effects of a communication transaction, the inquirer must usually present reasoned arguments in support of at
least three contentions: (1) the communicator's motives were
malevolent, or at least potentially malevolent; i.e., the communicator anticipated, or could have been expected to anticipate,
that harmful consequences would result from his or her messages;
(2) the messages were themselves likely determinants of the harmful
consequences; i.e., the events would probably not have occurred in
the absence of the communication; and (3) taken as a whole, the
consequences were, in fact, predominantly harmful; i.e., the negative effects on others outweigh the positive. Obviously, the inquirer

faces a formidable argumentative task, one embracing numerous thorny factual, value, and definitional questions.

Despite the difficulties associated with utilitarian approaches to ethical evaluations, this perspective has much to recommend it. After all, ethics is concerned with improving the quality of human existence, and the human condition is the essence of this task. Moreover, the quality of a person's communicative exchanges has a powerful impact on his or her social, economic, and psychological well-being. Small wonder, then, that many communication inquirers who seek to evaluate the moral quality of a communication transaction gravitate toward utilitarian assessment.

Rule-Governed Approaches to Ethical Evaluation

By rule-governed approaches to ethical evaluation we mean those ethical generalizations or theories that are usually labeled *formalistic. Such approaches argue that the morality of an action should be judged not on its effects but on its conformity to an ethical rule or principle.* Lest our liberty with the term "rule-governed" causes confusion, we should stress that utilitarian approaches to ethical evaluation are themselves based on an ethical principle, specifically, that an act should be judged by its effects or consequences. The rule-governed approaches discussed in this section stress *act* rather than *effect.* Thus, the moral injunction, "You should not lie," implies, in a formalistic sense, that any falsehood is wrong, *regardless of its effects,* because it violates an ethical rule.

There is another way that rule-governed approaches and utilitarian approaches are closely related. As Nilsen points out, "It seems probable that all ethical principles grew out of a recognition of the results of various forms of behavior" (p. 9). For instance, the Golden Rule rests on the assumption that if people treat others as they themselves would like to be treated, maximum positive effects will accrue for all parties.[13] Similarly, the moral injunction that people should not be treated as objects stems from the belief that such treatment produces harmful consequences for mankind. It seems fair to suggest, then, that the difference between the two approaches lies largely in the ethical flexibility manifested toward certain actions *qua* actions: *whereas the utilitarian would argue that particular communicative transactions may or may not be wrong depending upon their effects, the rule-governed theorist would contend these transactions are always wrong because they violate an ethical principle.*

At first glance, rule-governed approaches seem rigid and dogmatic, perhaps suggesting that they would be difficult, if not impossible, to defend. There are, however, several ways of defending these approaches to ethical evaluation. We will briefly consider two lines of argument: *the higher-moral-order* argument and the *fewer-harmful-cumulative-effects* argument.

If someone starts with the premise that human communication transactions should be governed by a set of ethical principles, the value of stipulating these principles as unambiguously and straightforwardly as possible seems apparent. Any time a principle is qualified by the term "unless" (as must be done when a utilitarian approach is followed) ambiguity is introduced and the opportunity for rationalization is created. A classic example which has provoked considerable controversy in recent years is the commandment, "Thou shalt not kill." From a rule-governed perspective, this commandment asserts that the act of taking another's life is wrong.[14] But a utilitarian approach introduces considerable uncertainty and concomitant margin for human interpretation. Is it permissible to take lives in defense of one's country? Is capital punishment (the taking of a life by the state as a deterrent to, or a punishment of, wrongdoing) morally justifiable? Is it morally defensible to take another's life in defense of one's own? Should a man be labeled a "criminal" if he kills for money to feed an impoverished family but a "coward" if he refuses to bear arms against the people of another country? The issues are legion, with most of them arising from efforts to distinguish morally among various motives for, and effects of, killing.

Thus, to avoid rationalization and endless ethical nitpicking, one could argue that the injunction, "Thou shalt not kill," reflects a higher moral order applicable to all of a person's transactions with other people. Although adherence to this rule, and others like it, may sometimes appear to result in harmful consequences for the rule-follower and/or other persons associated with the rule-follower, it is in the interest of the higher moral order for the principle to be obeyed.

The higher-moral-order argument can be joined with the fewer-harmful-cumulative-effects argument to defend rule-governed approaches to ethical evaluation. This latter argument answers the utilitarian theorist's emphasis on effects by contending that, in the long run, strict conformity with ethical principles results in fewer harmful cumulative effects. For example, if a communicator totally abstains from lying, occasional harmful consequences may result, but the cumulative effects will be predominantly positive.[15] Conversely, attempts to assess the ethical outcomes of lying are fraught with difficulties: the needs of the potential prevaricator may cause him or her to gauge the situation inaccurately (to rationalize the lie); the available information may be insufficient for a reasoned judgment of probable effects; subsequent events may invalidate the original assessment of the consequences, etc. As a result, the uncertainty and subsequent error associated with utilitarian approaches culminate in numerous harmful human effects, negative consequences that could be curtailed by following ethical rules scrupulously.

Despite the fact that rule-governed approaches to ethical evaluation can be reasonably defended, proponents of this general position face several formidable problems. The first lies in establishing the ethical superiority of particular rules, or principles. After all, there is a proliferation of moral rules, and sometimes they offer conflicting advice. Whether one should respond to a damaging falsehood or a cutting personal remark by turning the other cheek or by extracting a pound of flesh from the offender is itself a controversial issue. Consequently, the first step in the evaluative process centers on reasoned justification of the rule, or rules, which the inquirer has chosen to use when judging communicative transactions.

Moreover, the rule-governed approach often encounters a difficulty similar to one mentioned when discussing utilitarian approaches: *determination of whether or not a specific act violates an ethical rule hinges on assessment of the actor's motives.* Granted, for some rules motives are not an obstacle; if an inquirer can produce convincing evidence of falsehood, the rule against lying has been violated and the reasons for its violation are irrelevant. Some rules, however, do not always permit such unambiguous behavioral translation. Consider, for instance, a principle mentioned several times earlier: never treat other people as objects. Certainly, this rule seems to provide a useful ethical yardstick for evaluating many communication transactions. Yet by journeying again into the world of Kate and Fred, the difficulties encountered in its application can be illustrated:

FRED: "Boy did you hear that conversation behind us at the game? The old 'We've got to get to know each other as people' line. That guy was really trying to manipulate the girl and use her to his advantage with the stuff he was feeding her."

KATE: "I didn't have that feeling at all. In fact, I thought it was nice that he was trying to relate to her as a person. People don't really try to get close to each other much anymore. They're too threatened, insecure, or something."

FRED: "Don't tell me he took you in, too. Maybe the guy is more persuasive than I thought. He must be pretty effective at using others with that 'touchy-feely' routine."

KATE: "Your kind of cynicism explains why very few people can relate. I don't think the guy was trying to manipulate her. Why . . ."

The point of Kate's and Fred's conversation should be apparent. If Fred is correct in his assessment of the motives of his male neighbor at the game, the latter was behaving unethically; he was treating the girl as an object and trying to manipulate her with an interpersonal line. Conversely, if Kate's perceptions are valid, the male neighbor was acting ethically; he was trying to relate to his female companion as a person. It is frequently difficult to ascertain just *what* motives trigger an act, and, in the absence of convincing evidence, it is impossible to judge whether an ethical rule has been violated.

We end this section by emphasizing that any approach to ethical evaluation poses thorny problems for the inquirer. At best, the product of such inquiry is a convincing sample of reasoned discourse; as we have stressed repeatedly, the truth or falsity of moral judgments cannot be determined. But because of the centrality of ethical questions to every communication transaction, it is essential that inquirers continue to ponder them and to provide answers to them—no matter how tentative the answers themselves may be.

CASE 3. *Are the mass media socially responsible? A utilitarian analysis*

Nowhere is the utilitarian approach to value questions more apparent than in the continuing research efforts aimed at determining the behavioral impact of various types of mass media content. In particular, millions of dollars have been spent on studies investigating the effects of violent media content and probing the behavioral influence of erotic materials or pornography (Report of the Commission on Obscenity and Pornography, 1970; Report of the Surgeon General's Scientific Advisory Committee on Television and Social Behavior, 1972).

To be sure, most of the research itself deals with factual questions. But these questions are framed against a larger value backdrop; they relate to the ethical and, to a lesser extent, the aesthetic responsibilities of the mass media in our society. The researchers involved attempt to provide evidence concerning the value question: "Is it ethically defensible for the media to communicate violent and erotic content?" by assessing the behavioral effects of such messages on media audiences. The underlying assumption seems to be that if such content decisions contribute to undesirable behavioral consequences—e.g., if they increase the likelihood that a person privy to these messages will kill or rape someone—then the media are ethically remiss and should be constrained from communicating such material. Conversely, if the behavioral consequences are negligible or even positive (as in the case of the hypothesis that violent media content provides a catharsis and reduces the individual's desire to aggress against others) then the communication of violent and erotic content is permissible.

Two points concerning this utilitarian strategy merit emphasis. First, consistent with one of the major problems of utilitarian approaches mentioned in this chapter, it has proved exceedingly difficult to weigh the beneficial and harmful consequences of exposure to such media content. This is even true in the domain of factual questions: literally scores of studies have been conducted and they have yielded sharply conflicting findings about the behavioral effects of violence and eroticism. But even if it could be conclusively demonstrated that these messages stimulate no harmful actions against others, might not other undesirable consequences accrue from continued exposure to them? To what extent are public taste and sensibility retarded by a steady diet of such material? Should not the mass media aim at elevating the human spirit and condition, rather than pandering to humanity's baser instincts?

Questions such as these give rise to a second consideration: attempts to prescribe the ethical and aesthetic responsibilities of the media need not necessarily rest on a utilitarian foundation. A set of ethical and aesthetic rules could be formulated to guide the content decisions of media managers. Naturally, this approach would also suggest many thorny questions; for instance, *what* would these rules prescribe and *who* would do the prescribing? The important point, however, is that utilitarian attempts to deal with such value questions do not constitute the only alternative. Moreover, the complexity of such utilitarian ventures is amply documented in references such as the following:

Baker, R. K., and S. J. Ball (1969). *Mass Media and Violence: A Staff Report to the National Commission on the Causes and Prevention of Violence.* Washington: U.S. Government Printing Office.

Feshbach, S., and R. Singer (1971). *Television and Aggression.* San Francisco: Jossey-Bass.

Report of the Commission on Obscenity and Pornography. (1970). New York: Bantam Books.

Report of the Surgeon General's Advisory Committee on Television and Social Behavior. (1972). Washington: U. S. Government Printing Office.

Winick, C. (1970). A Study of Consumers of Explicitly Sexual Materials: Some Functions Served by Adult Movies. *Technical Reports of the Commission on Obscenity and Pornography.* Vol. 4. Washington: U. S. Government Printing Office.

THE INTRINSIC NATURE OF EVALUATION IN VALUE INQUIRY

Evaluation in value inquiry is intrinsic to the activity. Stated differently, the communication inquirer who pursues value questions has a direct scholarly concern with evaluation. Unlike the scientific inquirer, whose concern with values is extrinsic to the actual research questions, the value inquirer seeks answers—or at least, convincing arguments—concerning issues that are inherently evaluative. Speaking of the role of the communication critic, Fisher (1974) makes this distinction nicely, asserting that "the most fundamental task of the critic is to make evaluative judgments; the task of the scientist is to observe, measure, report and explain" (78).

This is not to say that students of value questions are immune from the extrinsic value judgments which face the communication scientist. Both groups of inquirers must choose from an enormous variety of potential research questions. Once students of value questions have chosen, however, their fundamental scholarly task also involves the rendering of value judgments about communicative events and environments. Formidable as the task may seem, concerned students of communication cannot shirk it, since the quality of our individual and collective communicative environments hinges upon our willingness to make informed, reasoned choices about our communicative values.

NOTES

1. We hope you will permit us a bit of latitude with this example. Whether the activities involved in writing this book constitute communication inquiry is questionable, since we are not so much adding to the store of available communication knowledge as we are synthesizing and pulling together already available information. Inquirers sometimes jokingly refer to this process as one of putting old bones into new caskets.
2. Of course, a Moslem's aversion to pork or a Hindu's distaste for beef do involve ethical considerations.
3. Recall our footnote in Chapter 4 dealing with reflexive prediction. We are alluding to this same problem here.
4. Operating from dissonance theory, a particular offspring of the family of cognitive consistency theories discussed in Chapter 2, Festinger and Carlsmith predicted that the one dollar, low justification subjects would report more positive ratings of the dull task. In this case, inconsistency would be generated by the

knowledge that one believes the task is dull but is telling someone else it is enjoyable. Payment of a large sum of money for
lying provides justification for the action and reduces dissonance; payment of a small sum increases the likelihood that one
will reduce dissonance by reassessing the attractiveness of the
task.

5. This question also has factual implications for inquiry, for if
   subjects consistently believe they will be deceived in a study,
   this belief may become a relevant variable in determining how
   they behave. (See Miller, 1970, pp. 101-102).

6. This study itself graphically illustrates the complexity of these
   ethical issues. If Walster *et al.* demonstrate that the harmful
   effects of a manipulation cannot be totally erased by debriefing
   (which they did), how can they ethically justify the use of such
   harmful manipulations in their own debriefing study?

7. We should note that the time, effort, and care devoted to debriefing subjects in the Milgram studies far exceeded the typical
   energy devoted to this activity in most research. Still, the logic
   of our argument holds no matter how much care is devoted to
   debriefing.

8. It should be easy to see how such a situation leads to measurement error. Subjects may choose the most socially desirable
   response rather than the one that most accurately mirrors their
   behaviors or attitudes. For example, one item on a widely used
   instrument for measuring anxiety asks about frequency of
   bed-wetting. It is not hard to see that bed-wetting adults will
   deem it socially undesirable to admit such behavior.

9. Specifically, NSF Grant #38398, *Effects of Videotaped Testimony on Information Processing and Decision-Making in Jury
   Trials.* A report on the findings of the first phase of this research
   is available in Miller *et al.* (1974).

10. Here, of course, we say science is self-correcting because of
    other researchers' inability to replicate bogus findings. The
    same assertion would hold true for honestly mistaken results.

11. We should note that this example is completely hypothetical.
    Not only have we shared the writing of the book, we have had
    no disagreements about such matters as order of authorship.

Nevertheless, we suspect that such problems often arise in collaborative undertakings.

12. This example is complicated by the possibility of a utilitarian theorist arguing that the harmful effects did not occur because of the original lie but rather because the untruthful guest *gossiped* about the meal with a third party. Had the potential consequences of the gossip been weighed, the host would not have learned that the guest had lied.

13. From a communication perspective, the Golden Rule suffers from another potential ethical defect. It is source-oriented; i.e., it assumes that others would necessarily like to be treated in the same way as the source. Thus, a masochist who enjoys being showered with verbal abuse could obey the Golden Rule by showering abuse on others. Perhaps a better form for the rule is, "Do unto others as you think *they* would like to be done unto."

14. Some would argue, of course, that this rule extends to any form of animal life. Although our discussion centers on human beings, we realize it could be broadened to include other animals.

15. Moreover, rules such as "You should not lie" are sometimes linked with more abstract ethical principles; e.g., "We should always do God's will." In such cases, the long-range effects of doing God's will are invariably postulated to be highly beneficial.

QUESTIONS AND EXERCISES

1. Listen to the conversations of a number of your friends and acquaintances. Is there some consistency about the topics they choose to discuss and to argue about? Can you identify the factors that influence their choices? Now try to observe some persons with whom you are relatively unacquainted. Do different topics come up? With which group do your own choices for conversation coincide most closely?

2. Miller and Nicholson argue that scientific inquiry about human communication can be value-free. Their analysis relies on defining key terms in certain ways. Prepare a short refutation of their argument, providing defensible alternative definitions of the

important terms. Can the two positions be translated into factual questions so that one or the other can be verified as true?

3. In making research decisions of your own, how would you define the following concepts, and what limits, if any, would you place on your prerogatives as a researcher when dealing with these concepts? You may decide to argue that some of the concepts are related:

   a. Deception of subjects
   b. Invasion of privacy.
   c. Informed consent of subjects.

4. How would you choose to respond to each of the following situations? Is your response based primarily on utilitarian or rule-governed ethical assessment? Can you distinguish clearly between the two approaches in each case and can you identify a consistent preference on your part for one approach or the other?

   a. A friend approaches you wearing an unattractive suit or dress and asks you how you like it.
   b. Your roommate asks you to tell a caller that their date is off for the evening because of a sudden home emergency when actually he or she is out with another person.
   c. A cab driver makes some insulting racial comments with which you disagree. (Here assume your choice is to remain silent or take issue with the remarks.)
   d. A friend asks to copy an "A" paper you wrote last term and turn it in for a related course he or she is taking this term.

5. *"Communication Inquiry: A Perspective on a Process* is an unethical book. It tells people how to learn more about the process of human communication which, in turn, permits greater manipulation and control of others. Since manipulation and control are bad, anything that increases the potential for such immoral actions is also bad." Attack or defend this argument, identifying and analyzing the key ethical premises on which it rests. Indicate how questions of definition, fact, and value all enter into the argument.

REFERENCES

Bramel, D. (1962). A Dissonance Theory Approach to Defensive Projection. *Journal of Abnormal and Social Psychology* **64**: 121–129.

Bramel, D. (1963). Selection of a Target for Defensive Projection. *Journal of Abnormal and Social Psychology* **66**: 318–324.

Carmichael, C. S., and G. L. Cronkhite (1965). Frustration and Language Intensity. *Speech Monographs* **32**: 107–111.

Festinger, L., and J. M. Carlsmith (1959). Cognitive Consequences of Forced Compliance. *Journal of Abnormal and Social Psychology* **58**: 203–210.

Fisher, W. R. (1974). Rhetorical Criticism as Criticism. *Western Speech* **38**: 75–80.

Kelman, H. C. (1968). *A Time to Speak: On Human Values and Social Research.* San Francisco: Jossey-Bass.

Lewis, S. (1925). *Arrowsmith.* New York: Harcourt.

Milgram, S. (1963). Behavioral Study of Obedience. *Journal of Abnormal and Social Psychology* **67**: 371–378.

Milgram, S. (1965). Some Conditions of Obedience and Disobedience to Authority. *Human Relations* **18**: 57–76.

Miller, G. R. (1970). Research Setting: Laboratory Studies. In P. Emmert and W. D. Brooks (eds.), *Methods of Research in Communication,* pp. 77–104. New York: Houghton Mifflin Co.

Miller, G. R., and M. Burgoon (1973). *New Techniques of Persuasion.* New York: Harper & Row.

Miller, G. R., D. Bender, T. Florence, and H. Nicholson (1974). Real versus Reel: What's the Verdict? *Journal of Communication* **24**: 99–111.

Nilsen, T. R. (1966). *Ethics of Speech Communication.* Indianapolis: The Bobbs-Merrill Co.

Ring, K. (1967). Experimental Social Psychology: Some Sober Questions about Some Frivolous Values. *Journal of Experimental Social Psychology* **3**: 113–123.

Simons, H. W. (1972). Persuasion in Social Conflict: A Critique of Prevailing Conceptions and a Framework for Future Research. *Speech Monographs* **39**: 227–248.

Walster, E., E. Berscheid, D. Abrahams, and E. Aronson (1967). Effectiveness of Debriefing Following Deception Experiments. *Journal of Personality and Social Psychology* **6**: 371–380.

Epilogue:
A Day in the Life of the Communication Researcher

If we accept the concept of process, we view

events and relationships as dynamic, ongoing,

ever-changing, continuous. When we label

something as a process, we also mean that it

does not have a beginning, an end, a fixed

sequence of events. The ingredients within a

process interact; each affects all the others.

—DAVID K. BERLO

The most fundamental of the fundamentals is

understanding the scientific process.

—JOHN WAITE BOWERS

We have acted as your tour guides for a short excursion into the world of the communication inquirer. For the most part, we have explored with you some of the important ingredients of the process of communication inquiry: framing questions; using theory; and defining, observing, and evaluating communication constructs and events. Each of these ingredients is crucial to sound inquiry. But as we have consistently stressed—and as the introductory quotations of this Epilogue emphasize—communication inquiry is a process, and all of its ingredients are inextricably related. Decisions reached about one matter have an impact on other matters; how inquirers choose to define influences how they observe; how they observe affects their judgment of certain ethical problems. Or, to avoid any implication of linearity, the inquirers' ethical predispositions may restrict the kinds of observations they are willing to make, which perhaps limits the definitional options open to them.

We feel the interrelatedness of the process of inquiry can best be reinforced by asking you to share a day in the life of the communication inquirer. Moreover, we believe that your brief visit will serve two other useful functions: first, it will illustrate once again that communication inquiry deals with events and situations which have a powerful impact on people's everyday lives; second, it will provide an opportunity for you to apply some of the concepts and ideas found in this book to the problem of asking significant communication questions and arriving at reasoned answers to them—after all, asking and answering questions is the essence of the inquiry process.

Since most of the day's activities are captured in dialogue, we must set the scene for you. Assume you have embarked on a scholarly apprenticeship with two communication inquirers: Mr. Fact and Ms. Value. Upon arriving at the office for your first day of training, you find your tutors engaged in a heated discussion:

MR. FACT: "You bet I'm interested in the effects of network television news programming on viewers. What I'm particularly concerned with are the ways that news programming influences viewer perceptions, knowledge, and attitudes. To use a far-fetched example, when a reporter ends a program by saying, 'And that's the way it is, Thursday, August 29, 1974,' are viewers left with the perception that they've been exposed to a complete report of all the newsworthy events that occurred that day?"

MS. VALUE: "Well, I'll grant that there are countless factual questions that could be asked, but to try to unravel all that complexity is like trying to kill elephants with popguns. What needs pursuing are the ethical responsibilities of the network news programmers. What intrigues me about the question you raise is whether the statement, 'That's the way it is,' can be morally defended. One could argue that it's a subtle falsehood."

MR. FACT: "Oh sure, we could speculate about that all day. But rather than a lot of armchair moralizing, I'd prefer to go out and get some facts, complicated as the situation may be. For instance, I wouldn't want to pass judgment on the ethics of that closing until I found out something about its effects on viewers."

MS. VALUE: "The world could collapse around us while you go on amassing trivia! We need some reasoned, informed values to guide our policy decisions *now,* not two or three hundred years from now."

At this juncture, you realize that Mr. Fact and Ms. Value are dangerously close to interpersonal swordpoint. Moreover, although they have raised some interesting questions, you know that the argument is pointless and ill advised. In your role as peacemaker, how would you resolve Mr. Fact and Ms. Value's dispute?

Fortunately, the protagonists must terminate their conversation because Ms. Value has to teach a 10 o'clock class. You accompany Mr. Fact to his office, where he shares with you some of his thoughts about the network television news problem:

MR. FACT: "You know, I couldn't bring myself to admit this to Ms. Value, but she really touched a sore spot with me. Conceptually, I have the feeling that network news programming has a profound influence on the ways that most people perceive and evaluate the world. Take the accounts of violence to which we're visually exposed each day—people being slaughtered in Vietnam, Cyprus, Northern Ireland, or the Middle East; disturbed persons planting bombs or indiscriminately killing others. Does this kind of fare make violence more acceptable to us? For that matter, don't such programming decisions as the events to be covered, the order in which they're presented, and the amount of time devoted to each one condition people's perceptions of what *is* newsworthy and important? But when I start trying to translate all this conceptual richness into things I can observe and measure, I get a real feeling of futility. Sure, I can ask people what their attitudes are about certain news events, or for that matter, how they feel about the medium of network television news. I can measure how much and what kinds of news information they retain. I can get verbal reports of their attitudes about violence, even though I realize such measures are probably contaminated by social desirability considerations. But if I were to create some violent situations and then observe how they behave, I'd run into some real ethical problems. Overall, then, when I finally do plan and conduct a study, I always end up feeling dissatisfied. Though Ms. Value says it's like trying to kill elephants with popguns, I usually end up feeling I've been slaying mosquitoes with cannons."

Mr. Fact has raised numerous interrelated questions about definition, observation, and evaluation. Not only do you wish to impress him with your interest and knowledge, you believe that you have some thoughts about these issues which may be helpful to him. How would you respond at this point; i.e., what would you say (or ask) about which issue to keep the dialogue moving forward?

A bit later, your conversation with Mr. Fact is interrupted by Ms. Value's return from class:

MR. FACT: "Well, Ms. Value, why don't you take our new apprentice to lunch? I've got a luncheon meeting with those representatives from the National Advertising Agency who want to fund some research on the persuasive effects of subliminal message cues."

MS. VALUE: "I'd avoid that research like the plague! All those guys are interested in is selling more soft drinks or new cars. Be careful of becoming a scholarly handmaiden for groups who are interested in manipulating others for their own financial gain."

MR. FACT: "I'll admit I've given that whole issue a lot of thought. Still, there are some interesting theoretical questions in the research that transcend the advertising profession. Moreover, I'm not sure that we're always fair in our judgments of such professions. Finally, the money from that research would permit us to bring in two more apprentices for training next year, and I'll bet our new member would consider that a worthwhile goal, right?"

Fact's question puts you on the spot. Of course you subscribe to the wisdom of providing research experiences for interested people like yourself. On the other hand, you realize that the problem being considered is a thorny one. What thoughts would you offer to prepare Mr. Fact for his luncheon meeting?

Over lunch, Ms. Value returns to her initial morning conversation with Mr. Fact:

MS. VALUE: "I'll have to admit Mr. Fact had a good point this morning. Any kind of utilitarian analysis of the ethical responsibilities of network television news programmers rests on an understanding of the effects of certain programming decisions. Furthermore, I guess the communication scientist is our best eventual hope for arriving at such answers. But the whole process moves at a snail's pace. We can't afford to suspend moral judgment on these questions until we have ideal data conditions. Still, I'm hesitant to fall back on rule-governed, formalistic ethical systems. And even if I did, I'd have a difficult time applying the rules to some network news transactions."

Obviously, Ms. Value has introduced some crucial thoughts about the relationship between factual and value inquiry. What advice would you give Ms. Value to reduce the conflict between her perceived need for factual data and her desire to come to grips immediately with some of the pressing ethical issues concerning network television news programming?

Ms. Value and you finish lunch and return to the office. Mr. Fact has also returned from his luncheon meeting with the advertising agency representatives:

MS. VALUE: "How did it go at lunch?"

MR. FACT: "We spent most of our time talking about the best way to measure persuasive effectiveness. The advertising people wanted to use a measure of increase in product sales, but I wanted to at least supplement that measure with some semantic differential items on attitudes toward the product."

MS. VALUE: "It seems to me that purchasing behavior is your best index. After all, a subliminal message cue like 'Buy Coke!' aims directly at influencing buying behavior. Moreover, I can't think of any theoretical reasons why such cues should change attitudes toward the product."

MR. FACT: "On the other hand, if this represents just a one-shot persuasive attempt with no carry-over effects it's not as theoretically interesting. Besides, if we run an experimental and control group design, we're stuck with a nominal level, buy/no buy measure, whereas the semantic differential gives us more powerful interval scaling. Finally, I think some attitude change theories would predict altered attitudes as a result of buying a product. For instance, some cognitive consistency theories . . ."

MS. VALUE: (interrupting) "Well, those questions aren't exactly my bag. I wonder how our new member would react to the problem?"

How would you react at this point? What issue would you center on to keep the dialogue moving constructively?

After the conversation has ended, Mr. Fact and Ms. Value give you some research materials to read for the remainder of the afternoon. But as you are about ready to depart for home, Mr. Fact appears at your office door:

MR. FACT: "Ms. Value and I have been talking about our initial dispute this morning, and we've decided that what's needed is not carping and backbiting but rather coordinated research activity. We'd like to launch cooperative parallel inquiries about the effects of network television news programming and the ethical responsibilities of television news programmers. Our problem is deciding where to jump into the stream. Would you give the whole matter some thought and be ready to provide any suggestions or ideas you have at a meeting tomorrow morning?"

What ideas and suggestions will you offer Mr. Fact and Ms. Value the next morning? Can you anticipate their questions and reactions to your ideas?

Perhaps this last question is the most crucial; since, as the ancient cliche tells us, tomorrow is another day. The process of communication inquiry is dynamic and ongoing. There is no beginning nor end to the search for knowledge and understanding of human communication. Consequently, even though we shall stop here, we hope the influence of this book does not end here. We are confident that it will not; for, formally or informally, part of every day of your life will be spent as a communication inquirer.

Index

AUTHOR INDEX

SUBJECT INDEX